POLICE DETECTIVES IN HISTORY, 1750–1950

Police Detectives in History, 1750–1950

Edited by
CLIVE EMSLEY
The Open University, UK

HAIA SHPAYER-MAKOV
University of Haifa, Israel

ASHGATE

© The contributors 2006

Published by
Ashgate Publishing Limited
Gower House
Croft Road
Aldershot
Hants GU11 3HR
England

Ashgate Publishing Company
Suite 420
101 Cherry Street
Burlington, VT 05401-4405
USA

Ashgate website: http://www.ashgate.com

British Library Cataloguing in Publication Data
Police detectives in history, 1750-1950
  1.Detectives—History 2.Criminal investigation—History
  I.Emsley, Clive II.Shpayer-Makov, Haia
  363.2'52'09

Library of Congress Cataloging-in-Publication Data
Police detectives in history, 1750-1950 / edited by Clive Emsley and Haia Shpayer-Makov.
   p. cm.
 Includes bibliographical references and index.
 ISBN 0-7546-3948-7 (alk. paper)
 1. Detectives—History. 2. Criminal investigation—History. I. Emsley, Clive. II. Shpayer-Makov, Haia.

HV7903.P63 2005
363.25'09—dc22

2005014116

ISBN-10: 0 7546 3948 7

Printed and bound by Athenaeum Press Ltd, Gateshead, Tyne & Wear.

Contents

List of Illustrations

List of Tables

List of Contributors with Affiliations

Beattie, John M. Professor Emeritus at the University of Toronto, Canada.

Brown, Howard G. Professor of History, Binghamton University, New York, USA.

Drabble, John. Visiting Professor, International Area Studies Teaching Program, University of California, Berkeley, USA.

Dunstall, Graeme. Lecturer in History, University of Canterbury, New Zealand.

Emsley, Clive. Professor of History, The Open University, UK.

Finnane, Mark. Professor of History and Dean of Graduate Studies, Griffith University, Brisbane, Australia.

Johnson, Eric A. Professor of History, Central Michigan University, USA.

Morris, Robert M. Former senior officer in the Home Office, currently research scholar, The Open University, UK.

Shpayer-Makov, Haia. Associate Professor of History, University of Haifa, Israel.

Sinclair, Georgina. School of History, University of Leeds, UK.

Wilson, Dean. Lecturer in Criminal Justice and Criminology, School of Political and Social Inquiry, Monash University, Melbourne, Australia.

Introduction

The Police Detective and Police History

Clive Emsley and Haia Shpayer-Makov

We learn that that mysterious body whose preterhuman sagacity and marvellous organization – the detective police [of London's Metropolitan Police] – actually consisted up to the middle of the year 1869, of 15 persons only, a number hardly sufficient to meet the constant demands made upon the force by Miss Braddon, Mr. Wilkie Collins, and others of the same school. The public, however, has gone on steadily believing, on the authority of novelists, in the wonderful organization of our secret police and the skill of its members – consoling itself for the impunity of the robber of real life by the speed and certainty with which the detective of fiction tracks out his imaginary criminals.[1]

The last quarter of the twentieth century witnessed a number of social historians turning their attention to questions of police and policing. In part this work emerged out of the need to know better who were the individuals that patrolled the streets of the nineteenth-century's burgeoning industrial towns and cities acting out the role of 'domestic missionary' and empowered to discipline the new working class with batons and, if necessary, more lethal weaponry.[2] More recently there has been a recognition that police officers were themselves generally recruited from the working class, that police institutions were some of the biggest employers of labour in the new nation states and that there is as much a need to study police officers as workers, members of families, recipients of benefits, welfare and

---

[1]   *Times* (after the *Pall Mall Gazette*) 5 October 1870, p. 5. Wilkie Collins remains well known for such mysteries as *The Woman in White* (1860) and *The Moonstone* (1868). Mary Elizabeth Braddon is much less known to modern readers but her sensational novels, most notably *Lady Audley's Secret* (1862), were immensely popular with the Victorian public.

[2]   The seminal articles here were Robert D. Storch, 'The Policeman as Domestic Missionary: Urban Discipline and Popular Culture in Northern England, 1850–1880', *Journal of Social History*, IX (1976) pp. 481–509, and idem, '"The Plague of Blue Locusts": Police Reform and Popular Resistance in Northern England 1840–1857', *International Review of Social History*, XX (1975) pp. 61–90.

pensions as any other group of the working class.[3] This historical research, however, even when it has looked beyond the policing of urban areas, has concentrated almost entirely on uniformed patrol officers. The aim of this collection is to begin redressing the balance by focusing on another type of police officer, one who has remained largely outside the current wave of historical research, the police detective.

The detective has become a prominent figure, almost a cultural institution, in much of the western world. He, less commonly she, is a central figure in novels, film and television dramas. Books about 'grey-celled wizards' or hard-boiled sleuths go back, in the former instance at least, to the early nineteenth century. In the second half of the twentieth century about one quarter of the most popular television programmes in Britain and a fifth of the films have been crime stories that generally involve a detective of some sort. Similar stories make up about a quarter of all fictional works sold in Britain and America.[4] The French *roman policier* has become as popular a topic for French cultural theorists as it is for the reading public.[5] The solving of a crime and the restoration of order is a positive outcome in most of these stories. Traditionally they provide the opportunity for showing a community re-establishing calm and neutralising disruptive elements. But, in recent years, it is possible to detect a shift away from intellectual mind-games to an engagement with political and social issues and increasingly the stories are less concerned with the mind of the detective and more with that of the psychopath. Moreover, while there are major police figures in detective stories – Maigret, Morse, Kojac to give just three examples – the detective is not always a police officer. Indeed among the common bit-part stereotypes there are often police detectives who behave either as clumsy foils before the rapier-mind of the intellectual sleuth or as rule-bound bureaucrats alongside the liberated, hard-boiled private eye. Several of the essays that follow in this collection touch on the police detective in literature and how police detectives themselves have contributed significantly to the traditional detective story and to the stereotypes. But, rather than literary and cinematic stereotypes, it is the men who

---

[3]   See, for example, Clive Emsley, 'The Policeman as Worker: A Comparative Survey c.1800–1940', *International Review of Social History*, XLV (2000) pp. 89–110, and Haia Shpayer-Makov, *The Making of a Policeman: A Social History of a Labour Force in Metropolitan London, 1829–1914* (Aldershot: Ashgate, 2002).

[4]   Robert Reiner, *The Politics of the Police* (3rd edn Oxford University Press, 2000) pp. 147–60. Reiner provides a useful typology here of the police/detective story.

[5]   See, for example, *Crime and Punishment: Narratives of Order and Disorder*, a special issue of *French Cultural Studies*, 12, no. 36 (2001); Sara Poole, '*Rompols* not of the Bailey: Fred Vargas and the *polar* as *mini-proto-myth*', *French Cultural Studies*, 12, no. 34 (2001) pp. 95–108; Annette Finley-Croswhite and Gayle K. Brunelle, '"Murder in the Metro": Masking and Unmasking Laetitia Toureaux in 1930s France', *French Cultural Studies*, 14, no. 40 (2003) pp. 53–80.

served as police detectives in the first century and a half of professional, bureaucratic police forces and the development of the institutions in which they served that constitute the focus of the volume.

Defining the police detective runs into the same problems as defining the police officer in general. In recent years it has been popular among some sociologists to see the right to deploy legitimate force in day-to-day dealings with the public as a key element that singles out the police officer from other agents of the state.[6] But the definition is by no means universally accepted, and it is not a definition that can be employed easily when distinguishing the police detective. Such agents might be identified as those police officers whose task it is to obtain information and evidence about offences committed against the law, to detect and apprehend the offenders and to present evidence against them in court. Their relationship to the police institution has to be stressed since there are other public servants engaged in similar activities working, for example, for customs and excise, for drug enforcement agencies or for immigration authorities but who are not attached specifically to institutions commonly labelled as police. There are also private inquiry agents who usually serve private interests and do not, as a rule, engage in criminal law enforcement or investigation. It is sometimes the case, however, that police detectives move into this line of the work when they retire from the police; Eugène-François Vidocq, whose name will recur in the chapters that follow, has a claim to being father of both the police detective and the private detective in France. Occasionally, also, as is described below by John Drabble in his chapter on the FBI, states have been known to employ or to recruit private agents for various policing tasks. The tasks of police detectives might also overlap with those of individuals in other state institutions when it comes to the political surveillance of enemies of the state (or those who were conceived as such) and guarding members of the state's elite. In sum, the police detective is best considered, loosely, as an agent charged with a particular set of tasks within the police institution.

Within the popular image of a modern police force, there is a further distinction between detectives, identified as those involved in the gathering of information, clandestine or otherwise, and other officers. Such a division is tied to a further popular difference between the two branches. Detectives are exempt from wearing a uniform on duty and are given the freedom to choose their clothing as it is demanded by the nature of their mission. This has led to much of the romance surrounding the detective and has been played upon in many of the literary and visual images as, for example, in the two contrasting photographs of Metropolitan

---

[6]   See, *inter alia*, David H. Bayley, *Patterns of Policing: A Comparative International Analysis* (New Brunswick, N.J.: Rutgers University Press, 1985) and Egon Bittner, *The Functions of Police in Modern Society* (Chevy Chase, MD: National Institute of Mental Health, 1970).

Police detectives taken around 1911 (see illustrations 0.1 and 0.2). The first shows the men in their Sunday best, the second shows them in disguise and, allegedly, ready to take to the streets of Limehouse to investigate drug smuggling. Historically, however, the demarcation line between detectives and other officers has not always been as clear cut as the popular image would suggest. Uniformed policemen occasionally undertook tasks associated with detection such as house-to-house inquiries, while detective work was often closely linked with the uniformed patrolman's task of prevention. Nor was the difference in appearance between detectives and uniformed officers always maintained. Initially American patrolmen did not wear a uniform. Their reluctance to put on 'livery' appears to have declined only gradually with broad changes within American society in the mid-nineteenth century that saw an increase in uniformed servants and in the aftermath of the Civil War when men had become accustomed to wearing uniform.[7] In Victorian England, as is noted below, uniformed officers were sometimes requested to disguise their identity and to work in plain clothes.

There are a variety of tasks within the police officer's trade: the prevention of crime and the detection of offenders are, perhaps, the most obvious, though they are not unique to the police officer. Prevention was specified as the central task for the new constables of London's Metropolitan Police when they first took to the streets in 1829. The creation of the New Police, as these new constables became known, was described by the old Whig historians as the beginnings of modern policing in England, if not the whole western world. They interpreted it as the logical outcome of a century of effort by far-sighted reformers to create a modern, effective police institution.[8] Yet, as John Beattie's chapter on the well-known, but hitherto little researched Bow Street Runners demonstrates, the New Police created by Sir Robert Peel for London performed rather different policing tasks from the men recruited and employed by reformers and improvers such as the Fielding brothers in Bow Street. The Runners were detectives, not patrolmen. There were also patrols working out of Bow Street as there were watchmen hired by the various London parishes. What Peel did was to centralise the system of patrols with the aim of prevention. The detective police in Bow Street and in the half-dozen other offices run by stipendiary magistrates initially functioned alongside the new police until they were abolished at the end of the 1830s. And at the moment of this abolition there were no serious plans on the table for any detective establishment within the Metropolitan Police.

---

[7]   Clive Emsley, *Policing and its Context 1750–1870* (London: Macmillan, 1979) pp. 111–12.

[8]   The books of Charles Reith, such as *The Police Idea* (Oxford University Press, 1938) and *British Police and the Democratic Ideal* (Oxford University Press, 1943) are among the most significant of these.

Illustration 0.1   London detectives in their Sunday best (1911).

Illustration 0.2   The same London detectives ready to take to the streets of Limehouse during an operation against drug smuggling (1911).

Across the United Kingdom considerable faith was invested in the idea of prevention, not least because of the concerns shared by many about police officers carrying out investigations in plain clothes. In the eyes of the freeborn Englishman such investigation smacked of spying and of the political intrusiveness ascribed to police institutions on continental Europe; no dividing line was perceived between such policing and provocation and entrapment. In addition, as Peel's new police took to the streets of London in 1829, so Paris was reeling from the scandal of its detective police being recruited from ex-convicts. The scandal of Vidocq and his ex-convict detectives, discussed in the chapters of both Howard Brown and Clive Emsley, was something of which the freeborn Englishmen who had beaten Napoleon and his police state less than a generation before became rapidly and smugly aware. But, as Dean Wilson and Mark Finnane point out below, in colonial Victoria the British authorities recruited their first detectives from men who had been transported as convicts, and for much the same reasons as the French. Moreover, English self-satisfaction over the Vidocq affair was short-lived since in 1833 Metropolitan Police Sergeant William Popay was exposed as having, on his own initiative, infiltrated the National Political Union and urged its members to radical and violent action. A parliamentary select committee investigated and Popay was dismissed. The select committee concluded that there was no objection to the occasional deployment of police in plain clothes 'strictly confined to detect Breaches of the Law and to prevent Breaches of the Peace, should these ends appear otherwise unattainable'. But it deprecated 'any approach to the Employment of Spies ... as a practice most abhorrent to the feelings of the People, and most alien to the spirit of the Constitution'.[9] A decade later when two police officers in plain clothes were recognised as attending a Chartist meeting in London they left rather than give fictitious names and addresses. They returned later in their uniforms and requested permission to be present.[10] But, while for some Englishmen it was easy to elide plain-clothes police and political policing, the problem of detecting serious criminal offenders could not be either wished away or ignored. Popay told the committee investigating him: 'all thieves know a policeman in uniform, and avoid him'. The comment was backed up by much of the evidence given by his superiors.[11]

Not every nineteenth-century English commentator, however, wished the detective police away. As Robert Morris explains below, there were commentators who lauded the police detective. Charles Dickens, for example, wrote several

---

[9] *Parliamentary Papers* 1833 (627), XIII, *Report from the Select Committee on the Petition of Frederick Young and Others*, p. 3.

[10] F.C. Mather, *Public Order in the Age of the Chartists* (Manchester University Press, 1959) p. 193.

[11] *Report from the Select Committee*, qq. 1127, 1759 and 1845.

journalistic pieces in praise of London's detectives, and notably of Inspector Field with whom he went on patrol into some of the dingiest rookeries of the poor.[12] In the 'stoutly-built, steady-looking, sharp-eyed man in black' – Inspector Bucket – in his novel *Bleak House* (1852–53), Dickens also created the first English police detective in fiction.[13] Memoirs, as Haia Shpayer-Makov shows, also boosted the image of the detective, and the memoirs of English and French police detectives were far more common than the memoirs of those officers who never got out of uniform. Indeed, the fascination with the detective and particularly with his need to penetrate the underworld, to know its ways, its language and its membership made him a significant literary figure from early on in the nineteenth century. The links between the police detective and the novelist is one of the central issues discussed in Clive Emsley's chapter on the French experience; and in France the police detective of literature tended to be much more sinister than his English counterpart. Such links have been picked up elsewhere by others who have explored other media in other periods and contexts. In the contexts of Britain and also of the British Empire well into the twentieth century and the years of decolonisation 'English methods' was a term used by British officers to denote open, upright and honest policing eschewing all subterfuge. The reality, as Georgina Sinclair emphasises below in the context of the end of empire, did not always measure up to the aspirations.

As Howard Brown points out below, while the role and skills of particular individuals have commonly been emphasised in histories that touch on detective policing, equally important in the nineteenth-century growth of the detective as hero was the growing fascination with physiognomy. Moreover, even if the detectives boasted about being able to identify criminals from their appearance, the bureaucratic record keeping of the new nineteenth-century nation state was central to their identification of recidivists. Record keeping remained an important part of the detective's armoury and from the mid-nineteenth century criminal files could carry a photograph of the offender. The collections of photographs appear rapidly to have become cumbersome and difficult to manage and they seem to have been rather more significant for the representation of scientific policing than for the

---

[12]   Charles Dickens, 'A Detective Police Party', *Household Words*, I (1850) pp. 409–14 and 457–60; idem, 'On Duty with Inspector Field', *Household Words*, III (1851) pp. 265–70. And for alternative, but equally favourable views, see, *inter alia* [W.H. Wills] 'The Modern Science of Thief-Taking', *Household Words*, I (1850) pp. 368–72 and Anon, 'Plain-Clothes Men', *Once a Week*, 3rd series IX (1872) pp. 479–82.

[13]   The emphasis here has to be on *police* detective. A case can be made for William Godwin, *Caleb Williams* (1794) as the first real detective novel; Philip Meadows Taylor, *Confessions of a Thug* (1839), a fictionalised account of the British campaign against the robber sect in India known as Thugs, has an official crime investigator as one of its characters.

serious business of detecting criminals.[14] Nevertheless, as the nineteenth century moved into the twentieth the champions of the police detective began to stress his growing use of science, technology and various forensic techniques. The photographs were a part of this, but they were augmented first by the system of scientific measurements established in France by Alphonse Bertillon and then by the use of fingerprints. These were also the years when the *scuola di polizia scientifica* was established in Italy by Salvatore Ottolenghi, a criminologist and pupil of Cesare Lombroso. From 1903 the courses at this school, situated in Rome's main prison, became compulsory for senior officers of the Italian police, the kind of men who, in Italy, were most likely to be involved in detective work. The school taught all of the latest methods of detection and a positivist perception of criminology based on the ideas of Lombroso. It acquired an international reputation and was ranked by Raymond Fosdick, the celebrated early twentieth-century commentator on police and policing, as one of the best training schools in Europe. Unfortunately Ottolenghi and his school still await a historian.[15] But it remains true that, while detectives across Europe, the European empires and the Americas might have sought to bask in the reflected glory of Sherlock Holmes and his brilliant use of logical and inductive reasoning, away from the novels and the stories the reality was invariably much more plodding and bureaucratic if, at times, scientific.

At first glance, given the fascination with detective memoirs, with detectives in novels, in the cinema and on television, the detective's general absence from police history is something of a puzzle. This absence has several explanations and these are not mutually exclusive. It is possible that the extensive attention given to detectives in literature tended to divert social historians away from them. Secondly, police detectives were always relatively few in number compared with the uniformed patrolmen. Admittedly, some detectives spied on radicals and working-class activists, but the romantic pursuit of criminal offenders had far less interest for social historians than the surveillance of working-class districts and of public space by uniformed officers. Most probably, perhaps, the absence of the police detective from the recent revisionist police history is explained by the initial focus of that history which concentrated on the domesticating and surveillance roles of the uniformed patrol officer. The uniformed patrolman was the individual publicly

---

[14] Jens Jäger, 'Photography: A Means of Surveillance? Judicial Photography, 1850 to 1900', *Crime, histoire et sociétés/Crime, history and societies*, 5, 1 (2001) pp. 27–51.

[15] See Mary Gibson, *Prostitution and the state in Italy 1860–1915* (2nd edn Columbus, Ohio: Ohio State University Press, 1999) pp. 121–22; Richard Bach Jensen, 'Police Reform and Social Reform: Italy from the Crisis of the 1890s to the Giolittian Era', *Criminal Justice History*, 10 (1989) pp.179–200: at p. 193; Raymond B. Fosdick, *European Police Systems* (New York: Century, 1915; reprinted Montclair N.J., 1969) pp. 190–93 and 329–30.

deployed to discipline the working class either at leisure or during economic
disorder. The uniformed patrolman, moreover, given his social origins, could also
be studied as a member of the uniformed working class; on continental Europe this
was usually after a period as a non-commissioned officer in the military. The ideal
patrolman was a model for the new industrial worker. He patrolled his beat at a
regular, steady pace under the periodic surveillance of his superiors. He gained
promotion by his own efforts. He had to be respectable, and so too did his wife and
family. While in Paris the first official detective squad, that of Vidocq, was
recruited according to the old adage of setting a thief to catch a thief, police
detectives in England were expected to be as respectable as their uniformed
counterparts. Their work practices, however, were less regimented and mechanical
than those of the uniformed patrolman.

It is not the aim of this book to give a social-economic profile of police
detectives across the western world, nor to trace, in detail, the development of
criminal investigation, but rather to shed light on some crucial aspects of the men
who worked at the institutional coal face during the development of detective
policing from the mid-eighteenth to the mid-twentieth centuries. Britain, and in
particular London, occupies a central place in the book. This is not because the
authors or editors here accept the traditional Whig history notion of the English
Police as the first modern police institution, nor because they accept the same
tradition's perception that the English system was in any way superior. Rather it is
to keep the volume manageable. The chapters that focus outside Britain and the
British Empire have been planned to show parallel developments in different kinds
of state, as with the essays on France, the comparisons and contrasts with detective
policing under a particularly authoritarian regime (Nazi Germany), and the role of
a centralised detective agency, the FBI, within a state that, traditionally, regarded
centralisation with even more suspicion than the English.

In the opening chapter John Beattie investigates the onset of organised
detection in eighteenth-century London – a metropolis which, according to the
traditional Whig historians, had very little in the way of police institutions.[16]
Individuals were involved in the detection of offences before the creation of the
Bow Street Runners, but the Runners' link with the police reformers, in particular
the Fielding brothers and Saunders Welsh, gives these men a special place in the

---

[16] This view is now under serious reappraisal, see, *inter alia*, Elaine A. Reynolds,
*Before the Bobbies: The Night Watch and Police Reform in Metropolitan London, 1720–
1830* (London: Macmillan, 1998); J.M. Beattie, *Policing and Punishment in London, 1660–
1750: Urban Crime and the Limits of Terror* (Oxford University Press, 2001); Andrew T.
Harris, *Crime and Legal Authority in London c. 1780–1840* (Columbus, Ohio: Ohio State
University Press, 2004). These books, however, all deal much more with watch and
constable systems rather than specifically with detective policing.

general history of policing. The next two chapters, by Howard Brown and Clive Emsley respectively, switch the perspective to France and show that, regardless of the Anglo-Saxon beliefs about a centralised police system and a powerful detective system, the realities of French policing were rather different. Even so, Paris appeared to provide a model when scandal required a reorganisation of London detectives at the end of the 1870s. Robert Morris discusses this reorganisation when he continues the London story, tracing the evolution of the detective department of the Metropolitan Police from its establishment in 1842 to the inter-war period. Haia Shpayer-Makov then rehearses at greater length some of the issues raised in the French context when she analyses the self-image of the London detectives as reflected in their memoirs.

There is a common assumption that the model for the policing structures of the British Empire was the gendarmerie-style institution that the British established in early nineteenth-century Ireland – the Irish, from 1867, the Royal Irish Constabulary. The truth of this assertion is still debated,[17] but it is also becoming apparent that the selection of models for imperial police forces was eclectic. The larger towns and cities, especially in the White Dominions, looked more to what was understood as a London/English model than to Ireland. The chapters by Dean Wilson and Mark Finnane and by Graeme Dunstall both indicate the continuing influence of what was understood as the English model in Australia and New Zealand, but also significant developments that are in line with the broad move to bureaucratic and technological detective policing. They also indicate the considerable differences between the contexts of policing even in the empire: Melbourne was a significant city, while so much policing in New Zealand (and indeed in Australia) saw officers thinly spread over vast areas of thinly populated land. Georgina Sinclair turns the spotlight on detective police in imperial trouble spots from the inter-war to the post-war period. The imperial territories that are the focus of her chapter were well away from the relatively pacific White Dominions. She notes the faith in a mild, English model but also how, in emergencies, this could be transformed into something far tougher and more aggressive with the deployment of military personnel. The focus on aggressive political policing prompts a further brief foray outside the English-speaking world with Eric Johnson's chapter on the generally positive image of the *Gestapo* in Nazi Germany and even in the post-war Federal Republic. The concluding chapter, by John Drabble, also addresses aggressive political detective work, but here in the context

---

[17]   Richard Hawkins, 'The "Irish Model" and the Empire: A Case for Reassessment', in David M. Anderson and David Killingray, eds, *Policing the Empire: Government, Authority and Control, 1830–1940* (Manchester University Press, 1991); Greg Marquis, 'The "Irish Model" and Nineteenth-Century Canadian Policing', *Journal of Imperial and Commonwealth History*, 25 (1997) pp. 193–218.

of the FBI and its attempt to establish a political consensus and to undermine organisations that it considered un-American on both the left and the right.

In as much as each of the individual chapters that follow focuses on a particular country, or in the case of Georgina Sinclair a particular empire, the book is not comparative. Significant comparisons and contrasts, however, can be drawn. The socio-economic profile of the detective officer has never been as clear as that of the working-class patrol officer, but while in the British and North American contexts a detective's police career generally began in the uniformed branch, this was rarely the case on continental Europe. Detectives everywhere, however, like the uniformed patrol officers, were required to possess the attributes of honesty and respectability. But it was much less easy to observe and supervise a man who, by virtue of the tasks with which he was entrusted, often needed to mix with those who were not respectable. The detective also acquired and often boasted of a professional mystique by which he was able to identify offenders by how they looked, by their *modus operandi*. Furthermore, as is evinced in the careers of the New Zealand detectives Bill Murray and Charles Belton, described by Graeme Dunstall, they liked to stress their abilities in interrogation and the way that they could coax an admission of guilt from suspects.

Since the beginnings of professional, bureaucratic police institutions in the late eighteenth and early nineteenth centuries the numbers of detectives have always been fewer than the numbers of uniformed patrol officers. Partly as a consequence, the detectives have invariably perceived of themselves as the elite. In their memoirs and in the way that they use the media, detectives commonly have liked to stress their knowledge of offenders, their shrewdness, their cunning and, in more recent times, their ability to deploy science and technology. But this cunning and this knowledge of offenders could also be an Achilles heel. Initially the borderlines between crime and law enforcement could be blurred. The recruitment of ex-criminals for the first police detectives in Paris was an extreme example of this, and the stigma was used by critics of the detectives in France for much of the nineteenth century and beyond. But in London also, eighteenth-century thief-takers and then the Bow Street Runners did not refrain from dabbling in lawbreaking or in deriving income from their connections in the criminal underworld. The pressure of public opinion contributed to the end of such recruitment practices, but so too did the authorities' desire to have police institutions that were efficient and effective. Police institutions, even in authoritarian regimes such as Nazi Germany, have difficulty in functioning without a degree of popular support; the *Polizeitag* (Police Day) established by the Nazis in 1934 was specifically designed to encourage the population to see the police officer as *Freund und Helfer* (friend and helper).[18] Even after the departure of Vidocq and his men from the Paris

---

[18] Robert Gellateley, *Backing Hitler: Consent and Coercion in Nazi Germany* (Oxford

Prefecture, detectives in Paris and elsewhere, still maintained contacts with criminal environments and used informers from within those communities stigmatised as criminal. The authorities played down the links between detectives and the criminal world (unless as a key part of their attempts to protect society) and resorted to a strategy which emphasised the implementation of proper procedures and the honesty of detectives. Robert Morris notes how in London the police authorities as employers were concerned about their ability to exercise control over their employees. The nature of detective work often made it difficult to maintain such control and the potential difficulties have not gone away. Scandals exposed among Metropolitan Police detectives in the late twentieth century have demonstrated the problems in setting police officers on relatively modest incomes to investigate high-earning entrepreneurs dealing in, for example, drugs and pornography. Detective officers in such situations are exposed to dangerous levels of temptation and the potential for serious corruption. And especially when the detectives regard themselves as elite, superior to uniformed officers who work regular shifts under a much greater degree of surveillance.[19] Shortly after these revelations a sociological investigation of the 'ducking and diving' and 'wheeling and dealing' of detectives in the East End of London showed their behaviour to be almost interchangeable with that of the small-scale entrepreneurs, who often worked on the fringes of legality.[20]

The detective in literature and other forms of media production has been mentioned at some length in this introduction, and it is a theme that recurs in many of the following chapters. Howard Brown, for example, dwells on the role and importance of the press even at the end of the eighteenth century, while Haia Shpayer-Makov concentrates on detective memoirs at the end of the nineteenth and beginning of the twentieth century. Detectives, much more so than uniformed police officers, wrote about their professional lives from the Bow Street Runners onwards. John Christie is described by Dean Wilson and Mark Finnane as a particularly striking example of the colourful, self-glorifying detective autobiographer. Christie's autobiography also appeared in the years addressed by Shpayer-Makov when a great many commentators were expressing concerns about moral decay and about the dangers of working-class culture and of female emancipation and liberated sexuality. These concerns were projected on to the burgeoning towns and cities by both intellectual commentators and the popular press. No wonder then that the detective, who claimed in his memoirs and through

---

University Press, 2001) pp. 43–45.

[19] Barry Cox, John Shirley and Martin Short, *The Fall of Scotland Yard* (Harmondsworth: Penguin, 1977).

[20] Dick Hobbs, *Doing the Business: Entrepreneurship, the Working Class, and Detectives in the East End of London* (Oxford University Press, 1988).

the press to be able to perceive and control the threats to respectable, law-abiding folk and hence, by extension, to civilisation itself, became such a powerful figure and often sought and enjoyed a special relationship with the media. There were spectacular successes, and detectives and police authorities liked to play upon these. But there were also spectacular failures that drew much criticism and, in the English-speaking world, could see such labels as the 'defective police' humorously and disparagingly applied.[21]

Protecting the respectable has never meant guarding people from theft and murder alone or simply detecting the perpetrators of such offences. The English might have disliked the idea of political police. The Home Secretary could stand up in Parliament on the eve of the First World War to deny tartly that such a police existed in Britain, but protection and detection even then could involve the surveillance and pursuit of political activists.[22] Just as, according to one of the senior officers interviewed in the Popay inquiry, 'a man in uniform will hardly ever take a thief',[23] so a man in uniform was not best able to maintain a surveillance of political suspects. Nineteenth-century France, with its Bonapartists, royalists (legitimists and Orleanists) and republicans (moderate and Jacobin) always appeared under threat. Nazi Germany, with its desire to establish a pure *Volksgemeinschaft*, also found scores of internal political enemies, and its *Gestapo* subsequently became the byword for sinister, oppressive political police. But as several of the chapters that follow show, political policing has never been confined to continental Europe or the non-English speaking world. Political and terrorist threats at the beginning of the twenty-first century are, potentially, on a much bigger scale than before, but governments have always worried about internal threats and have always seen police detectives as one instrument of protection in this respect.

---

[21] Criticism was particularly extreme in London during the Jack the Ripper Murders, see L. Perry Curtis, Jr. *Jack the Ripper and the London Press* (New Haven and London: Yale University Press, 2001).

[22] *Hansard*, LXI (30 April 1914) col. 1874 and LXII (5 May 1914) col. 121. For the development of the 'political police' in nineteenth-century England, see Bernard Porter, *The Origins of the Vigilant State: The London Metropolitan Police Special Branch before the First World War* (London: Weidenfeld & Nicolson, 1987).

[23] *Report … on the Petition of Sir Frederick Young*, q. 1127.

Chapter One

Early Detection: The Bow Street Runners in Late Eighteenth-Century London

J.M. Beattie

Of the two crime-fighting functions of policing – surveillance on the one hand, detection and prosecution on the other – only the first has had a long history in England. In eighteenth-century London, the parish constables were charged with keeping the peace and dealing with any disorderly or criminal behaviour that came to their attention, and the night watch with guarding the streets after sunset. It was of course hoped that their presence on the streets would discourage potential offenders. Beyond that, constables called to the scene of a crime or watchmen coming upon an offence in progress could be called upon to assist the victim in apprehending the offenders and taking them before a magistrate. But there were severe limits as to the help victims of crime could expect to receive from such officials. For their part, the constables continued to a considerable extent to be ordinary citizens serving in the post for a year as an aspect of their civic duty. Such men were never likely to take more on themselves than custom demanded, and neither they nor the nightwatchmen had ever been expected to provide more than immediate help to victims of property crime or violence. There was no expectation that they would help victims to discover the identity of offenders who could not be immediately apprehended, to search for clues, or to interview witnesses, and so on. In a system of prosecution that depended fundamentally on the energy and resources of the private citizen, detective work was very much left to the victim. Presented with a magistrate's warrant to arrest someone within their jurisdiction, the constables were obliged to do so. But neither constables nor magistrates thought it their duty to do anything more than respond to information supplied by others.[1]

---

[1]   Douglas Hay, 'Using the Criminal Law, 1750–1850: Policing, Private Prosecution, and the State', in Douglas Hay and Francis Snyder, eds, *Policing and Prosecution in Britain, 1750–1850* (Oxford University Press, 1989) pp. 16–25.

This was to change in the eighteenth century as a number of men in London became involved in the business of detection and prosecution. That they did so was largely a consequence of a striking increase in the amount of reward money being offered by the state for the conviction of certain offenders and by victims of property crime for the return of their stolen goods. Men known as 'thief-takers' can be found in London in the early seventeenth century, but their numbers were much increased after 1689 when Parliament established statutory rewards of £40 for the conviction of offenders charged with a number of offences that were causing particular anxiety – robbery on the highways and on the streets of London, burglary, and coining. Both private and state rewards became even more common and more valuable in the first half of the eighteenth century, facilitated by the growth of newspapers and by a government decision to increase by royal proclamation the reward for the conviction of a street robber in London by the addition of £100 over and above the £40 established by statute. Over the quarter century between 1720 and 1745, and again briefly between 1750 and 1752, the reward for the conviction of a robber in London was £140, a sum that approached three or four years' income for even a skilled workman.[2]

These interventions by Parliament and the monarch were undoubtedly intended to encourage the victims of offences to make an effort to catch and prosecute those who stole from them and to encourage those with knowledge that would lead to the apprehension and conviction of offenders to come forward – including accomplices, who were additionally encouraged by the offer of a pardon.[3] They may have done so. But they also had the larger effect of prompting significant changes in policing in London by encouraging the activities of private thief-takers prepared to seek out, capture, and prosecute offenders whose conviction promised such rewards.[4] Despite the corruption that rewards inevitably encouraged, belief in their usefulness and in the value of detection and of the certainty of prosecution and punishment as deterrents to crime strengthened over the first half of the eighteenth century. Such convictions lay behind the major innovations in policing

---

[2]   J.M. Beattie, *Policing and Punishment in London, 1660–1750: Urban Crime and the Limits of Terror* (Oxford University Press, 2001) pp. 376–84.

[3]   This was the objective of the reward of a certificate granting the holder lifetime relief from service in all parish offices (a 'Tyburn Ticket') for the conviction of shop-lifters, a device clearly intended to encourage the shopkeepers of London to go to the trouble and expense of prosecuting offenders as a way of diminishing what was thought to be a growing problem.

[4]   Beattie, *Policing and Punishment*, chapter 5; Tim Wales, 'Thief-takers and their clients in later Stuart London', in Paul Griffiths and Mark S.R. Jenner, eds, *Londinopolis: essays in the cultural and social history of early-modern London* (Manchester University Press, 2001) pp. 67–85; Ruth Paley, 'Thief-takers in London in the Age of the McDaniel Gang, c. 1745–54', in Hay and Snyder, eds, *Policing and Prosecution*.

introduced by Henry Fielding in the middle years of the century and developed thereafter by his half-brother, John, innovations that made their house in Bow Street, Covent Garden, a centre of magisterial activity and policing.

Henry Fielding moved to Bow Street in 1748, encouraged by a government stipend of £400 to carry on the active magisterial work of his predecessor, Sir Thomas DeVeil, who had made his house well known as a place where the public would be able to find a justice of the peace with some regularity. Fielding arrived at Bow Street just as the War of Austrian Succession was coming to an end and as the rapid demobilisation of the large army and navy was producing seriously high levels of crime in the metropolis. He responded to the threat of violence on the streets and the highways leading into the metropolis by bringing together the first body of officers dedicated to catching and prosecuting offenders. In his four-and-a-half years as the chief magistrate of Westminster – before ill-health forced his withdrawal in 1754, and indeed caused his death soon thereafter – Fielding initiated practices and won government approval for a plan that was to make Bow Street the leading centre of policing in the metropolis.

Fielding was preoccupied from his first days at Bow Street with the consequences of the crime wave. He developed strong views about its causes and how it might be diminished, views expressed most notably in a pamphlet published in 1751 entitled *An Enquiry into the Causes of the Late Increase of Robbers*. In this wide-ranging analysis of the process of criminal administration he criticised the way the criminal law was administered, blaming the increase in crime in part on the timidity of juries, the harmful effects of too many pardons, and the carnival atmosphere surrounding executions at Tyburn, which, he thought, had become more of an encouragement than a deterrent to crime.[5] But perhaps the most original sections in his *Enquiry* were those in which he discussed policing issues of the kind that were arising from his practice at Bow Street. For in the winter of 1749-50, with reports increasing of violence in the streets of London, Fielding had taken what was to turn out to be an important initiative by persuading a group of men, including constables and ex-constables, to devote themselves to seeking out and apprehending serious offenders and bringing them to Bow Street for examination and commitment to trial. The need for such a body, as he saw it, sprang from the reluctance of victims to undertake prosecutions and the difficulties they faced if they chose to do so, particularly the difficulties of apprehending members of gangs who were frequently armed and prepared to use violence to rescue any of their associates in danger of being taken. Victims got little help, he recognised, from the existing policing forces. The impunity with which London robbers acted, the indifference they showed to the consequences of their actions, exposed, in

---

[5] Henry Fielding, *An Enquiry into the Causes of the late Increase of Robbers* (first published 1751), ed, Malvin R. Zirker (Oxford University Press, 1988) pp. 154–59.

Fielding's view, the serious weakness and incapacity of the civil authorities. A more vigorous response was required, of the kind that Fielding was organising at Bow Street, the success of which would depend on public support of men willing to undertake the dangerous task of finding and apprehending violent offenders. And because the force that he was assembling included men who were not sworn peace officers, it also required a proper understanding of the powers available under the law to ordinary citizens to bring felons to justice. The two long passages of the *Enquiry* in which Fielding discusses these issues – and in which he developed a defence of thief-taking and an analysis of the right of the ordinary citizen to make arrests – bear fundamentally on his efforts to establish a police presence and police authority at Bow Street.[6]

One other issue turned out to be crucial: how were his men to be supported? If they were going to devote time to the business of thief-catching they would have to be paid in some way: it had to be made 'worth their while', Fielding said, 'to apply themselves entirely to the apprehending Robbers ... .'[7] Occasional parliamentary or private rewards could not be counted on to sustain a stable force of half a dozen men, not to speak of the administrative and other miscellaneous staff that the Bow Street office required. When he published his *Enquiry in 1751*, Fielding had not as yet devised a way of financing the Bow Street office and his experiment, as a consequence, came close to failing.[8] When an opportunity arose he was thus eager to suggest to the government an alternative way of supporting his officers and a much cheaper way of encouraging effective prosecutions than through massive proclamation rewards.[9]

The decisive initiative came in the fall of 1753 as violent offences in and around London continued at such levels that the government was desperate to find a solution. The Pelham administration was clearly reluctant to renew the £100 supplementary reward for the conviction of robbers in London, almost certainly for the reasons that had led them to bring it to a temporary end in 1745: the corruption it encouraged, and the significant and unpredictable costs involved. During the two

---

[6]   Ibid, pp. 145–54.
[7]   Huntington Library: HM 11617, 'Memorial' written by Fielding in late 1753 or early 1754.
[8]   Ibid.
[9]   Fielding continued to argue, nonetheless, that the basic state rewards – those established by Parliament – were not distributed in a way that was fair to his men (National Archives/Public Record Office, London [hereafter NA], SP 36/125, ff. 23, 91). Asked for his advice, the Attorney General supported the practice that had developed over the first half of the century by which those who provided information or who played any role at all in the taking, prosecution, and conviction of the offender had some entitlement to a share in the reward. The case and Attorney General Ryder's answers are at NA, SP 36/153, ff. 10–11 (misdated 12 January 1753 for 1754).

years in which it had recently been in force, the proclamation reward had cost the Treasury £4,600 in 1750 and £6,500 in 1751 and the first half of 1752 at a time when the government was striving to reduce the massive national debt incurred in the recent war.[10] In any case, the drain on the Treasury had done little to stem the violence on the streets of London, and by the fall of 1753 ministers were desperate for new ideas and a new response that might do something to control the streets of the capital. They were willing to pay, but they wanted the costs to be more modest and to be known, not open-ended as they were under the system of proclamation rewards.

Asked for his advice, indeed for a new plan of policing, Fielding provided them with a scheme designed to encourage and support his Bow Street officers.[11] As an alternative to the proclamation rewards, he proposed that he be given a sum of money (beyond his own stipend) to be used for two purposes. One was to encourage rapid reporting of London offences to Bow Street by offering to pay for their immediate advertising, with descriptions of the offenders and of the goods taken; the advertisement would also include the offer of a reward, if the victim was willing to pay, as a way of encouraging information from pawnbrokers and others with knowledge of the offenders. The second was to support his officers with fees for services – with payments at his discretion for their expenses and their 'trouble' in going after and attempting to apprehend serious offenders and indeed carrying out other policing tasks for which no state or even private rewards would be available. This was at the heart of the Bow Street system. Without a staff of officers prepared to seek out and catch accused offenders, Bow Street would have remained simply a magistrates' court, no doubt an active magistrates' office in which the public would have been able to register their complaints and obtain warrants at most hours of the day, but just a magistrates' office nonetheless. And without the government subvention Fielding's men would have remained simply thief-takers for whom even state rewards would not have encouraged continuity and permanence of service. Payments from the office supported not only their efforts to catch robbers and other serious offenders, but more general policing efforts too; and such payments also made it possible for them to go on any duty within the metropolis or indeed anywhere in the country or even abroad. In the first year, Fielding was given £200 for these purposes above his own £400 stipend.[12] His men, though not themselves in receipt of an annual stipend, began for the first

---

[10] NA, SP 36/153, f. 16: 'An Account of what Sums have been paid by the Treasury in Rewards for Apprehending Highwaymen and Street Robbers for the Six last Years, Viz From the Year 1748 to the Year 1753, both inclusive'.

[11] Martin C. Battestin, *Henry Fielding: A Life* (London: Routledge, 1989) pp. 577–78.

[12] NA, SP 36/153, f. 16.

time to earn income from the office for their expenses and trouble – in addition to public and private rewards and payments from government departments.

Within months of his plan being accepted, ill-health forced Fielding to resign and leave the development of the thief-taking force to his half-brother, John, who was to remain at Bow Street for a quarter of a century, the chief magistrate of Westminster, indeed the pre-eminent magistrate in the metropolis, and the architect of a system of policing that made the detection and apprehension of offenders a central task of the peace-keeping establishment.

John Fielding and the emergence of the Bow Street office

The Treasury's support of the Fieldings' policing plan, increased to £600 by 1765, enabled them not only to reward officers for their work, but also to support the kind of clerical staff that was centrally important to their conception of the office, especially to John, who had been blind since he was nineteen and who was clearly dependent on records kept by others. He also had a passion for information and a strong belief in the importance of keeping track of known and suspected offenders. From the early years he charged one of the leading officers to keep an alphabetical 'Register of Robberies, Informations, Examinations, Convictions, suspicious Book, and Newgate Calendars'.[13] In having such detailed information collected – including a book in which rumours about men suspected of committing offences were recorded for future reference and one in which the outcomes of trials at the Old Bailey were collected so that offenders ordered to be transported could be monitored – Fielding was perhaps compensating for his blindness; it must certainly help to explain why he was thought to have had a prodigious memory for criminal suspects. But mainly it is testimony to his determination to carry out, and indeed to expand on, Henry Fielding's ideas about the need for effective prosecution if serious crime was to be confronted in London.[14]

Unfortunately, all of these records, and indeed all the records of the work of the Bow Street magistrates, were destroyed during the Gordon Riots in 1780, and those of subsequent decades were apparently abandoned when the magistrates' court moved into a new building in the 1880s. In 1792 the Middlesex Justices Act created seven additional 'public offices' on the model of Bow Street and

---

[13]   NA, T 1/449, f. 33, no. 15.

[14]   For John Fielding's ambitious efforts to create a national system of criminal information, see John Styles, 'Sir John Fielding and the problem of criminal investigation in Eighteenth-Century England', *Transactions of the Royal Historical Society*, 5th ser., 33 (1983) pp. 135–49; and *idem*, 'Print and Policing: Crime Advertising in Eighteenth-Century Provincial England', in Hay and Snyder, eds, *Policing and Prosecution*, pp. 55–111.

introduced an administrative system that has left a complete run of financial accounts.[15] But for the years before that we have to depend for knowledge of the Bow Street office on seven annual financial reports submitted by John Fielding to the Treasury in the 1750s and 1760s when he applied for renewal of his annual subvention, descriptions of the office by insiders (in 1777 and 1783), and fragmentary evidence from newspapers and trial records. Though we are left to speculate about some matters, this evidence reveals a good deal about the Bow Street officers and the main work they undertook in the four decades before the 1792 act changed the character of London policing.[16]

The basic structure of the office remained over that period roughly as it had emerged in the early years, certainly with respect to the officers who bore the brunt of the policing work. An account of its staff and work, probably written in the spring of 1783 by Sampson Wright, chief magistrate at Bow Street following John Fielding's death in 1780, suggests that the same administrative arrangements and modes of operation were in place as are revealed by the financial accounts of the 1750s and 1760s.[17] Six principal officers were 'attached' to the office and responded to the magistrates' orders and instructions, though they were not formally admitted to an established post nor paid a salary, not even an annual retainer. They maintained a certain freelance character, since they were able to take up work on their own behalf when someone came to the office to lodge a complaint. They performed a variety of duties with respect to the administration of the criminal law: investigating offences and making arrests in the metropolis and its environs, mainly, though not exclusively, felonies; responding to calls for help from magistrates around the country for the same purpose; gathering evidence; and occasionally undertaking more menial tasks such as serving summonses or distributing hand bills. Wright identifies another small group of a half dozen or so men who can also be discerned in the financial accounts of the 1750s and 1760s and who occasionally helped with the frontline work of apprehending suspected felons, but were more likely to be called upon to collect witnesses or take suspects back and forth between Bow Street and one of the gaols in which they were held

---

[15] Ruth Paley, 'The Middlesex Justices Act of 1792: its origins and effects', PhD, University of Reading, 1983. The post-1792 accounts are at NA, T 38/673.

[16] The office accounts are at NA, T 38/671 (a bound volume containing the accounts for 1756, 1757, 1759); T 1/387 (1758); T 1/414 (1762); T 1/449 (1766); T 1/454 (1767). Descriptions of the office are in the National Library of Ireland [hereafter NLI], Ms 15929 (3), dated 1777; and Ms 15930 (1). The latter is undated and unsigned, but internal evidence suggests that it was written by Sampson Wright in 1783. (I owe my knowledge of these documents to Simon Devereaux.) John Fielding also published two pamphlets on the origins of the office: *A Plan for Preventing Robberies* (1755) and *An Account of the Origin and Effects of a Police set on Foot ... in the Year 1753 ...* . (1758).

[17] NLI, Ms 15930 (1).

for trial. What these officers should be called, particularly the front-line men, was obviously something of a problem. Although both Henry and John Fielding claimed that their officers were either constables or ex-constables – in an effort to clothe them in a certain respectability and to distinguish them from the private thief-takers – this was far from being the case. Some were indeed constables of Westminster parishes, and their attachment to the office must have been crucial in certain situations, because while ordinary citizens could make arrests when acting under a magistrate's warrant (as Henry Fielding was at pains to make clear in his *Enquiry* in 1751), they did not have the authority to break down doors in search of accused offenders and similar powers that the oath of office conferred on constables. But the officers could not all have been referred to as Bow Street constables, and it seems likely that that is why they came to be called 'Runners'. There was a good deal of hesitation and circumlocution at first about what they should be called. John Fielding initially talked about them as 'real thief-takers', but some serious corruption scandals involving private thief-takers in the mid-1750s made that less than useful. As for the public, the Bow Street officers were generally known in the early years as 'Mr Fielding's men'; and they often simply said of themselves that they were 'attached' to the Bow Street office. By the late 1770s they were being called 'Runners', a term that had usually been used to denote men who escorted prisoners between magistrates' courts and gaols or who worked for bailiffs, conducting those arrested for debts to a 'sponging house'. It was used in that sense in 1755 about an assistant at Bow Street who was said to be 'a runner at Mr. Fielding's office to carry persons backwards and forwards' to and from Newgate.[18] Two decades later, it was beginning to acquire the meaning that it retained into the nineteenth century when it came to refer to the officers who did most of the heavy work of seeking out and apprehending suspected offenders. It was almost certainly not meant to be complimentary, but it stuck because it solved a problem by providing a name for a new kind of peace officer.

Although the office retained the same basic structure over its first four decades, there was a distinct change in the character of the officers who carried the main burden of work, or at least in their incomes and consequently in their willingness to make that work something of a career. In the early days in the office, before the government provided a subvention, and in John Fielding's first few years when the grant was no more than £400, it seems clear that there was insufficient money to provide even a small regular income for the six officers who did most of the serious policing work. This no doubt explains why in the first decade or so there was a good deal of turnover among the officers and why some of those who did stay on for a number of years were also employed in other areas of criminal administration. William Pentlow, one of Henry Fielding's most valuable early

---

[18]   *Old Bailey Proceedings* [hereafter OBP], April 1755 (#s179–81, Pryer et al).

recruits, was appointed, on Fielding's recommendation, as keeper of the New Prison in 1751, presumably to ensure that he could continue as a Bow Street officer, which he did through the 1750s.[19] Several others of the early Bow Street men were also prison officers – or were given such posts as a means of support when they proved to be useful to the work of the office.[20] Others in the early years were valuable because they had knowledge of the criminal world from having had close contact with it: Edward Wright, for example, kept an alehouse in the notorious Black Boy Alley (described as 'nothing but a den of thieves'[21]) and was a suspected receiver; Leonard Yates had been closely enough associated with pickpockets to have given evidence for the Crown in four cases at the Old Bailey.[22] At Bow Street he was first employed to distribute handbills, and in a job for which he was peculiarly suited – watching for pickpockets. Within a few months he was chasing highwaymen and footpads.[23] William Darvall, who was an active officer for a year or two in the late 1750s (until he shot and killed a man guarding a stage coach, having mistaken him for a highwayman) had himself been an active highwayman before being apprehended by Bow Street men and turning King's evidence to convict his accomplice. Within months he too was working on the other side of the law.[24] There was some stability in the office in the 1750s, but also a great deal of turnover. Few of the men recorded as receiving payments for some form of activity in 1757, for example – the first year in which they are named in Fielding's financial accounts – were still on the books in 1762, when the next account is available.[25] By the late 1760s and in the 1770s and subsequent decades, continuity among the Bow Street officers was much more striking, as the office became better known, more work came their way, and as other resources and thus incomes increased. Sampson Wright said in 1783 that the Runners had been 'enabled to procure a very comfortable Livelihood with Reputation to themselves and Benefit to the Public'.[26] Their livelihood and reputation were almost certainly being enhanced in the 1780s by the increase in prosecutions (and thus in both

---

[19] Battestin, *Fielding*, pp. 511–12.

[20] They included three of Pentlow's turnkeys at the New Prison: Robert Saunders, Thomas Street and Edward Gaul. One of the officers of the Palace Court, William Norden, was also an active Bow Street man.

[21] OBP, April 1755 (#s179–81, Pryer et al).

[22] OBP, February–March and April 1757, #s 104, 105, 122, 164 (Gorman, Jones, Walker [twice, at successive sessions]).

[23] NA, T 1/387, pp. 1–5.

[24] Payments for the pursuit and capture of Darvall are scattered throughout the Bow Street accounts for 1757 (NA, T 1/671). His trial for murder is at OBP, April 1761 (#148, Darwell [*sic*] and Marsden); he was convicted of manslaughter.

[25] NA, T 1/671; T 1/ 414.

[26] NLI, Ms 15930 (1).

public and private rewards) following the conclusion of the American war, as well perhaps by their more frequent engagement in significant provincial criminal cases as a result of the broadening contact and the increased flow of information between Bow Street and magistrates outside London.[27] Some of the Bow Street men also began to work regularly for major institutions like the Bank of England and, following George III's first illness in 1788 and the threats on his life in the 1790s, Bow Street officers were being paid to guard him and other members of the royal family. Their names became well known to the public through the newspapers and through their appearances as witnesses at the Old Bailey, and by the length of tenure in the office of so many of them. Long careers became the norm in the last three decades of the eighteenth century. Several of the men whose work can be documented in the financial accounts of 1766 and 1767 remained active in the 1770s and some into the 1780s, including John Heley (until 1778), William Haliburton (1782), and John Noakes who retired in 1785, after a 28-year career. They were joined and gradually replaced in the 1770s and 1780s by a new group of active men, some of whom were to serve well into the next century. They included most notably John Clarke (1771?–1790?), Nicholas Bond, who was active by 1771 and who was to become one of the three Bow Street magistrates by 1786, Charles Jealous (1774–94), Moses Morant (1776–93), Thomas Carpmeal (1779–1808), Patrick McManus (1781–1816), John Townsend (1784–1832) and John Sayer (1784(?)–1832).

The Runners at work

With respect to their work in the early decades of the office, the most active men were sent on a variety of policing tasks by the Fieldings. They investigated a range of offences, not all of which were likely to produce a statutory reward, and from time to time performed more routine tasks like distributing handbills about particular offences or taking suspects to and from Newgate and other prisons. In their more private capacities, they also frequently responded to requests for help from victims of offences of all kinds. Their work was never to be restricted simply to the most serious offences or to those for which statutory rewards had been created. But whenever there was concern about rising levels of crime in London,

---

[27]   Peter King has found that six Bow Street officers were involved in the conviction of felons at the Essex assizes between 1783 and 1787 (Peter King, *Crime, Justice, and Discretion in England 1740–1820* (Oxford University Press, 2000). The work of the Bow Street Runners outside the metropolis is being investigated by David Cox, ' "A certain share of low cunning": the provincial activities of Bow Street principal officers 1792–1839', PhD, University of Lancaster, in progress.

the balance of their work moved decidedly towards dealing with felons, most especially those who threatened harm to their victims. In the early years of the office, this involved a certain amount of preventive patrolling in and around the metropolis. The office budget could not, however, sustain the heavy drain on the funds that sustained patrolling required. The Bow Street men continued to mount short-term patrols over several days and nights looking for particular offenders, but efforts to institute permanent patrolling on the streets and highways from the office in the 1760s failed for want of funds. For the most part, the Runners went after robbers and other suspected felons once an offence had been reported to the office. John Fielding's account to the Treasury in 1767 of the way he had spent the £600 subvention over the previous year (the last such account that survives before the Middlesex Justices Act of 1792 introduced a new financial system) reveals that about 70 per cent of the budget was devoted to the central task of searching out highwaymen, footpads, to a lesser extent shoplifters, gangs who stole from coaches, and on occasion murderers.[28]

Bow Street's involvement in a case – in a robbery or any other criminal offence – generally began with the arrival of the victim in the office or a messenger bringing news of an event. The allegations made and, if possible, descriptions of the offenders, were recorded. The Fieldings encouraged such reporting by rewarding the messenger (a shilling became a standard amount) and by paying for the advertisement that would appear in the following day's newspapers, sometimes in more than one paper, but most often in the *Public Advertiser*, the successor to the *Daily Advertiser*. John Fielding believed strongly in the importance of the rapid dispersal of information – in the metropolis and indeed throughout the country – if goods were going to be found and offenders apprehended. Frequently a handbill would be printed even ahead of advertisements and be distributed to pawnbrokers and other likely places by some of the Bow Street men.

In cases of robbery or other serious offences the Runners commonly became engaged as soon as a report of an offence reached the office, especially if a victim could supply descriptions of the suspects and clues as to where they might be found. They would set out to broadcast information about the offence and to tap their most promising sources. In replying to Lord Hardwicke's inquiry in 1783 about how the office was trying to discover who had broken into and stolen from Lord Grantham's house in Whitehall, Sampson Wright, Fielding's successor as chief magistrate, made it clear that their efforts to detect and apprehend such offenders depended on the collection and organising of information. He told Hardwicke that

---

[28] NA, T 1/454. I analyse this account in greater detail in my forthcoming study, provisionally entitled *The First English Detectives: the Rise and Fall of the Bow Street Runners*.

Hand Bills, containing a Description of the several things stolen, have been delivered at all the Pawnbrokers, Silversmiths, and other Shops, where the Property taken is, from the Nature of it, likely to be disposed of; and Advertisements, offering His majesty's pardon to any One of the Offenders who will surrender and give an Account of his Accomplices, have been published in the Gazette and Daily Papers, and every other Step taken that appeared likely to produce Information; but, I am sorry to say, without Success.

Some Persons who were violently suspected of the Robbery have been taken up and examined in hopes of their making Discovery, and have been committed and kept in Prison as long as the Law would justify, and for want of sufficient Evidence to authorise their further Confinement have been set at large ... .[29]

To make their appeal for information as speedy as possible, the office kept up-to-date lists of pawnbrokers, silversmiths, and 'Cloaths Shops' in order to deliver handbills to them.[30] The offer of a royal pardon to entice one of the offenders to turn king's evidence and betray his accomplices, would almost certainly be understood in a case like burglary to be in addition to a share of the parliamentary reward, which, depending on the numbers convicted, could be very large. Beyond that, the Runners had a good deal of information in their records about people they suspected of committing offences and of those who had been charged but escaped conviction and punishment. The office kept track of the 'Night-houses and disorderly Houses to which Offenders generally resort', along with lists of known and suspected offenders,[31] and in the Grantham case the Runners had rounded up some of these men, committed them for the three days the law allowed, and no doubt tried to induce one of them to confess. What Wright did not say in his letter to Hardwicke was that the Runners were almost certainly hoping to get a lead from some of the people they paid to pass on information and rumours about recent offences.

Some accused offenders seem to have been arrested because they were in the book as suspects to be watched, if not actually in the records collected at Bow Street then in the officers' shared memory and experience. The most useful information from which the Bow Street officers built up their knowledge of offenders and criminal associations came from informers – people in a position to overhear talk about offences committed or planned. That kind of information was acquired piece by piece from those willing to cooperate with police officers for a price, passing on gossip and their more direct knowledge of offences. There can be no doubt that informers were an indispensable weapon, especially against

---

[29]   British Library, Additional MS 35621, f. 229.
[30]   NLI, Ms 15929 (3).
[31]   NLI, Ms 15929 (3); Ms 15930 (1).

highwaymen, street robbers, burglars and gangs of other serious offenders, indeed perhaps the Runners' most important weapon.

How many informers – snitches, or 'noses' – were in the pay of Bow Street officers is impossible to document. But that they were crucial to their work of detecting and apprehending the most serious offenders, indeed offenders of all kinds, is certain. Connections between them were largely established and maintained in the alehouses and taverns in the crowded and dangerous sections of town, especially in pubs like the Nag's Head, the flash houses that were the common resort of men who engaged in theft and robbery and who were likely to talk about it, even to brag and boast about their exploits, in the only centres of sociability available to them. Some of the officers active in the 1780s gave evidence about their use of informers to the 1816 and 1817 Commons committees investigating the police of the metropolis. They all agreed that informers and the flash houses they gathered in were crucial to their work. A visit to a notorious house might turn up someone they had been looking for, or they might pick up a scrap of intelligence over a drink and a chat with the keeper or a group of patrons. Such houses were indispensable, they said, in maintaining contact with men willing to earn a little by passing information on to them. One of the Bow Street men, Samuel Taunton, told the committee that 'thieves are a set of men who are apt to talk and open their minds a little to each other; and if we have any body that we can obtain information from, it is from conversations at those times'.[32] Such talk, passed on to Runners who could match it to reports of offences recently committed, made robbers vulnerable, and perhaps helps to explain why, not infrequently, arrests were made within days, even hours, of a complaint received at Bow Street.

Important as they were, informers must have been responsible, however, for the detection and apprehension of only a portion of the offenders prosecuted by the Bow Street police officers. Robbery and other offences like housebreaking that threatened violence and were thought to be especially serious for this reason loomed large in the work of the Runners, but they also went after shoplifters and pickpockets and minor thieves of all kinds, few of whom are likely to have talked about their offences in the way robbers were prone to do, or to have fallen under the gaze of the sorts of informers with whom the Bow Street men had regular contact. Indeed, that must have been true of the wide range of other offences that they were sent to look into by the magistrates or for which they were engaged by private prosecutors. Investigating offences about which no inside information was

---

[32] *First and Second Reports from the Committee on the State of the Police of the Metropolis* 1817, vol. VII, pp. 233 and 484 (In Irish University Press series of British Parliamentary Papers, *Crime and Punishment: Police*, 4 vols [Shannon, 1969] vol. 2) *Second Report*, p. 393.

forthcoming and in which advertisements produced no leads, required an effort to turn up evidence from pawnbrokers and other dealers who might have taken in stolen goods, or to uncover witnesses who could help to identify and locate suspects. It was rarely disclosed at the pretrial hearing or at the Old Bailey how the Runners found witnesses, how they persuaded them to give them crucial evidence and then testify in court. Their experience and knowledge of the taverns and night houses in the right parts of town provided leads, and one can only speculate that their threats of prosecution as an accomplice induced some people to talk, and the temptations of a reward others. The general public knowledge that the Runners were active investigators may in itself have induced some witnesses to come forward. There is abundant evidence in the Old Bailey trial accounts that the Bow Street office was known as a place where people could go who were inclined to report their suspicions, for whatever reason – out of fear or greed or simply a sense of civic duty.

With experience, the Runners developed useful detective skills, rudimentary no doubt in modern terms, but much more effective than any group of officials charged with policing duties had ever brought to bear on London crime. They were full-time policemen, some of them by the late eighteenth century with decades of experience of investigating crimes and chasing suspects across the metropolis and indeed across the country. They must have acquired a considerable knowledge of the topography of crime in the capital as well as of the forms and characteristics of the offences they dealt with day in and day out. Several developed expertise in some areas – if only in examining crimes scenes and interrogating witnesses. William Garrow made a joke in court about Charles Jealous's ability to tell the difference between city and country dirt on a highwayman's boots and also of his claim to be able to remember faces and conversations at long remove, but his doing so nonetheless speaks to Jealous's reputation, or at least his own claims, as an investigator.[33] Some Runners brought expertise to the job. It was an undoubted benefit to the Bow Street policing of coining in the 1770s and 1780s that the man who led the raids in those decades, John Clarke, had apprenticed to a silversmith or silver-canehead maker and knew about dies and stamps and the tools and processes involved in metalwork in general. He had been employed by the Mint to track down coining operations even before he became a Runner. Like other Runners who took up private work or work for government departments, he continued to be 'employed by the Mint', as he said in court on several occasions, used by them as an organiser of raids on coiners and an expert witness at trials.[34] He brought to

---

[33]   OBP, December 1783 (#2, Roberts).

[34]   He said at the Old Bailey in 1782 that he had been 'employed for the Mint thirteen years' (OBP, January 1782 [#100–3 John Morgan, et al.], that is since about 1769). His ongoing connection with the Mint was confirmed in a 1786 uttering case when a

coining cases, in particular, an ability to manage the collection of evidence and to speak about it in court with the kind of authority that made such prosecutions more effective than they otherwise might have been – which helps to explain why Clarke appeared at the Old Bailey in about half the coining cases between 1771 and 1793, and why in the cases in which he gave evidence the conviction rate was 82 per cent as against a rate of 40 per cent in those in which he did not testify.

In the 1770s and 1780s, the Runners appeared regularly in the witness box at the Old Bailey giving evidence for the prosecution. Being frequently in court and having to deal with the aggressive questioning of defence counsel must have developed their sense of the kind of evidence that was useful in court and thus what to look for in investigating offences. I presume that this is what Sampson Wright meant when he said in 1783 that the Runners' 'Experience and Knowledge of the Law of Evidence' made them 'ten times more useful than the [parish] Constable ever can be' when it came to catching and prosecuting felons.[35] Undoubtedly, he had in mind not only the kind of specialised expertise that John Clarke brought to coining cases, but more general skills, deriving mainly from experience – skills in examining crime locations, finding and interviewing witnesses, and checking alibis more carefully and systematically than had been done in the past. These were skills acquired mainly by experience, from a commitment to solving crimes and devoting time to it, and, as Sampson Wright also said, 'by acting and conversing with those of long Practice'.[36]

Conclusion

What effect the presentation of prosecution evidence by these more professional witnesses had on the character of trials at the Old Bailey is an issue I will have to leave for another occasion. Here we might simply speculate that juries may have come to expect more substance and detail in the evidence of witnesses who were appearing in trials in virtually every session by the 1780s. The jurymen were themselves experienced and sensitive to the bearing and consequences of evidence in particular circumstances, given the complexity of the law and the range of their own discretion. Two sets of jurors heard all the trials of the accused from Middlesex, and twelve men typically sat on all the cases from the City of London.

Clerkenwell magistrate to whom it had been initially reported by an informer sent him to the Mint Solicitor, Vernon, who in turn sent him to Clarke. The latter used the informer to trap the suspect into committing the offence again, made the arrest, and managed the prosecution (OBP, April 1786 [#425, Thomas Bassett]).

[35] NLI, Ms 15930 (1).
[36] NLI, Ms 15930 (1).

Each juror not only heard dozens of cases in a matter of a few days, but many of them returned to serve again at future sessions several times over.[37] They must have become familiar with the Runners. Whether they trusted their evidence more than say that of a parish constable making a very occasional appearance is impossible to say. Defence counsel certainly thought that they could undermine the Runners' credibility as witnesses by reminding juries about the bias that rewards might introduce in cases in which parliamentary rewards would be paid to those involved in the prosecution if the defendant were convicted. But that was countered by their growing respectability. The jurors knew that they were active and knowledgeable investigators – as a foreman revealed when, at a burglary trial, he asked one of the Runners if they had examined the crowbar they had taken from a defendant's house to see if it matched marks on the door frame of the house that had been broken into.[38] That kind of investigation was expected of them, part of the persuasion that they possessed skill and special knowledge. It was presumably those assumed qualities and their experience – and perhaps their courage – that made the Runners attractive to the dozens of provincial magistrates, government departments, and private victims who called on them to investigate crimes in order to get their stolen property returned and to deter future offenders. Their frequent appearances at the Old Bailey giving evidence for the prosecution may also have had an important influence on the remarkable increase in the number of defendants who decided in the 1780s that it would be prudent to seek the assistance of counsel. It seems likely that the sudden spurt in the engagement of lawyers on the defence side was a consequence of a change in the effectiveness of prosecutions and a consequent imbalance in the courtroom. If that had been the case, the more frequent appearance of Bow Street men in the witness box may have been at least part of the reason.[39]

It is worth reflecting, in conclusion, on the place of the Runners – and the place of the work of detection and pursuit, apprehension and prosecution – in the changes taking place in London policing in the late eighteenth and early nineteenth centuries, in particular when the initiative that began in Bow Street in the 1750s was broadened by an act in 1792 that created seven police offices on the model of Bow Street, each presided over by paid magistrates and each with a group of full-time, paid constables.[40] These developments have yet to find their place in the

---

[37] For jurors at the Old Bailey and for trial procedure more generally, see Beattie, *Policing and Punishment*, pp. 259–77; John H. Langbein, *The Origins of Adversary Criminal Trial* (Oxford University Press, 2003).

[38] He hadn't. OBP, April 1785 (#430, William Harding).

[39] For defence counsel, see Langbein, *Origins of Adversary Criminal Trial*, ch. 5; Allyson N. May, *The Bar and the Old Bailey, 1750–1850* (Chapel Hill: University of North Carolina Press, 2003).

[40] Sir Leon Radzinowicz, *A History of English Criminal Law and its Administration*

modern history of London policing perhaps because they seem to have had a separate and relatively short-term existence and because, as I suggested at the beginning, they played little part in the development that has been at the centre of policing history – the creation of the Metropolitan Police by Robert Peel in 1829. That force was based on the night watch and constabulary, both of which had undergone considerable changes over the course of the eighteenth century.[41] The New Police also took up the policing tasks that had been at the centre of the work of the watchmen and constables and that amounted to a commitment to the prevention of crime through surveillance, through a constant and unremitting watch. Detection and prosecution played no part in the policing schemes devised by the new commissioners of the Metropolitan Police in 1829. The constables in the seven public offices created in 1792 were absorbed into the new force. The Bow Street men were not. They remained briefly as rivals but were disbanded ten years later.

It seems clear that so long as policing history in the eighteenth century is conceived as a single reform narrative centred on 1829, the Runners will always remain outside the story – an interesting, curious, but essentially fringe subject. But for eighty years by then they had in fact played a crucial role in the policing of London and thus it seems to me necessary to recognise that two parallel policing practices developed in the eighteenth century. The Runners need to be seen not as a failed attempt to create 1829, but as the outcome of a process that began in the late seventeenth century as a response to particular policing problems that were dominant then and remained dominant for more than a century.

They were the outcome of concern about the levels of violent crime that could not be discouraged by increasing penal severity: robbery and burglary were already subject to capital punishment. Despite various suggestions of ways to make capital punishment more gruesome and thus more terrifying, the only real strategy available to the authorities was to manipulate the number of people being hanged by managing the incidence of pardon – a matter that had been turned over to the cabinet in the 1690s. That had limited efficacy. Thus the determination from the late seventeenth century to catch, convict and punish more of the serious offenders; and thus the rewards for conviction. The Bow Street Runners were a product of those beliefs in the necessity of detective policing and more effective prosecution. Their success in their own time explains why in 1792 seven similar police offices were created in the metropolis (with paid magistrates and detective constables) in

---

from 1750, 4 vols (London: Stevens, 1948–68) iii, chapter 5; Paley, 'The Middlesex Justices Act of 1792'.

[41] Reynolds, *Before the Bobbies*; Ruth Paley, '"An Imperfect, Inadequate, and Wretched System"? Policing London before Peel', *Criminal Justice History*, 10 (1989) pp. 95–130.

which all criminal prosecutions were concentrated. This statute, coming exactly a hundred years after the first reward statute, was the culmination of one of the two streams of policing developments in eighteenth-century London.

Why the belief in the necessity of detection collapsed so quickly in the subsequent thirty years and found no place in the so-called New Police in 1829 is an important question – but a question for another occasion.

Chapter Two

Tips, Traps and Tropes: Catching Thieves in Post-Revolutionary Paris

Howard G. Brown

Si les brigands, à l'approche de l'hiver, redoublent d'audace, le bureau central saura aussi redoubler d'énergie et de surveillance, et aidé par le concours des bons citoyens, il ne négligera rien pour assurer la tranquillité publique et garantir la sûreté des personnes et des propriétés.[1]

L'Ami des lois, 23 vendémiaire VIII (15 October 1799)

A crude *Almanach national de l'an IX* (1800–1) printed at Basel and sold throughout the Helvetic Republic contained a variety of items ranging from a soldier's *bon mot* in the sixteenth century to an excerpt from Mungo Park's account of his voyage to the interior of Africa. Among these sundry items was the story of a gruesome killing in faraway Paris in the autumn of 1799. According to the *Almanach*, three well-dressed men entered a jewelry shop just after the owner left on an errand. One of the men distracted the lone clerk, while the other two carefully scrutinised the doors, windows, and shutters. However, the owner's young son had observed their odd behavior and later reported it to his father. Certain that a robbery was planned for that night, the jeweller persuaded several friends to lie in wait inside the shop. As expected, the three suspicious men, now accompanied by a fourth man, returned to the jewelry store at midnight. One of them managed to open a shutter, reach through the bars and unlatch a window. The men inside suddenly seized his arm and he blurted out, *Je suis pris* (I've been nicked). Without hesitation, an accomplice drew a large knife and lopped off the man's head. This shocking scene is depicted in a wood-block print (see illustration 2.1). In the background is a slumping, headless body with one arm stuck in a barred window and streams of blood spurting from the neck. In the foreground are three

---

[1]   If brigands increase their audacity at the approach of winter, the Bureau Central will know how to increase its energy and surveillance, and aided by the support of good citizens, will neglect nothing in order to ensure public tranquility and guarantee the safety of persons and property.

Illustration 2.1   Representation of a singular and very remarkable killing. *Almanach national de l'an IX* (1800).

men running up the street with one of them carrying the head. The jeweller and his friends tried to track the thieves by following the trail of blood, but lost them in the twisted streets and narrow alleys of Paris. But the story does not end there. The police spent several days on the case without producing any leads. Without a head, the captured corpse could not be identified, and his pockets were devoid of clues. Several days later, however, a fisherman on the Seine caught the head in his nets and took it to police headquarters. There a clerk in the Bureau Central recognised the head and said that it belonged to a man who was said to have left town a few days earlier to return to southern France. The clerk even knew the man's Parisian address. Supplied with this information, agents of the Bureau Central went directly to the victim's appartment where they found his accomplices dividing up the contents among themselves. The robbers were promptly arrested and duly executed.[2]

This report of a 'singular and very remarkable killing' received the same prominence in the Swiss *Almanach* as stories on Pope Pius VI dying in French captivity at Valence and First Consul Bonaparte deftly escaping Austrian capture while traversing the Alps. Why did 'The Horrible Murder' become one of the *Almanach*'s three feature stories of the year? What about this story resonated with readers who lived so far, physically and culturally, from the great French metropolis? It would appear that bringing together ruthless criminals and successful police work via the trope of beheading, all in post-revolutionary Paris, was irresistible. It struck too many chords to be ignored. Whether the story was true or not, it captured both the extraordinary level of violent crime at the time and the emergence of a popular image of police efficiency. Thus, the publication of this item embodied an important cultural moment in the history of police work in France.

In order to understand the full resonance of this story, in order to get it, not as a joke, but as an important cultural signifier, we need to explore a variety of issues ranging from banditry to bureaucracy. By the time we return to the *Almanach national de l'an IX* at the end of this chapter, it should be apparent that it was during the last years of the First Republic that a modern image of police detection first emerged. As we will see, this story represents the turning point in the shift from outlaw hero to detective hero, the point at which criminals still strove for the picaresque, but were too frightening to be the subject of heroic treatment, and the police began to achieve an admirable new efficiency, but without emerging as individual heroes. This shift is not to be found either solely in the realm of quotidien police practices, or principally in the arena of literary representations; rather, it is the interplay of these two, the relationship between practices and perceptions, that defined a new era.

---

2   Archives Nationales (hereafter AN) F[7] 7805, d. 129, p. 40.

Given the unusual structure of this article, it is worth providing a quick overview of its component parts. First, a brief examination of the two most prominent figures in the history of policing in the early nineteenth century, Fouché and Vidocq, will reveal the distortions that their self-representations have introduced into scholarly interpretations. Thereafter, the demise of a colourful bandit and his brutal associates provides a case study in the interaction between novel aspects of policing and altered public perceptions. Such an approach has the advantage of combining actual police work with the role of newspaper coverage in shaping perceptions. This knowledge, once integrated with key features of 'The Horrible Murder', exposes the central tropes that emerged around cops and robbers at the turn of the century. Finally, an analogy to changes in the medical profession in France offers a useful context in which to understand the changed nature and perception of police work.

In the shadows of Fouché and Vidocq

Two figures cast large shadows over the history of policing in the early nineteenth century – Joseph Fouché and Eugène-François Vidocq. The first incarnates the awesome effectiveness of political policing under Napoleon; the second established his renown as a career detective. The tendency to view policing through the lenses of Fouché and Vidocq has distorted perceptions of police detection, both in their own day and ever since. Moreover, the change in perspective from Fouché, the master of political policing, to Vidocq, the master of criminal detection, tends to miss the most significant changes that overtook ordinary policing during the same years.[3]

Historians have long been in thrall to the 'myth of Fouché' as the machiavellian master of an all-powerful imperial police with a tentacular network of spies and informants. This image is as much the work of nineteenth-century novelists and memorists as it is of historians.[4] Whatever the origins, it has kept the focus on the great man at the expense of his many minions.[5] In the three years following his

---

[3]   Clive Emsley, *Policing and its Context, 1750–1870* (London: Macmillan, 1983) is a notable exception; however, as a wide-ranging comparative study it is necessarily brief on actual police practices.

[4]   Jean Tulard, 'Le mythe de Fouché', in Jacques Aubert et al., *L'État et sa police en France (1789–1914)* (Geneva: Droz, 1979) pp. 27–34. Typical of the distortions raised by an excessive focus on Fouché is Henry Buisson, *La police: son histoire* (2nd ed. Vichy: Wallon, 1950).

[5]   Note the emphasis in this summary statement by Ernest d'Hauterive in *Napoléon et sa police* (Paris: Flammarion, 1943) p. 10: 'He gave [the police] a reputation for extraordinary perspicacity and this reputation constituted part of its power, on its equalling a

appointment as Minister of General Police in the summer of 1799, Fouché's reputation for police efficiency grew so rapidly that he appeared to threaten Bonaparte's hold on power. Therefore, when the First Consul transformed the regime into a personal dictatorship in the summer of 1802, he removed Fouché from power by disbanding the entire police ministry. After a two-year hiatus, during which the Cadoudal-Pichegru conspiracy revealed the regime's continuing vulnerability, the newly proclaimed Emperor restored both Fouché and the Ministry of General Police in July 1804. The next six years as minister only served to embellish his reputation as the consumate policeman. Scholarly attention has remained disproportionately distracted by the drama of the *haute police*.[6] Thus, the myth of Fouché is largely based on his success against the murky world of political opposition and cloak-and-dagger conspiracies.

Since Fouché's reputation grew out of his success against political opposition, and since this was established during his first stint as minister, it is worth noting the methods that led to his greatest successes. These do not reflect well on the minister and indicate the dubious tactics employed by the police at the time. The much exaggerated Jacobin 'conspiracy of daggers' was given a forceps birth by *agents provocateurs* and the related 'Chevalier plot' was hatched with a police spy on the inside. In another famous case, Fouché managed to free the kidnapped Senator Clément de Ris simply by using the Comte de Bourmont as an intermediary to arrange favourable terms with the kidnappers. This became 'une ténébreuse affaire' only because Bourmont was in no position to explain his role and Fouché insisted on staging a dramatic, but fake, rescue of the senator in order to burnish his reputation as a master policeman.[7] Fouché's greatest triumph came when the police unravelled the conspiracy to blow up Bonaparte on Christmas Eve 1800. However, his glory was due largely to having insisted from the start that it had been the work of royalists. The crime itself was solved solely by the meticulous work of the prefecture of police.[8] None of these unflattering facts were

---

lot of agents'.

[6] See Louis Madelin, *Fouché, 1759–1820*, 2 vols (Paris : Plon et Nourit, 1901); Hubert Cole, *Fouché: the Unprincipled Patriot* (London: Eyre and Spottiswoode, 1971); Pierre-Marie Desmarest, *Quinze ans de haute police sous le consulat et l'empire*, edited by Léonce Grasilier (Paris, 1900).

[7] Gustave Gautherot, *Gentilhomme de grand chemin: le maréchal de Bourmont (1773–1846) d'après ses papiers inédits* (Paris : Presses Universitaires de France, 1926) pp. 135–40; Honoré de Balzac, *Une ténébreuse affaire* (1843), Rose Fortassier, ed, (Paris, 1999) pp. 11–12, insists that Fouché arranged the kidnapping in the first place.

[8] For an introduction to the actual resolution of these various plots, see Henri Gaubert, *Conspirateurs au temps de Napoléon 1er* (Paris: Flammarion, 1962) pp. 36–121. See also Jean Rigotard, *La police parisienne de Napoléon: la préfecture de police* (Paris : Tallandier, 1990) pp. 73–94, who notes that the only information Fouché had contributed to the investigation proved useless.

allowed to become public at the time. Thus, Fouché, like Napoleon himself, was able to fashion a personal myth based on the most convincing evidence of all, success itself, however it was achieved.

As a result of the many intrigues woven around the political police, far less attention has been paid to either the popular perceptions or actual practices of ordinary policing in the age of Napoleon. It is not until the emergence of Eugène-François Vidocq, appointed head of a new *brigade de sûreté* in 1812, that historians of the period begin to take an interest in the methods of fighting ordinary crime.[9] As the lead character suddenly changes, so too does the angle of vision. The necessary context shifts from the intrigues of political policing to the heroics of criminal detection. The *Mémoires de Vidocq* (published in 1828–29) has been seen as the bridge between the traditional literature of roguery stretching back to the Spanish *picaro* and the modern crime novel usually centred on a brilliant detective.[10] The first two volumes of the *Mémoires* trace the criminal adventures of Vidocq, a real-life thief and forger whose repeated escapes from prison and the *bagne* made him famous in the underworld. Tired of being relentlessly on the run from the authorities, he decided to offer his services to the Prefecture of Police as a prison informant. The last two volumes recount his role in helping to found the *brigade de sûreté* in 1812 and his numerous triumphs while director of this ever-expanding squad until his ouster fifteen years later. The *Mémoires de Vidocq* were immediate best-sellers. Having acquired almost instant fame and fortune, he worked hard to keep his name in the public eye by publishing numerous other works on the criminal world he knew so intimately.[11] Thus, Vidocq's publications took his remarkable conversion from unsuccessful recidivist criminal to successful thief catcher and elevated it to something with even greater appeal: the transformation of a sympathetic outlaw into a master detective. It is the literary element of this transformation that should be underscored. Vidocq's brilliant innovation was more in literary genre than in police techniques.

---

[9]   Vidocq began to agitate for the creation of an independent security force while employed as an *agent particulier* of the Prefecture of Police in 1811 (and may even have described himself as the *chef de sûreté* as part of his initiative), but an actual *brigade de sûreté* was not created until 1812. This has led to inconsistency in dating the birth of the detective branch later known simply as the *sûreté*. Compare Jean Savant, *La vie fabuleuse et authentique de Vidocq* (Paris: Hachette, 1950) pp. 160 and 168–69; Samuel Edwards, *The Vidocq Dossier: The Story of the World's First Detective* (Boston: Houghton Mifflin, 1977) pp. 46–49, and Jean Tulard, *Paris et son administration (1800–1830)* (Paris: Ville de Paris Commission des Travaux Historiques, 1976) pp. 149–51 and 178.

[10]   Frank W. Chandler, *The Literature of Roguery*, 2 vols (New York : Houghton, Mifflin and Co., 1907) ii. 524–28.

[11]   *Supplément des mémoires de Vidocq* (1830); *Les Voleurs: Physiologie de leurs moeurs et de leur language* (1837); *Éclaircissements donnés au commerce sur les manoeuvres captieuses des filous* (1840); *Quelques mots sur une question à l'ordre du jour* (1844); *Les vrais mystères de Paris* (1844); *Les chauffeurs du Nord* (1845–46).

Biographers of Vidocq rarely treat his publications with much skepticism, especially considering the role his ghost-writers are known to have played in fabricating various parts of the narrative.[12] Nonetheless, the *brigade de sûreté* is widely considered the first official detective bureau in European history; furthermore, Vidocq also formed the first private detective agency in France in 1833. However, Vidocq's many successes did not come from remarkable powers of logic and inductive reasoning nor from the development of new investigative techniques. In fact, there is very little 'detection' evident in Vidocq's writings. Usually he simply disguises himself as a criminal of one sort or another, spends time in various taverns where the crime is likely to be discussed, insinuates himself into the chief suspect's social circle, earns his confidence, weedles incriminating information out of him, then springs the trap and sends him to jail. If there is any genuine 'detection' involved, it is based on a thorough knowledge of the criminal world. In fact, this was also the key to his literary success. The monotony of describing numerous cases is alleviated not by the cleverness of the detective work, but by a myriad of realistic details about life among the 'dangerous classes' of proletarian Paris. It is this same insider's knowledge that filled his later publications. As Régis Messac has noted, there is very little about the methods of Vidocq that resembled those of Sherlock Holmes.[13]

Since the police practices described in Vidocq's memoirs apparently made him the first modern detective, it is worth pausing to consider the methods used to resolve his many cases. Apart from his rare talent for infiltrating criminal milieux, Vidocq's success in catching criminals was based on more pedestrian elements. Chief among these was extensive record keeping. The success of Vidocq's private detective agency owed a great deal to the voluminous files he had assembled during his time running the *brigade de sûreté*. By 1842, his agency had accumulated information on 30,000 crooks. This has been called the 'first step towards developing a system for the rapid identification and retrieval of information about criminals'.[14] In fact, however, it was simply a legacy of the

---

[12] Maurice Descombres wrote the first two volumes and L.F.J. L'Héritier the last two. The extent of their fictionalisation has never been subjected to much scrutiny, but it is known that L'Héritier borrowed entire passages from such works as Patrick Colqhoun, *Police of the Metropolis*, and simply transcribed names and places into French. See, Régis Messac, *Le 'detective novel' et l'influence de la pensée scientifique* (Paris: Bibliothèque de la Révue de littérature comparé, 1929) pp. 277–79. As for biographies, see especially Jean Savant, *La vie fabuleuse*, and Philip John Stead, *Vidocq: A Biography* (London: Staples, 1953).

[13] Messac, *Le 'detective novel'*, pp. 279–85.

[14] Cited in Paul Metzner, *Crescendo of the Virtuoso: Spectacle, Skill, and Self-Promotion in Paris during the Age of Revolution* (Berkeley, Cal.: University of California Press, 1998) p. 106.

mania for collecting individual data on suspects generated during the First Republic. For example, during his second ministry, Fouché developed his own specialised data base on *chouans* and brigands in western France, which he called a topographical and biographical 'dictionary'.[15] Equally important to Vidocq's success was visual memory, his ability to put a name to a face. Before fingerprinting, anthropometry, or the daguerreotype, the police of the early nineteenth century were forced to rely on verbal descriptions of suspects. These could be hopelessly vague and of little practical value unless the individual in question had unusual distinguishing characteristics. Even then, such descriptions were more useful in ruling out suspects than in actually picking one out of a crowd.[16] As one would expect from a master of disguises and criminal role-playing, Vidocq possessed remarkable powers of observation. He exploited this talent to the full by memorising faces and systematically associating them with the names in his files. He and his agents would regularly visit prisons in order to fix the identity of as many prisoners as possible for future reference.[17] Experience proved the efficacy of such methods. They did not, however, constitute a breakthrough in criminal detection.

In addition to massive record keeping and the deliberate cultivation of visual memory, Vidocq's success against crime relied upon a more extensive police force and the centralised coordination of law-enforcement officials. Elaborating on these elements would not have made very compelling reading, however, either for contemporaries or later historians. Hence their absence from his literary output and general neglect by subsequent scholars. Even his most serious biographers have done little to investigate the evolution of police practices in the early nineteenth century. Instead, they have succumbed to hagiographic interpretation of Vidocq's significance in the history of policing by accepting the claims he made for himself. This suggests that historians have been rather naive in accepting what is a milestone in the history of literature as a milestone in the history of policing.

Not only is the history of policing more prosaic, but so too is the history of public perceptions of policing. It did not take until the publication of Vidocq's memoirs for the public to begin to see the police in a new light. In other words, seeing Vidocq as the transition from outlaw hero to detective hero has an enduring power because it offers both a pleasing inverted symmetry and a well-defined

---

[15] See AN F^{7*} 2261–2270 and Madelin, *Fouché*, i, 495–96.

[16] The greatest utility of such verbal pen-portraits was for domestic passports. Here is a typical physical description, in this case of Barthélemy Ponsy of Gignac (Hérault): '1.77 mètres tall, light brown almost blond hair and eyebrows, fine forehead, blue eyes, aquiline nose, nice mouth, small and smiling, round chin, oval face, in general good looking, carrying himself well and swaying slightly when he walks'. Archives départementales de l'Hérault, L 6731*, 21 germinal VII.

[17] *Mémoires de Vidocq*, iii, 405.

historical turning point. But there are many indications that the most important changes in both public attitudes and police methods took place during the later years of the First Republic, while Vidocq was still a criminal.[18] It was the great crime wave at the turn of the century and the state's response to it that ultimately found expression in Vidocq's memoirs. Vidocq is given credit for being the first detective chief, but he was not really a detective at all. He simply personified the nature of the preventive system that emerged in the aftermath of the French Revolution, with its emphasis on penetrating the underworld, using entrapment, keeping extensive records, and coordinating police pursuit.

La bande à Baudoin

A close look at the demise of a single group of brigands operating around Paris during the Directory provides a window onto the real world of banditry and police prosecution and allows us to pay particular attention to the issues of public representation. It is evident from this case that crime and punishment gripped the public's imagination during the late 1790s. Thus, 'France's worst crime wave in modern times'[19] became the catalyst for a new perception of the police.

Young Louis Baudoin alias Fortin might have had a certain vulgar, popular appeal. He was a tall, handsome, prosperous looking fellow who cultivated the image of a flashy scofflaw. A garish tiger-skin cap adorned with tricolor ribbons, an aqua blue vest, and a hussard's sabre combined to give him a picaresque air. Rather than prowling the countryside on his own, Baudoin travelled *en famille*. He and his mistress rode in a stylish two-horse carriage accompanied by two enormous dogs. These mastiffs were often harnessed to a small cart bearing the couple's young son. Baudoin further amused onlookers by giving the boy handfuls of silver to finger as they rolled into town. The outlaw also cultivated his image with a verbal flare. When finally arrested in late 1799 and interrogated about why he had eluded the gendarmerie on a previous occasion, he impertinently replied, 'I escaped because I had a faster horse than they did'.[20] This would not be surprising. He had entered the cavalry before the Revolution under the name of Louis Fleury *cadet*, perhaps hoping to be taken as the lesser scion of a great family. Later, when he entered a new regiment, he changed his name to the romantic sounding Louis

---

[18] In fact, the irony may be that it was changes both in the efficacy of the police and popular attitudes towards it that persuaded Vidocq to join the other side.

[19] Gordon Wright, *Between the Guillotine and Liberty: Two Centuries of the Crime Problem in France* (Oxford University Press, 1983) p. 34.

[20] Archives de la Guerre (hereafter AG) C[18] 2, interrogation of Baudoin by the capitaine-rapporteur du 1er conseil de guerre de la 17e division militaire, 26 pluviôse VIII.

Delisle Damour. Finally, like tens of thousands of other young soldiers, Baudoin deserted the cavalry in 1795. He changed his name to Etienne Cholet. He changed it again, this time to Louis Fortin,[21] after becoming an itinerant horse merchant who did not always buy the horses he sold. A conviction for horse-thieving and an impressive escape from the jail at Châteaudun (Eure-et-Loire) consolidated his place in the world of crime. Once free again, Baudoin joined forces with other Normans who had gone from stealing horses to invading farmhouses.

Baudoin's self-presentation and career trajectory indicate that he had a romanticised image of himself as something of an outlaw hero. The genre was well established in eighteenth-century France by the literature on such bandits as Cartouche and Mandrin, and even by lesser figures such as Poulailler. These famous brigands of the *ancien régime* had become popular outlaw heroes celebrated in anonymous pamphlets, handbills, and chapbooks. Such men stood out from garden variety thieves and highwaymen by the force of their personalities and the scale of their activities. Louis-Dominique Cartouche (1693–1721) had captured the popular imagination with his bold effrontery, almost magical sleight-of-hand, and ability to organise hundreds of thieves into a coherent criminal network. The often humorous and always charming Louis Mandrin (1725–55) was likewise the 'captain' of an impressive criminal organisation. His audacity helped to turn extensive smuggling activities and raids on tax farmers into something of a regional rebellion. Finally, 'the famous Poulailler' (d. 1786), according to a broadsheet being hawked in Paris at the time of Baudoin's early exploits, had been the captain of a band of some 500 men and was believed by 'ignorant and vulgar folk' to have supernatural powers to elude the authorities. Perhaps more important, he was said to have stolen from the rich, aided the poor, and harmed no one in the process.[22] Although certain accounts emphasised the violence and brutality of these outlaws, most popular renditions simply made them picaresque anti-heroes. They appeared as sympathetic rogues with the cunning to outwit social superiors and invert the patterns of an unjust social order.[23] It is from this perspective that they became role models for the likes of Baudoin.

Baudoin had obvious charisma, but his potential popularity suffered when he got involved with other ex-soldiers and horse thieves whose real business was brigandage. It was no doubt his experience in battle together with his re-arrest and

---

[21] He was able to forge his own papers using an official *cachet* he had stolen and thus was guilty of much the same crime as Vidocq was sent to the *bagne* for committing.

[22] In fact, Poulailler (i.e. 'the poultry man') had a band of no more than five men and had only barely graduated from the theft of livestock to armed burglary when his career was cut short by the authorties. Julius R. Ruff, *Violence in Early Modern Europe 1500–1800* (Cambridge University Press, 2001) pp. 21–22 and 30; Richard Cobb, *Reactions to the French Revolution* (Oxford University Press, 1972) pp. 272–75.

[23] Metzner, *Crescendo of Virtuoso*, pp. 86–88.

escape from the gendarmerie in December 1797 that propelled him into the world of violent crime.[24] A few weeks after his second escape, Baudoin joined five other men in robbing the proprietor of the 'ferme de Folie' near St-Just in the prosperous plains of the Oise north of Paris.[25] This served as a fillip for him and his new-found friends to execute another, more violent, armed robbery a month later. One night in March 1798, two men pretended to be searching for deserters in order to gain entry into the large farmhouse of St-Rémy-l'Abbaye near Clermont (Oise). As soon as the door opened, Baudoin grabbed the guns from over the fireplace and cried out, 'To me, hussards!' Immediately, another ten armed men swarmed into the house and overpowered the men on hand. All the inhabitants were soon bound and blindfolded. The intruders proceeded to beat and torture the owner and his wife. In the growing custom of the day, known as *chauffage*, the bandits thrust their victims' feet into the burning hearth to get them to reveal their hidden cash and jewels. The robbers then gorged themselves on food and wine, smashed all the furniture and dishes, and finally raped the owner's wife and a domestic servant. The owner, Pierre-Antoine Pillon, later died of his injuries. His wife Vachette had her feet so badly burned that even a year later she could not make the one-day journey to Paris to testify against her assailants.[26]

Despite its gratuitous cruelty, such an assault on a rich republican purchaser of 'national properties' may have been broadly approved in parts of the West or the Midi where counter-revolutionaries and draft-dodgers made up the bulk of brigand bands. After all, the attack at St-Rémy-l'Abbaye appeared to have political overtones. The first man to burst into the farmhouse, young Louis Lamarre, claimed to be the bastard son of the late Duc de Choiseul, France's leading minister in the 1760s. 'As an émigré', Lamarre announced, 'he was forced to rob in order to live' and further observed 'that it was a good occupation'.[27] His claim apparently lacked substance, which makes his motives interestingly ambiguous. Was Lamarre trying to mask the gang's crime as royalist retribution against a prosperous *fermier* who supported the Revolution because he had profited from it? Or was Lamarre mocking aristocrats by playing on their notorious sexual license and perceived dishonesty? Either way, as a purported émigré, he painted himself as a victim of the revolution and thereby justified his depredations as so many blows

---

[24] AG C[18] 3, directeur de jury de Clermont (Oise) au capitaine–raporteur du 1er conseil de guerre de la 17e division militaire, 30 nivôse VIII. Immediately after his break from the gendarmerie, Baudoin began assembling his stylish transportion by stealing a horse and dog from an innkeeper at Petit-Crèvecoeur.

[25] AG C[18] 2, interrogation of Baudoin by Béhourt, JP du 11e municipalité de Paris, 12 pluviôse VIII.

[26] *Ami des lois*, 3 germinal VII; *Le Moniteur*, 3 germinal VII; AG J2 247, jugement du 5 ventôse VIII.

[27] AGC[18]2, 'procédure instruite contre François Boullanger [et al.]'.

against an iniquitous new regime. Thus, both Baudoin and Lamarre tried to create exculpatory personas for themselves in the eyes of the populace – Baudoin as a flamboyant outlaw hero in the eighteenth-century tradition, and Lamarre as first a social and then a political outcast, forced into a life of crime. In this sense, they assumed the twin faces of banditry in the wake of revolutionary upheaval.[28]

Other participants were less inclined to disguise the motives for their crimes. If they did project distinct identities, it was as pseudonymous characters in the vast underworld of itinerant trading, fenced goods, petty theft, and armed robbery. The most violent member of the band was a stalky cattle merchant named François Petit alias Nezel but better known as *le Petit Boucher*. One of his colleagues, a livestock trader named François Mariotte alias Gueroult, gained his criminal notoriety as *le Normand* or *le Petit Louis,* whereas the sometime clothing peddler François-Charles Lolivret was widely known as *le Gros François.* Men such as these not only found it prudent to have an alias to deflect law-enforcement officials, their acquisitions of *noms de guerre* indicated a certain status in the criminal community. And there is no doubt that Baudoin's associates had considerable notoriety by the time he became involved with them.[29] But it was not easy to carve out a distinctive identity as a bandit. France was swarming with them during the Directory and Consulate.

Thus, if Baudoin imagined himself as the stuff of popular legends, his choice of timing and criminal métier were not propitious. The *ancien régime* had seen its share of violent criminality. However, Baudoin lived at a time when the sheer number of brigands militated against any one of them acquiring more than a local reputation. Many scores, if not hundreds, were described, like Baudoin, as the 'terror of our district',[30] and yet they remained only regionally notorious. Moreover, banditry had become so pervasive that it cast doubt on the state's ability to stabilise a post-revolutionary social order. Under these conditions, the populace was far less inclined to transform gang leaders into heroes struggling against social

---

[28] On the relationship between political and criminal banditry, see especially Gwynne Lewis and Colin Lucas, *Beyond the Terror: Essays in French Regional and Social History* (Cambridge University Press, 1983) pp. 152–231.

[29] For example, Lolivret had been condemned to death *in absentia* in the Calvados in October 1793; then, under a false name, to 24 years in irons in the Orne in May 1794. After serving less than a year, he escaped from the *bagne* at Brest. Later, apparently without knowing his full criminal past, the court of the Calvados put him on trial for another farmhouse robbery. However, this time he escaped from the prison at Rouen in September 1796 before being convicted (*in absentia*, of course) and sentenced to eight years in irons. Mariotte had a similarly long list of convictions under at least two other pseudonyms. For these and many other details, see AG C^{18} 2, public prosecutor of the Seine-Inférieure to JP Béhourt, 25 floréal VI.

[30] Ibid, commissaire du gouvernement à Chateaudun (Eure-et-Loire) au capitaine-rapporteur du 1er conseil de guerre à Paris, 13 pluviôse VIII.

injustice. They may have remained the object of a morbid fascination, especially if they perpetrated their spectacular violence at a safe distance. What better way to experience a *frisson* of fear than to be in Basel when reading about criminals in Paris carrying off the severed head of their erstwhile accomplice? Although potential subjects were hardly in short supply, almost none of the common-law criminals, as opposed to the more political ones, became the material for picaresque fiction. On the contrary, the sheer numbers and bloody-minded violence of the bandits who ravaged the French countryside in the late 1790s, especially as explicitly political motives gradually gave way to criminal ones, seemed to discredit the idea of popular outlaw heroes, at least temporarily. It was this same phenomenon that opened the possibility for the police to become the subject of popular admiration.

Bandits and bureaucrats

It is instructive to follow the demise of Baudoin and his companions. Each of the stages in the unraveling of his 'band' reveals the changing nature of crime and responses to it at the turn of the century. When historians discuss the machinery of justice during the First Republic, they usually do so in terms of inept gendarmes, pusillanimous magistrates, sympathetic juries, and intimidated witnesses. Such an image ignores the rapid progress made in restoring law and order in the years 1797 to 1802. The handling of crime around the capital in these years illustrates this trend. Although banditry tends to thrive on the geographic and institutional periphery of society, the criminal chaos of the early Directory meant that proximity to the capital made little difference. The police of Paris even reported that brigands in the region put up notices promising a daily stipend of fifty livres to anyone who joined them.[31] Although this suggests an impressive organisation of criminal activity, the degree of cooperation between the various groups of *chauffeurs* operating in the Isle-de-France remains unclear. Certainly there was no single leader, no criminal master-mind such as Cartouche or Mandrin. By all standards of criminal organisation, the brigandage around Paris was largely inchoate. Brigand bands were both real and plentiful, but few were as large or as organised as republican officials believed them to be. Nonetheless, authorities in the region were afflicted with the same 'banditry psychosis' that prevailed in other parts of the country. This led them to see large criminal conspiracies where there were only loose affiliations. Such assumptions played a major part in the prosecution of the

---

[31] Report by Bureau central on 25 frimaire IV, in Adolphe Schmidt, *Tableaux de la Révolution française publiés sur les papiers inédits du département et de la police secrète de Paris*, 3 vols (Leipzig, 1867–70) ii, 546.

so-called 'bande d'Orgères' which operated in the *pays de Beauce* west of Paris. Now famous as the largest criminal organisation of the period, it was, in reality, a judicial amalgam of several disparate groups, each of which had a distinct nebula of especially intrepid malefactors. If one explores beyond the prosecution's sensationalist claims, it quickly becomes apparent that most of the criminals associated with this 'bande' were in fact undisciplined delinquents who came and went largely as they pleased.[32] Much the same was true of other criminal networks, including the one with which Baudoin associated.

The prevalence of the 'banditry psychosis' among law-enforcement officials in Paris had the disadvantage of sometimes saddling the wrong persons with responsibility for major crimes. For example, an otherwise routine case of highway robbery south of the capital grew into the famous 'affaire du courrier de Lyon' due to the conviction and execution of Joseph Lesurques, a shifty land speculator who was almost certainly a victim of mistaken identity when he appeared before a juge de paix (JP) in Paris. How could such a massive heist have been successfully executed, thought the investigating magistrate, without a clever dandy like Lesurques to mastermind it?[33] The police's prevailing suspicion that most major crimes were the work of a large criminal conspiracy could also have its advantages. Their fervent belief in the 'bande noire', a vast criminal organisation that supposedly extended from the Loire Valley to Bordeaux and Marseille, was based on little more than a common underworld *argot* and the ever more grandiose 'revelations' of a highwayman hoping to save his neck. And yet, the officials' unrelenting efforts to connect the dots, even where there were no direct connections, helped to bring several dozen criminals to justice.[34] This is precisely how the authorities eventually caught and executed Baudoin.

Local authorities came to believe that a spate of violent farmhouse robberies

---

[32] André Zysberg, 'L'Affaire d'Orgères: justice pénale et défense sociale (1790–1800)', in Michel Vovelle, ed, *La Révolution et l'ordre juridique privé: rationalité ou scandale?* 2 vols (Paris : Presses Universitaires de France, 1988) ii, 639–51; Richard Cobb, *Reactions to the French Revolution* (Oxford University Press, 1975) pp. 178–215. The indictment presented to the Criminal Court of the Eure listed 118 individuals (Cobb, p. 186), but a staggering 64 individuals (out of more than 300 imprisoned at Chartres in connection with this case) died in prison before the trial (Zysberg, p. 645).

[33] Georges-André Euloge, *Histoire de la police des origines à 1940* (Paris: Plon, 1985) pp. 98–102. For another case of shoddy prosecution, in which the aged *abbé* Solier was condemned to death and executed by a special military commission as 'one of the principal organisers of the system of brigandage in the departments of the Ninth Military Division and one of the principal leaders of the bands that committed the robberies of public funds, other thefts, and assaults', see Howard G. Brown, 'An Unmasked Man in a *Milieu de Mémoire*: The Abbé Solier as Sans-Peur the Brigand-Priest', *Historical Reflections/Réflexions historiques* 26 (2000) pp. 1–30.

[34] AN F[7] 4282, d. 12 (bande noire); BB[18] 733, DD 4521.

committed in the early months of 1798 north and east of the metropolis were the work of a single criminal gang. Several indications, including timing and method, pointed in that direction. The same brutal *modus opperandi* used at St-Rémy-l'Abbaye had been employed only a few weeks before at Bailleul-le-Soc (Oise) where a half-dozen bandits badly abused the aging landowner Pierre-Denis Queste and came away with 3900 francs in gold, 900 francs in silver, four horses, and an enormous treasure of silver tableware, gold and silver ornaments. Another brutal attack, this time at the Frangeallé farm near Château-Thierry (Aisne) displayed a similar pattern. All of the brigands rode horses; they employed deadly force (Mme Thevenin was killed by gun shot and her wagon-driver was clubbed to death); and they targeted a rich farmer (the thieves took 5000 francs in gold, over 600 francs in silver, and several sacks full of silverware and jewelry). Even though this attack occurred 100 kilometres from the previous assaults, it came less than a week after the atrocities at St-Rémy-l'Abbaye and so the two crimes naturally became associated.[35]

As is so often the case in police work, it took a combination of criminal carelessness and simple luck for the authorities to begin tying these crimes together. The day after the attack at Frangeallé, two gendarmes from Château-Thierry, tired from a day of searching, stopped for a drink at a tavern at Laferté-Milon. There they stumbled upon five of the perpetrators. An arrest and hasty search revealed blood-stained clothing. Definitive proof of guilt came shortly thereafter when one of the culprits tried to dispose of incriminating evidence by dropping a sack of gold louis and silver ornaments into the latrine of the local JP. As unpleasant as the retrieval may have been, it proved more than worth the effort.

From luck followed good police work. This required quite remarkable cooperation across jurisdictional and institutional boundaries. Rather than send the robbers to the district prosecutor at Château-Thierry, the JP at Laferté-Milon sent them to Reims in the neighbouring department of the Marne where the captives had planned to rendez-vous with other associates. Three days later, the wife of one bandit and the mistress of another were arrested at Monchenot south of Reims. A day after that, another pair of gendarmes arrested three women and a child travelling together in a carriage east of Châlons. Those arrested included the wife and daughter of Jean-Charles Fontaine, who had just hanged himself in jail at Reims, as well as the wife and child of Louis Baudoin, one of two men who had managed to flee on horseback. Within a few days, these four men and five women were all concentrated in the hands of the district prosecutor at Château-Thierry.[36]

---

[35] AG C^{18} 2 and 3 contain the investigation.

[36] These were: Petit, Lolivret, Chemin and Mariotte; Jeanne-Marguerite Guerrier (marchande forraine de bestiaux, résident of Compiègne, aged 24, wife of Chemin), Claire Leture (marchande forraine aged 22, mistress of Petit), femme Fontaine, fille Fontaine,

In addition to recent improvements in the quality of the rural constabulary, the eventual punishment of these bandits owed much to cooperation between civilian authorities and the rigours of military justice. The prosecutor at Château-Thierry realised that the nature of the crime at Frangeallé meant that the recent anti-brigandage law of 28 January 1798 made them all subject to a court martial.[37] Apparently convinced that they were connected to the brigand band headed by Jean-François Salembier, a criminal gang recently prosecuted at Lille (and made famous fifty years later by Vidocq in *Les chauffeurs du Nord*), the prosecutor at Château-Thierry transferred his clutch of prisoners to the military court at Lille. By the time they arrived at Lille, however, the Parisian police had convinced the Directory that these *chauffeurs* and their women folk were part of a different criminal organisation, one deemed responsible for a variety of crimes throughout the Isle-de-France. This made them justiciable by the military courts of the 17th Military District headquartered at Paris. Therefore, on 3 April 1798, the Directory ordered the nine prisoners at Lille transferred to the capital where they would be amalgamated with numerous other accused brigands already in prisons throughout the city. This ability repeatedly to transfer a batch of prisoners between several different locales, where they could be registered, viewed, questioned, and even shown to possible witnesses, should not be underrated. Such actions would have been unthinkable in many parts of the south and west where escape attempts and roadside rescues were common obstacles to law enforcement.

The growing number of brigands presumed to be part of the same organisation made the logistical aspects of prosecution increasingly challenging. The investigation proceeded along numerous tracks. Following up scores of clues wherever they led took extensive cooperation, especially from the various justices of the peace and district prosecutors scattered across a half dozen departments. It was especially important that the military and civilian elements of the prosecution worked well together. This had clearly become the case in Paris by early 1798.[38] The rules of military justice obliged the military prosecutor to conduct his own questioning of the accused and the relevant witnesses before the case went to trial. These rules had to be followed despite the fact that those accused of brigandage could only be sent before a military court after a civilian investigation had been conducted and the civilian prosecutor had formally found the accused subject to the

---

Grénot (femme Baudoin) and a child (aged 6).

[37] This law made housebreaking and armed robbery into capital crimes and specified that if such crimes had been committed by more than two people, the accused, as well as their accomplices, would experience the summary justice of a military court. A guilty verdict brought a death sentence. The decision to turn suspects over to military justice had first to be made by a civilian district prosecutor (*directeur du jury*).

[38] Schmidt, *Tableaux*, ii, 306, Mathieu, commissaire du Directoire de la Seine, au ministre de l'Intérieur, 22 ventôse VI.

law of 18 January 1798. These stipulations meant that the JP for the Thermes district and the *Bureau central* above him served to coordinate the investigation of the *chauffeurs*.

The Paris Bureau Central has received little more than denigration from most historians. The standards of comparison have always been the *lieutenant générale de police* in the *ancien régime* and the *préfecture de police* created under Napoleon. These both had the advantage of being headed by single individuals who enjoyed considerable security in office. In contrast, the three positions on the Bureau Central were filled by sixteen different men during its brief life span from 1796 to 1800. Shared leadership and instability in personnel are taken as *prima facie* evidence that the policing of Paris during the Directory was clunky and inept. We should not forget, however, that the Bureau Central replaced a far more confusing and decentralised system of law enforcement in the capital.[39] In contrast, the three members of the Bureau Central were appointed by the Directory, were required to work closely with an appointed government commissioner and were watched over directly by the Ministry of General Police. Under this enhanced executive control, the Bureau Central exercised considerable powers. These included issuing police subpoenas, interrogating suspects, and assigning criminal investigations to JPs, who then acted as the *police judiciare* in preparing the basis for criminal prosecutions. The Bureau Central also obtained the right to appoint *commissaires de police* from lists presented by each district. Further down the hierarchy, it controlled the *officiers de paix*, who in turn managed the system of inspectors and informants. Thus, the Bureau Central had greater authority and autonomy than any of the previous police organs of Paris during the Revolution.[40]

As a result of its extensive police powers, the Bureau Central developed a large and complex administrative structure. About half of its employees had served in the old *lieutenance générale*, notably Henry, the redoutable head of the *bureau de sûreté* and known as the 'ange malin'. It was he who took charge of anti-bandit operations.[41] The staff of the Bureau Central included specialists of every stripe, from professional interrogators to low-level copyists. The elaborate duplicities and apparent venality of an inspector general like Pierre-Hugues Veyrat complemented the brutish tactics of other investigators such as Bertrand, who favoured the use of

---

[39] During the Convention, each of the 48 sections had a surveillance committee, a justice of the peace, and commissioner of police, all empowered to issue appearance subpeonas and arrest warrants. If this was not confusing enough, the municipality had both a Department of Police and a Surveillance Committee. Furthermore, national organs such as the Committees of Public Safety and of General Security and the Commission for the Police and Courts intervened heavily in the policing of the capital, and frequently did so with little regard for hierarchy.

[40] Schmidt, *Tableaux*, ii, 440–42; Tulard, *Paris et son administration*, pp. 55–65.

[41] Rigotard, *Police parisienne*, p. 88.

flintlocks and thumbscrews to speed interrogations.[42] More important than the tactics of seduction and intimidation was the elaborate record keeping established in the Bureau Central. Paris was one of the few places in France where the revolutionary system of issuing and checking passports for domestic travel was consistently enforced. In addition, numerous registers recorded crimes, arrests, physical descriptions, names of vagrants and flop-house residents, etc. Because it was based on registers, a system of cross-referencing was essential. However, the constant need to update led to an exponential growth in documentation. By the time the Prefecture of Police replaced the Bureau Central in 1800, there were some 400 large registers in use.[43] This mania for recording the criminal and marginal population in and around Paris arguably became the greatest weapon in the arsenal of the police (and the precursor to the vast data sets of Fouché and Vidocq). It was the large number of clerical staff and the voluminous records they generated that made it possible for the Bureau Central to integrate the pursuit of the *chauffeurs* from Château-Thierry into the larger pursuit of brigands whose crimes took place well beyond the capital.

The concentration of policing in Paris had ramifications for its physical aspect as well. The public impression this created was one of overwhelming scale and complexity, especially compared to the modest and scattered offices of the former Lieutenancy General. The Bureau Central and its attendant staff soon overflowed its main headquarters (the former residence of the First Presidents of the Parlement) and spilled into the eclectic heap of ramshackle buildings that surrounded it. As a result, those who had business with the police had to enter a labyrinth of corridors, narrow passage-ways, dead-end staircases, and dimly lit rooms. Inside their cramped offices, employees piled boxes and bundles in every available corner. Waiting rooms were invariably filled to overflowing and friends and relatives often overheard interrogations even when they did not get rough.[44] This appearance of confusion and chaos was belied by the considerable achievements of the Bureau Central. Though staggeringly prolific in 1796, the number of 'grands crimes' such as murders and robberies dropped sharply thereafter.[45] By the autumn of 1799, journalists could reassure the public that the

---

[42]   Ernest d'Hauterive, *Mouchards et policiers* (2nd ed. Paris : Gallimard, 1936) pp. 139–55; Tulard, *Paris et son administration*, pp. 132–33.

[43]   Charles-Louis Limodin, *Réflexions générales sur la police, par le citoyen Limodin* (Paris, frimaire V); Tulard, *Paris et son administration*, p. 135.

[44]   Georges Lenôtre, *Two Royalist Spies*, trans. by Bernard Miall (London: T.F. Unwin, 1924). According to the publication of a senior employee (Limodin, *Réflexions*), 'in the space of seven months, the Bureau Central's *Chambre d'arrêt* alone had seen two thousand forty-seven persons, ranging from thieves and conspirators to émigrés and prostitutes, without counting the house searches, which sent two thousand individuals there'.

[45]   See reports for the autumn of 1798 published in Schmidt, *Tableaux*, iii. 291–97 and 330–38.

Bureau Central would know how to deal with any potential increase in banditry.[46] This was not whistling in the dark, as the role of the Bureau Central in bringing *chauffeurs* to justice indicates.

The steady influx of *chauffeurs* into the prisons of Paris between the initial arrests near Château-Thierry and the actual trial a year later exacerbated already overcrowded conditions. As much as 20 per cent of all prisoners in France at the turn of the century were detained in the capital, whereas only 2 per cent of the French population actually lived there.[47] The concentration of so many violent malefactors in one city, and especially in certain prisons, came to pose the risk of a coordinated escape attempt. Large prison break-outs were distressingly common elsewhere in the country.[48] Therefore, the Bureau Central responded by having a set of leg irons fastened to a dozen of the *chauffeurs* detained at the Conciergerie.[49] This cruel and unusual precaution further marked them out as high profile criminals. As the case grew, other special arrangements became necessary as well.

By the time the case went to court in April 1799, it had grown into the largest criminal trial conducted in Paris between that of the September massacres in 1796 and the Cadoudal-Pichegru affair of 1804. There would eventually be twenty-eight defendants, nine of whom were women. This trial of a large criminal gang before a military court was representative of numerous such trials being held all over France at the time. Although the largest gang trials took place before regular criminal courts, the use of military courts to try civilians was fast becoming a large and integral part of the republic's war on banditry.[50] As was the case elsewhere, the unusual size of the trial being planned in Paris presented certain logistical difficulties. The Minister of Justice prohibited the military court from using the Conciergerie, on the ground that holding this trial in a prison would create the wrong impression, or any of the courtrooms in the Palais de Justice, because they

---

[46] See the quotation that opens this chapter.

[47] This is based on budget allocations due to the lack of statistics on actual prisoners. See Jacques-Guy Petit, *Ces peines obscures: la prison pénale en France, 1780–1875* (Paris: Fayard, 1990) table on p. 120.

[48] To cite but two examples, 56 of the 204 prisoners incarcerated at Villefranche (Haute-Garonne) escaped in the spring of 1797 and 12 of 31 prisoners arrested for rioting in the Tarn escaped from Albi in early 1798. AN BB[18] 329 and 864.

[49] AG C[18] 3, commissaire du Directoire près le Tribunal Criminal de la Seine au capitaine-rapporteur du 1er conseil de guerre du 17e division militaire, 27 brumaire VII.

[50] The Criminal Court of the Pas-de-Calais pronounced verdicts on 41 associates of François Salembier; the Criminal Court of the Seine-Inférieure put 83 members of the 'bande Chandelier' on trial; and the Criminal Court of Eure-et-Loire decided the fate of 113 accused members of the 'bande d'Orgères'. Though military courts rarely handled more than a dozen defendants at a time, they prosecuted several thousand bandits and rebels across France during the two years that the law of 18 January 1798 remained in effect. See my forthcoming book, *Ending the French Revolution: Violence, Justice, Repression*.

were already fully booked. Instead he authorised the trial to be held in the great hall of the Hôtel de Ville. The increased space was needed to accommodate the large number of defendants and their lawyers, as well as to provide tables to hold several hundred objects, most of them stolen, to be used as evidence against the accused. The larger venue was not intended to accommodate a larger audience, however. The government did not want this to become a show trial and insisted on enforcing the regulation in the code of military justice that allowed only as many spectators as there were judges.

The military prosecution of rural bandits in the heart of the capital did not go unnoticed, however. Although excluded from the courtroom itself, the public learned about the great trial of *chauffeurs* from the daily press. Newspaper coverage of crime had grown markedly during the Directory and helped to generate a growing sense of insecurity even as crime itself was being reduced. In contrast to the more expansive and sensationalist press of the nineteenth century, newspapers in the late 1790s rarely provided more than the slimmest details for any particular crime. Even as the frequency of reports increased, individual newspaper items tended to remain no more than two or three lines long. In this respect, reporting on the trial of *chauffeurs* in Paris was unusual and served as something of a precursor to later reporting techniques. For example, the sheer wickedness of the accused held a great fascination for the Parisian press. According to one paper, the accused displayed 'an audacity and calm that should only belong to innocence'. Equally fascinating was the heinousness of their crimes. 'The entire audience shuddered with horror upon learning the details of the misdeeds committed by these villains'. 'Those who attended the court sessions wondered how human beings could attain such a degree of villainy as these wretches', commented another journalist, who then regaled his readers with the details of the *chauffage* at St-Rémy-l'Abbaye. He also claimed that the rape victims had been infected with venereal disease, an apt metaphor for the violation and pollution of society spread by bandits during the period.[51]

After several days of hearings, the military court sentenced seventeen of the accused to death.[52] An attempted suicide by one of the condemned temporarily

---

[51]   Quotations are from: *L'Ami des lois*, 30 ventôse VII; *Le Publiciste*, 30 ventôse VII; *Le Moniteur*, 3 germinal VII.

[52]   Those condemned to death were François Petit dit Nezel ou *Le Petit Boucher*, François Guerrier dit Boulanger, François Mériotte, Gilles Chemin, François-Charles Lolivret dit *Le Gros François*, Pierre-Félix-Edouard Dion, Garnier dit *Le Petit Gars*, Hyacinthe Sénéchal dit Toto, Pierre Monier dit Bizet, Louis Lamarre, Louis Baudoin dit Fortin (contumax); les femmes Claire Leture (concubine de Nezel), Jeanne-Margueritte Guerrier (femme de Chemin), veuve Thérèse-Julienne Fontaine, Rose Fontaine sa fille, Marie-Louise-Adelaide Grénot (femme de Baudoin). The 11 persons not sentenced to death were sent back to prison in order to be tried by regular criminal courts for crimes committed

delayed the executions.[53] An appeal resulted in further delay. The bulk of documentation made this a longer procedure than usual, but the military review panel upheld all of the convictions. Finally, on 24 April 1799, a month after the verdict, fifteen of the now infamous *chauffeurs* were guillotined in mid-afternoon on the *place de Grève* in front of the Hôtel de Ville. Though the guillotine had not operated there during the Revolution, the *place de Grève* had long been the traditional site of executions and thereby symbolically linked the *chauffeurs* to the great criminals of the *ancien régime*. Journalists underscored the extraordinary criminality of those who perished that day as a necessary precaution in an age of widespread suspicion about government persecution. It was reported that the *chauffeurs* 'generally showed the same audacity on the scaffold as they had showed in court and in the course of their crimes'. Even more importantly, 'indignation against them was universal because people knew they had dipped their hands in blood a thousand times'.[54] Such a description was clearly intended to exclude them from the popular image of heroic outlaws who stole only from the rich and did so without maiming or murdering them. In announcing the verdict, journalists elaborated on the world of crime from which they came. The *chauffeurs* supposedly belonged to 'an organisation so vast and coordinated that it would be difficult to extirpate without the greatest vigilance ... Their police is the most severe; the least insubordination is punished with death. Among them high birth adds to the hierarchy of ranks ... Former brandings are important recommendations [and] they appear to play with death, which they call *la boule*'.[55] The presence of women among those executed also provided a nexus between elements of the underworld. It was noted that Thérèse-Julienne Fontaine had been widowed twice; her first husband having been hanged during the *ancien régime* and her second husband having hanged himself in jail at Reims. Furthermore, her eldest daughter and her husband had been condemned to death and executed for brigandage by the same military court only a few months before. Finally, the widow Fontaine's other daughter, Rose, who was noted for her prettiness, was guillotined along with her mother.[56] Thus, journalists did their best to smother any notion that these bandits might be the fit objects of popular admiration and at the same time helped to trumpet the achievements of police detection and judicial retribution.

As the reader will have noticed, only fifteen of the seventeen individuals condemned to death by the military court were executed on the *place de Grève*. The two others were Jeanne-Marguerite Guerrier and Louis Baudoin. Their

---

before the law of 18 January 1798.

[53] *Clef du Cabinet*, 10 germinal VII.
[54] *L'Ami des lois*, 6 floréal VII.
[55] *Clef du Cabinet*, 7 floréal VII.
[56] *L'Ami des lois*, 5 germinal VII; AG J2 247, verdict of 22 messidor VI.

individual fates further illustrate the general nature of investigative policing in the period. Even after a year in a female prison in Paris, Guerrier avoided the fate of her husband, Gilles Chemin, by claiming to be pregnant. In the meantime, a female informant in the Madelonettes prison convinced the Bureau Central that Guerrier could be persuaded to divulge information about other brigands. She began by revealing the false identity and real whereabouts of Louis Baudoin. When he was arrested at Evreux and transferred to Paris, Guerrier confirmed his true identity. Guerrier's pregnancy turned out to be a hoax, as proved by nine months of menstrual rags hidden in her straw mattress, and she again faced execution. However, Guerrier managed repeatedly to defer her date with the guillotine by continuing to cooperate with the authorities. This included making trips out to various provincial courts in police wagons. In this way she helped to bring to justice ten 'robbers, killers, and *chauffeurs*' over a two-year period.[57] It was exactly her sort of insider information and confirmation of identities that the police needed to close cases.

In the meantime, Louis Baudoin, also known as Fortin, became something of a curiosity in Paris. Though confined to prison, he seemed to belong to the ménagerie of attractions being brought in from the provinces at the time. These included such oddities as the 'wild boy' from the Aveyron, the gentle giant from Perpignan, and the dwarf who cost 10 centimes to see beside the café des Grands-Hommes on the Boulevard Montmartre.[58] Although dozens of witnesses from a variety of robberies did not recognise him, a handful of victims from St-Rémy-l'Abbaye did make a positive identification. In addition, despite Baudoin's many pseudonyms, his appearance had made a lasting impression on innkeepers, a half-dozen of whom came to the capital to identify him. This was enough to send him before the first military court.

Once on trial, Baudoin was unable to resist the temptation of fame. He not only admitted to belonging to the infamous band of *chauffeurs*, but insisted that he had been one of its key organisers. Thus, it was as the band's 'treasurer' and would-be 'squadron leader' that he was judged. During the trial, Baudoin displayed 'the calmness of a man familarised with crime; all of his actions and all of his words revealed his ferocity'. Mindful of his potential for posthumous popularity, Baudoin joked with the judges and spectators alike. According to the press, 'he appeared to have only one regret, not to be able to pursue the course of his atrocities'.[59] Once condemned to death, he followed the lead of Jeanne-Marguerite Guerrier and

---

[57]   AG C¹⁸ 3, Béhourt, JP de la11ᵉ municipalité de Paris, au capitaine-rapporteur du 1ᵉʳ conseil de guerre, 2 messidor IX.

[58]   *Le publiciste*, 10 ventôse VIII.

[59]   *L'Ami des lois*, 9 ventôse VIII.

promised to help arrest a thousand others like him in exchange for a reprieve.[60] The authorities refused to make this deal. Therefore, on the afternoon of the day his conviction was confirmed, Baudoin *dit* Fortin was guillotined on the *place de Grève*.

The contrasting fates of Guerrier and Baudoin are instructive. Guerrier's utility as an informant kept her alive. In fact, she survived until March 1815 when the government commuted her death sentence to twenty years in prison, or little more than time served.[61] On the other hand, Baudoin was promptly executed despite a similar willingness to cooperate with the police in exchange for his life. No doubt his use of the trial to cultivate his notoriety made it impossible for the authorities to delay his execution. But there were other issues at stake as well. The ubiquitous use of criminal informants, whether in or out of prison, gave the police a thoroughly unsavory air. Not only did the police need the cooperation of criminals to make cases, but they often played the role of *agents provocateurs* to set traps for the criminally inclined.[62] This badly tarnished the reputation of the police in general and made almost any slander against them credible. So murky was this area of police work and so shaky was the regime's credibility that the Directory categorically refused to allow magistrates to commute death sentences in exchange for service as police informants. The republic had enough trouble establishing its legitimacy without having known felons in its employ. Thus, on one hand, Guerrier survived because the police depended on informants, she was female, relatively unknown, and more of an accomplice than a perpetrator. On the other hand, Baudoin perished because he was a deserter, armed robber, and murderer, and a failure to execute him would have led to suspicion of police corruption, no matter the quality of his information. Authorities were surely also concerned about their ability to hold onto him for a long time because 'he possessed to a supreme degree the art of escaping from prison'. Given his colourful character and criminal notoriety, any escape from prison would have greatly boosted his potential as an outlaw hero. Therefore, it was imperative that Baudoin die at the hands of 'the public executioner of the department of the Seine in the presence of the people'.[63]

This triumph of the forces of order, and the impression of efficient policing it created, was due to several factors not prominent before this time. First, these people committed their crimes after the draconian law of 18 January 1798 and

---

[60] Bulletin de police, 9 ventôse VIII excerpted in Alphonse Aulard, *Paris sous le Consulat: Recueil des documents pour l'histoire de l'esprit public à Paris*, 4 vols (Paris, 1903–13) i, 182.

[61] AG C[18] 3, chef de l'état-major de la 1ère division militaire au capitaine-rapporteur du 1er conseil de guerre, 6 mars 1815.

[62] d'Hauterive, *Mouchards et policiers*.

[63] AG C[18] 2, jugement du conseil de révision, 15 ventôse VIII.

were therefore the subject of military justice. Because the 17th Military District covered the entire Isle-de-France, and because the military and civilian authorities at Paris worked well together, it was possible to envelop a large number of *chauffeurs* in a single trial, whether or not they all belonged to a single gang. Second, the police system proved remarkably efficient. Even though the culprits came from a half dozen departments and were arrested in separate groups, they passed smoothly through the hands of innumerable detachments of the gendarmerie, several justices of the peace, at least three civilian district prosecutors, and two military prosecutors, as well as the increasingly powerful Bureau Central at Paris before ending up partitioned on the *place de Grève*. Although Fortin got away the first time, he was condemned to death *in absentia* and tracked down nine months later. Third, the guilty were punished because witnesses (and not just victims) from three departments had the courage to testify against brigands known as *le Gros François* and *le Petit Boucher* at the same time as Baudoin and his principal partner remained at large. Fourth, the conviction and execution of the *chauffeurs* at Paris received an unprecedented level of newspaper coverage. Though nothing was reported about the methods of police detection, success spoke for itself and helped greatly to improve the image of the police.

Tropes in image and action

This detailed examination of the character and prosecution of Louis Baudoin and his fellow *chauffeurs* gives us the evidence we need to understand the publication by the Swiss *Almanach de l'an IX* of a major story about a failed robbery at distant Paris. In this light, it becomes clear that this story constituted an important sign of the times. Violent crime had reached unprecedented levels in the latter half of the 1790s. Groups of robbers both large and small preyed on the prosperous, whether travelling in stage-coaches, living on isolated farms, or running urban businesses. As newspaper reports on the trial of *chauffeurs* indicate, the most common features of these criminals was their planning, audacity, atrocity, *sang-froid*, and persistent life of crime. 'A Horrible Murder' is a remarkably concise compilation of these different tropes. The robbers examined the jeweler's shop from the inside before attacking it; they targeted this shop despite it being located 'on one of the busiest streets of Paris'; they did not hesitate to kill even if one of their own; they had the chilling presence of mind to lop off his head and take it with them; and they preferred to commit another crime – stealing the personal effects of their dead accomplice – rather than keep a low profile or even leave the city. Moreover, such a combination of manifest failure, cold cruelty and simple stupidity made these particular villains so thoroughly unattractive that they could never be associated with popular outlaws. To be sure of this, the wood-block print portrayed the fugitive who carried the head as a well-heeled dandy wearing thigh-hugging breaches, a tail coat and top hat. Thus, the dominant tropes associated both with the *chauffeurs* and with the jewelry shop robbers consistently foreclosed the possibility of popular appeal. The everyday reality of organised crime was obviously too widespread and too threatening to generate anything more than fascinated fear.

General revulsion at the level of violent crime opened the way for the police to become the subject of popular admiration. Here too the significance of the *Almanach* story is suggested by the fate of the *chauffeurs* at Paris, in particular that of Baudoin. Several more tropes are worthy of note: criminal elusiveness, ineffective pursuit, sheer luck, police knowledge, and judicial punishment. Observe the parallels: at first the would-be jewelry store robbers eluded the police just as Baudoin had done when his companions were seized; the fisherman's lucky find of a head in his nets proved the start of a successful pursuit in the same way the gendarmerie from Château-Thierry had first to stumble upon several *chauffeurs* in an inn at Laferté-Milon. Perhaps most striking of all is the pivotal role of the Bureau Central in the effectiveness of the pursuit. That a clerk recognised the head, had heard of the man's supposed travel plans, and knew his address in Paris would not be read as mere coincidence. It had a strong air of authenticity. As we saw with Vidocq, the Paris police cultivated the study of criminal faces. Furthermore, an unseemly number of agents employed by the Bureau Central had one foot in the criminal underworld, either past or present, and, therefore, knew a great deal about the movements of dubious characters. Finally, extensive record keeping, together with constant surveillance of flop-houses and cheap rentals, provided the Bureau Central with a veritable directory of suspects' addresses. Thus, only an effective police agency could turn serendipity into arrests and executions.

If there is one part of the *Almanach* story that does not offer a symbolic summary of the major features of law enforcement at the time, it is the abrupt conclusion in which executions follow immediately from the arrest. This elides what was usually a substantial effort on the part of the *police judiciare* to assemble a case before finally putting suspects on trial. This could mean extensive correspondence with other law-enforcement officials, numerous transfers and subpoenas, and scores of interviews. In Baudoin's case, for example, the pre-trial documentation totaled 423 items, including dozens of notebooks full of interrogations and depositions.[64] This literally spoke volumes about the investigative capacity, as well as the basic practice, of the Paris police during the First Republic. They had only the most primitive techniques of acquiring forensic evidence and so relied almost exclusively on what the modern espionage community calls 'human intelligence'.

---

[64] AG J2 99.

The trope of decapitation also played its part in telling the story of crime and punishment in the period. Despite the fact that more people died by military firing squad during the Terror than by guillotine, it was images of the latter that captured the popular imagination. In fact, it is almost impossible to find contemporary depictions of firing squads.[65] In contrast, all of Europe, Switzerland included of course, had seen images of the guillotine. The most common such image was that of Louis XVI's execution. The many renditions of this scene almost always showed the executioner grasping the king's dripping head by the hair and holding it up for the crowd to see. Much the same image is incorporated into the *Almanach*'s wood-block print. Rather than depicting the head tucked under the arm of the fleeing murderer, the artist has him holding the severed head by the hair out in front of him, just as Louis's head was held. Thus, the image as presented in the wood-block print subliminally maps the murder of a robber onto the great crime of revolutionary regicide. It is even possible that this scene, situated in Paris as it was, also brought to mind the execution of such leading revolutionaries as Brissot, Hébert and Danton. In each of these executions, the ruthless leaders of a political faction decapitated an erstwhile partner in revolution in order to pursue their life of political criminality. The similarities are indeed striking.

By the time the *Almanach* was published in 1800, the daily use of the guillotine throughout France in the context of ordinary criminal justice was gradually eroding its exclusive association with Jacobin terror. After all, by the turn of the century, the republic was carrying out over 800 criminal executions each year. This was at least three times the number of executions per annum during the peak years of the *ancien régime*.[66] It should be noted that the other two robbers shown fleeing the scene in the *Almanach* are depicted looking at the man carrying the head. Thus, they both draw the viewer's attention to the grizzly head and constitute a small audience. This increases the similarity with public executions by invoking the gaze of an approving crowd. In such a context, the headless body of the thief stuck with his arm through the bars of the jewelry shop window clearly symbolised the fate of armed robbers who had the misfortune of being seized by the authorities. Whether convicted by a civilian or military court, their bodies were rendered limp and headless by the 'blade of justice'.

---

[65] For a rare example, see Abbé Ferdinand Gaugain, *Histoire de la Révolution dans la Mayenne*, 4 vols (Laval, 1918) insert in vol. 4.

[66] Howard G. Brown, *Ending the French Revolution: Violence, Justice, Repression*, chapter 13 (forthcoming).

Conclusion: Dissection and detection

As bizarre as it may sound, finding individual body parts such as a severed head in the Seine was not an uncommon experience at the turn of the nineteenth century. The alarming increase in human flotsam in the river led citizens of the capital to fear that it was another sign of the spectacular level of violent crime in their city. In fact, however, as newspapers explained, it was the result of a mania for human dissection and the surreptitious disposal of well-used cadavers. Medical students unable to obtain one of the limited places in the Practical School of Dissection (founded at Paris in 1797) were forced to learn their techniques from private instructors. Thus many medical teachers took to procuring their own corpses, conducting dissections in make-shift 'amphitheatres', and then disposing of the remains in the Seine.[67] No doubt, such practices greatly complicated the task of an official in the Bureau Central asked to identify a head caught in a fisherman's net. Apart from these practical concerns, however, the new direction in medicine, as well as scholarly assessments of it, has more important implications for our understanding of police work in post-revolutionary Paris.

The sudden enthusiasm for dissection was part of a major shift towards 'pathological anatomy' as the basis of medical diagnosis in France. Many historians consider this the birth of modern medical science. Akernknecht emphasised the use of statistical data based on numerous autopsies whereas Foucault distilled the changes into the idea of a novel *regard*, or gaze. Such emphases helped to reify the concept of a Paris School which transformed the practice of medicine in the early nineteenth century. However, focusing on the achievements of the so-called Paris School distorts our view of how medicine was actually practiced in France at the time. In fact, despite important changes to the structure of the medical profession in the years 1794–1803, the education of doctors did not change as much as previously claimed. As a result, the nature of medical practice across France remained a fluid mix of clinical training, traditional remedies, and outright quackery.[68] The lesson here is that a thorough understanding of changes in general practices and public perceptions in any field of endeavour requires looking beyond the emergence of new institutions and a few famous practitioners.

---

[67] Dora B. Wiener, *The Citizen-Patient in Revolutionary and Imperial Paris* (Baltimore and London : Johns Hopkins University Press, 1993) pp. 181–83.

[68] Laurence Brockliss and Colin Jones, *The Medical World of Early Modern France* (Oxford : Clarendon Press, 1997), pp. 802–26; Elizabeth Haigh, *Xavier Bichat and the Medical Theory of Eighteenth-Century France* (London : Wellcome Institute for the Study of Medicine, 1984); L. W. B. Brockliss, 'L'Enseignement médical et la Révolution: essai de réévaluation', *Histoire de l'education* 42 (1989) pp. 79–110; Matthew Ramsey, *Professional and Popular Medecine in France, 1770–1830* (Cambridge University Press, 1988).

As the evidence in this chapter indicates, our improved understanding of changes in French medicine offer a clear lesson for the study of police detection in the same period. By paying too much attention to structural changes in policing brought about by Fouché's emphasis on political policing or Vidocq's appointment to head the *brigade de sûreté* (the 'Paris School' of policing), we distort the evolutionary changes in ordinary police work. There is no doubt that a greater attention to physiognomy – in other words, a new *regard* – grew out of requiring passports for domestic travel, devoting time to studying criminals in prison, and circulating suspects among various authorities. These practices combined with an explosion in record keeping by the police. Though not used to calculate statistically significant correlations (as was the case with autopsies in medicine) the many registers kept by the Bureau Central and the Ministry of General Police did serve a diagnostic function by tracing the identities and likely source of criminal pathogens at work in the social body. All the same, these novel abilities did not so much replace traditional methods as complement them. Police detection continued to rely heavily on turncoat informants and police agents who could pass as criminals themselves. The combination of methods enabled the police to obtain impressive results in treating the epidemic of violent crime that afflicted France in the 1790s. The unprecedented attention newspapers devoted to this struggle altered public perceptions. Widespread reporting of heinous crimes such as the *chauffage* at St-Rémy-l'Abbaye helped to forestall popular admiration for picaresque outlaws like Louis Baudoin. Moreover, the growing success of the authorities enhanced the image of policing. This was an important first stage on the way to genuine popularity as detective heroes. In short, novel institutional practices combined with the tips and traps of traditional policing to yield modern tropes of fighting crime.

Chapter Three

From Ex-Con to Expert: The Police Detective in Nineteenth-Century France

Clive Emsley

Detectives and the French police system

The detective, both the private detective and the police detective, has become a central figure in modern escapist, popular culture. He, and occasionally she, is the character who walks murky mean streets protecting us from the criminal 'other'. He and she can mingle with the 'criminal' other, knows its ways, can occasionally be corrupted by it, but more often solves crimes and, by dealing with offenders, prevents other crimes. Individuals working to solve crimes and who pursued offenders were not creations of the nineteenth century. Nevertheless, the growth of a mass-reading public during the nineteenth century probably contributed to the growth of thrilling adventure stories, of which detective literature constitutes one genre. Moreover, the development of bureaucratic, professional police forces, also a phenomenon of the nineteenth century, contributed to the development of professional bureaucratic detectives. By the end of the century police detectives were claiming a professional expertise for their *métier*, and none more so than in France where the police detective had been transformed from a reformed, though often still suspect member of the criminal classes to a respectable professional worker claiming special skills.

Un détective is not a specific rank or post in the contemporary *Police nationale*; nor was it at the beginning of the nineteenth century. Indeed, the word was only introduced into France during the 1870s and then in the context of English police detectives.[1] This, in itself, is an interesting linguistic development given first, the

---

[1] *Trésor de la Langue Française* (Paris: Editions CNRS, 1979) defines the old meaning of the word as 'Policier anglais, specialisé dans les enquêtes', and gives as an example of the first use in French, the English police detective Fix in Jules Verne's *Le tour du monde en 80 jours* (1872). Between 1907 and 1909 a journal called *Le Détective* was published, described as 'étude d'épuration sociale, organe hebdomadaire des fonctionnaires de la Préfecture de Police'. *Détective Magazine*, 'revue hebdomadaire de police' began in

English suspicion about detective policemen, a suspicion that was to be found even in the highest ranks of London's Metropolitan Police, and second, the reorganisation of the Metropolitan Police detectives at the end of the 1870s was carried out by a man, C.E. Howard Vincent, who based his knowledge of detective work on a relatively brief study of practices in the Paris Prefecture.[2] In France agents of *la police judiciaire* were, and are, charged with investigating crimes, apprehending and bringing the perpetrators to justice, but they are not necessarily members of one of the two principal police organisations in France, *la Police nationale* and *la Gendarmerie nationale*. The most obvious example here is the *juge d'instruction* who investigates offences and who can direct agents from one or other of the two police organisations to assist in his or, from the late twentieth century, in her enquiries. Of course, the agents from police organisations claim expertise in such investigative service work as they provide for the *juge* and they are essentially the equivalent of, and carry out very similar tasks to the police detectives in modern Britain or the United States.

During the nineteenth century there was no specialised judicial policing system outside of Paris, and even in Paris, for much of the century, the system remained fluid. Members of the *Gendarmerie nationale*, the military police that patrolled the main roads of France and was the first line of defence against popular disorder, occasionally acted in plain clothes. They undertook such service particularly in the pursuit of brigands and refractory conscripts during the Napoleonic period. But while such operations were often successful, they also raised serious procedural questions, the most notable being whether individuals could be prosecuted for resisting gendarmes who were not readily identifiable as such because they were not wearing their uniforms. In 1805 the *Cour de cassation* declared that gendarmes out of uniform should not be considered as undertaking their police functions. The Gendarmerie Ordinance of 1820 made a similar ruling; but the renewals in 1854 and 1903 suggest that the regulation was not always obeyed.[3] By the end of the nineteenth century, the *Gendarmerie* was stressing the image of its men as honest, uniformed soldiers of the law in contrast to the detective police and their sinister *missions occultes* (secret missions). The detective police, in turn, characterised the

---

1909, and the highly successful *Détective*, modelled on New York's *Detective Fiction Weekly*, in 1928.

  [2] Stefan Petrow, 'The rise of the detective in London, 1869–1914', *Criminal Justice History*, 14 (1993) pp. 91–108; and more generally, Clive Emsley, *The English Police: A Political and Social History* (2nd edn., London: Longman, 1996) pp. 72–73, 104–7 and 236.

  [3] Clive Emsley, *Gendarmes and the State in Nineteenth-Century Europe* (Oxford University Press, 1999) pp. 72, 91, 104, 111, 125 and 156–7; Louis Larrieu, *Histoire de la Maréchaussée et de la Gendarmerie, des origines à la Quatrième République* (Ivry-sur Seine: Phénix Éditions, 2002) pp. 530–32.

gendarmes as rural plods, who might arrest unfortunate tramps, but lacked the flair for dealing with real criminals.[4]

On occasions police detectives from Paris could be loaned to a provincial town or district faced with a particular problem. In 1889, for example, on the request of the *parquet* of Epinal, *inspecteur principal* Jaume was sent to Pont-à-Mousson where he tracked down and apprehended a former gendarme named Dauga responsible for a series of crimes in the area.[5] The traditional Whig perspective of the French police, that still informs much of the Anglo-Saxon perspective, assumes that there was a system centrally controlled and directed. There were *commissaires* appointed by central government in the larger towns dating back to the Revolution. Throughout the first half of the nineteenth century these *commissaires* were appointed by the minister of the interior from a list of local worthies prepared by the departmental prefect; legal or policing expertise was not always considered essential for appointment – political loyalty was what mattered. There was a gradual shift, however, as the century wore on and by 1900 the *commissaires* were developing into a trained, professional body with a growing sense of professional identity.[6] But if the *commissaires* of provincial towns and cities were centrally appointed, the size and structure of the rank and file police officers who served under them depended not on the government in Paris, but principally on what the local municipality was prepared to establish and fund.[7] Only with reference to political subversion did central government become seriously involved in investigation and surveillance outside Paris. The agents of this political police were closely linked to the railway network as it spread during the 1840s; the railway was seen as offering new opportunities for both crime and police intelligence. The *commissaries spéciaux de surveillance des chemins de fer* were established in 1846; there were 33 of them by 1860 with 70 subordinate *inspecteurs*. There were similar *commissaires* on the frontiers and others charged with inspecting books. In 1889 there was a reorganisation dividing these agents into *Police spéciale de la*

---

[4] Laurent López, 'Les relations entre policiers et gendarmes: À travers leurs représentations mutuelles sous la troisième République (1875–1914)', in *Figures de gendarmes*, special edition of *Sociétés et Représentations*, edited by Jean-Noël Luc, 16 (2003) pp. 213–27.

[5] Jean-Marc Berlière, 'L'institution policière en France sous la troisième République', Thèse pour le doctorat, 3 vols, Université de Bourgogne, 1991, iii, 1185; for the special *commissaries* charged with, among other things, political policing, see Howard C. Payne, *The Police State of Louis Napoleon Bonaparte* (Seattle: University of Washington Press, 1966) pp. 222–32.

[6] See, for example, M.L. Pélatant, *Rapport sur le service de la police* (Grenoble, 1906). Pélatant, a notable example of the professional policeman, was Commissaire central of Grenoble when he wrote this pamphlet.

[7] Clive Emsley, 'A typography of nineteenth-century police', *Crime, histoire & sociétés/Crime, history and societies*, 3, 1 (1999) pp. 29–44.

frontière and *Police spéciale de l'intérieure*. Six years later, on a wave of anxiety over anarchist outrages, their numbers were increased and they were unified into, simply, *Police spéciale*.[8] Aside from these essentially political policemen, it was not until 1907 that a specialised *police judiciaire* was established outside of the Paris police. The aim of this chapter is briefly to chart the development of detective police agents in nineteenth-century Paris, and to explore both their literary image and their self-image.

Set a thief...

There was a long tradition of police in early nineteenth-century Paris. Initially, the French word *police* had been virtually synonymous with civil government, but during the seventeenth century it became more associated with the government of a city. The broad meaning was reflected in the range of tasks carried out by the agents of the old régime's *lieutenant générale de police de Paris* which, in addition to crime and public order, covered, among other things, the supervision of markets and wetnurses, street-cleaning, street-lighting and fire-fighting. Dealing with crime was a relatively small part of the tasks of the police; the men responsible for the detection and pursuit of offenders had been relatively few under the old régime, and were not many more under Napoleon. The Prefect of Police in Napoleonic Paris had a broad responsibility, like his predecessors, for the smooth running of the city. Spread across the city under his command were 48 *commissaires de police*, each one with a small office situated in one of the 48 *quartiers*. There were also 24 *officiers de paix* who had a roving commission, and who were assisted by *inspecteurs*. None of these men wore a uniform, though the *commissaire* had a tricolour sash and the *officier de paix* carried a distinctive baton. Any one of them could be involved in the detection and pursuit of a criminal offender, but their tasks continued to range much wider than simply the suppression of crime. From 1800, when the Prefecture was created, the central administration of the Paris Police, situated in the rue de Jérusalem, consisted of some 100 men divided into three divisions.[9] Within the second division was the *bureau de sûreté* whose task was dealing with the crimes committed in the city. The *bureau* maintained links with

---

[8]   For these political agents, see Jean-Marc Berlière, *Le monde des polices en France* (Brussels: Éditions Complexe, 1996) pp. 19–22, and for the late nineteenth century, Marie Thérèse Vogel, 'Les polices des villes entre local et national: L'administration des polices urbaines sous la III République' (Thèse pour le doctorat, 2 vols, Université Pierre Mendès France, Grenoble II, 1993) ii, chapter 7.

[9]   Clive Emsley, 'Policing the streets of early nineteenth-century Paris', *French History*, 1 (1987) pp. 257–82.

both the *commissaires* and the *officiers*, but initially its personnel consisted largely of clerks and register keepers. Its first administrator was Monsieur Henry, known as *l'ange malin*, a veteran of the old régime police of Paris who had continued to serve in his chosen *métier* throughout the Revolution. *Mouchards*, or informers, had been employed under the old régime, though probably not in the numbers often assumed, and Henry continued to employ men who were known to have committed offences to inform on other offenders. The *mouchard* was unpopular and feared; at times he probably acted for the police under coercion and to keep himself out of prison. But *mouchards* were also to be found in prisons, reporting to Henry on the plans of fellow prisoners. In 1812 a significantly new step was taken when Henry, after discussion with the Prefect, appointed one of these informers to command a squad of other ex-convicts whose specific responsibility was to be the detection and pursuit of criminal offenders.[10]

Eugène-François Vidocq was the man appointed by Henry. Vidocq's *modus operandi* has already been discussed in Howard Brown's chapter above, but it is worth briefly revisiting his career at this point so as to underline the impact that its future revelation was to have on the image of detective police in France during the nineteenth century. Vidocq had been born in Arras in 1775, and had enjoyed a long, varied career as baker, thief, soldier, deserter and an escaped convict from the *bagnes* of both Brest and Toulon. He had begun working for Henry as an informer in the Paris prisons of Bicêtre and La Force in 1809. In March 1811 his release was arranged, and this was initially disguised as yet another escape during a transfer from one prison to another. Before the end of the year Vidocq was established at the head of a group of four ex-convicts like himself who were to be Henry's new detective squad. By the 1820s, the squad had grown to 28 and was settled in 6 rue Saint-Anne, behind the Prefecture building. The squad was *of* the Prefecture, but significantly it was not *in* the Prefecture; moreover, it was financed from secret funds rather than openly through the Prefecture's budget. Prefect Pasquier, whose agreement had been necessary for Henry to establish the squad, claimed that Vidocq would never have been permitted to cross the threshold of his office.

The *officiers de paix* and other policemen treated the new criminal detectives with disdain and even downright hostility, and there were other critics who found in the existence of Vidocq's band another stick with which to beat the police. 'L'existence publique du chef de ces individus, *le nommé Vidocq*, est une

---

[10] Jean Tulard, *Paris et son administration (1800–1830)* (Paris: Ville de Paris Commission des Travaux Historiques, 1976) pp. 134–35 and 149–51; on the old régime detectives (three *inspecteurs* were responsible for dealing with crime from 1750 to 1776, and four thereafter until the Revolution) and *mouchards*, see Alan Williams, *The Police of Paris, 1718–1789* (Baton Rouge, La.: Louisiana State University Press, 1979) pp. 104–11 and 228–31.

monstrosité qui pèse enormément sur la police', declared Louis Guyon in his contemporary and highly critical study of the *commissaires* and *officiers de paix* in Paris.[11] Yet Vidocq and his men appear to have achieved a considerable degree of success in solving crimes and apprehending their perpetrators; and the notion persisted that the best way to catch a thief was to use a thief, preferably an ex-thief. When Vidocq resigned for the first time in 1827 he was replaced by one of his subordinates, another ex-convict, named Barthélemy 'Coco' Lacour. Vidocq himself appears to have maintained links with the Prefecture, especially following the July Revolution, and in April 1832 he was recalled as chief of what was, since the prefectoral order of 28 September 1830, officially known as the *brigade du sûreté*. During a sensational case of attempted robbery heard at the assize court of the Seine at the end of September 1832, Vidocq's agents were accused of acting as *provocateurs*. The scandal contributed to his second resignation; his letter of resignation probably pre-empted dismissal by the Prefect of Police, Henri Gisquet.

Vidocq left the service of the Prefecture to set up a private detective agency that specialised in investigating the creditworthiness of individuals for businessmen. He can thus claim to be a founding father of both police and private detectives in France.[12] With Vidocq's departure from the police Gisquet set about reorganising the *sûreté*; he appointed a capable *officier de paix*, Pierre Allard, as its new chief, brought the funding of the bureau under the municipal budget, and forbade the recruitment of men with criminal records. At the same time, new quarters at 5 rue de Jérusalem symbolically confirmed the break with the past.

Literary images

While there were court cases like that of September 1832, Vidocq's notoriety was really established by his colourful memoirs which, understandably, emphasised his personal abilities and successes, but which were also quite open about his sinister past. The memoirs, which first appeared in Paris in 1828, caused a sensation.[13]

---

[11] 'The public existence of the chief of these individuals, the man named Vidocq, is a monstrosity that weighs heavily on the police'. Louis Guyon, *Biographie des Commissaires de Police et des Officiers de Paix de la Ville de Paris* (Paris, 1826) p. 229.

[12] Dominique Kalifa, *Naissance de la police privée: Détectives et agences de recherches en France, 1832–1942* (Paris: Plon, 2000) chapter 1, and see also pp. 281–86 for the regulations of Vidocq's private firm.

[13] Eugène-François Vidocq, *Mémoires de Vidocq, chef de la police de sûreté jusqu'au 1827*, 4 vols (Paris, 1828). These memoirs have gone through many editions. The most recent edition, which also includes his volume on criminals, is E-F Vidocq, *Mémoires: Les Voleurs*, introduction by François Lacassin (Paris: Robert Laffont, 1998). There have also been a variety of often romantic biographies; see, *inter alia*, Jean Savant, *La vie fabuleuse et*

They contributed to the unfavourable image of the Paris police already established by writers like Guyon, and, incidentally, they confirmed all of the worst prejudices that Englishmen possessed against French policing.[14] The memoirs also probably encouraged Prefect Louis Debelleyme's determination to clean up the organisation, to relieve 'Coco' Lacour of his duties, and to put some police agents into uniform as *sergents de ville* so as to make the police more visible, less sinister, and generally more approachable for the population. The sensation of the memoirs probably also contributed to Gisquet's decision to reorganise the *sûreté* in 1832. However, the memoirs seem to have been rather more sensational than Vidocq had intended, since they were expanded and elaborated by two writers employed successively by the publisher to make Vidocq's own narrative more exciting and fantastic for the reader. The first of these, variously identified as Maurice Descombres and Emile Morice, was dismissed on Vidocq's insistence after the appearance of volume one. Vidocq agreed to put his name to the second and third volumes, revised and expanded by L.F. L'Héritier de l'Ain, but refused to sign off the same writer's fourth volume. Yet this unfortunate experience did not stop Vidocq from collaborating with other authors for the novels *Les vrais mystères de Paris* (1844) and *Les Chauffeurs du Nord* (1845–46).[15] He also produced a survey, based on his own experience, of early nineteenth-century French criminality, *Les Voleurs, physiologie de leurs moeurs et de leur langage* (1836) and which focused particularly on the offenders' *argot*. Together these books did much to shape the image of the detective policeman in early nineteenth-century Paris and also the representation of the criminal offender. But the most significant literary projection of Vidocq himself came with Vautrin, the fantastic and superhuman criminal/policeman created by Honoré de Balzac.

Balzac knew Vidocq and it is generally accepted that he modelled Vautrin on his acquaintance. Vautrin first appeared in *Père Goriot* (1834–35) but it is in *Splendeurs et misères des courtisanes* (1837–47) where he is the dominant character. A master of disguise Vautrin appears in the novel in successive guises, as Jacques Collin, as the Spanish priest Carlos Herrera, and, among his underworld associates, as *Trompe-la-Morte* (Death-dodger). At the end of the novel, after a

---

authentique de Vidocq (Paris: Seuil, 1950); Philip John Stead, *Vidocq: A Biography* (London: Staples, 1953); Eric Perrin, *Vidocq: Roi des voleurs, roi des policiers* (Paris: Perrin, 1995); James Morton, *The First Detective: The Life and Revolutionary Times of Eugène-François Vidocq, Criminal, Spy and Private Eye* (London: Ebury Press, 2004).

[14] Vidocq's memoirs first appeared in English in 1828–29, and in July 1829 the Surrey Theatre presented *VIDOCQ! The French Police Spy*. See, Stead, *Vidocq*, p. 123. London was then in the process of establishing the Metropolitan Police whose first constables took to the streets in September 1829.

[15] These books were published under Vidocq's name, but the authors were, respectively, A. Lucas and Auguste Napoléon Vitu.

series of adventures which in some instances mirror those of Vidocq, he is recruited as a detective in the Paris Prefecture. But while he is the best known, Vautrin was not Balzac's only sinister policeman. Equally dangerous, though without a criminal pedigree and specialising rather more in political skulduggery than in the pursuit of thieves and murderers, was Corentin – again a character in *Splendeurs et misères des courtisanes*, but also in *Les Chouans* (1829–45) and *Une ténébreuse affaire* (1841–46). Disguise, subterfuge and courage were essential to Balzac's police detectives. But then they needed these qualities and abilities as they were required to mingle, undetected, with brave royalist counter-revolutionaries and with the dangerous criminal underworld that was portrayed as a kind of counter-society, at war with ordinary civil society – 'Paris est, pour eux, ce qu'est la forêt vierge pour les animaux féroces'. Balzac's criminal underworld had its unfortunates among those poor and destitute through no fault of their own; but it also had its professional thieves and murderers with their own hierarchy, their own code, and, of course, their own language in which each word was 'une image brutale, ingénieuse ou terrible'.[16] This picture was reflected also in Eugène Sue's *Les mystères de Paris* (1842); here the character of *Bras Rouge*, a central figure of Sue's fantastic underworld, is ultimately revealed as a police spy. Twenty years later, with the publication of *Les Misérables*, Victor Hugo introduced the reading public to a police agent as horrifying as Vautrin in the merciless Javert.

Javert had been born in prison; his mother was a fortune teller (*une tireuse de cartes*) and his father a convict. Javert himself was not a criminal but, because of his origins, he felt himself to be an outsider.

> Il remarqua que la société maintient irrémissiblement en dehors d'elle deux classes d'hommes, ceux qui l'attaquent et ceux qui la gardent; il n'avait le choix qu'entre ces deux classes; en même temps il se sentait je ne sais quel fond de rigidité, de régularité et de probité, compliqué d'une inexprimable haine pour cette race de bohèmes dont il était. Il entra dans la police.[17]

He had also developed an obsessive tunnel vision when it came to enforcing the law. In many ways Javert was the ideal police functionary; he was courageous and determined, and if he was mistaken in his single-minded and endless pursuit of

---

[16] 'Paris for them is as the virgin forest for fierce animals'. '… an image brutal, clever, or terrible'. The quotations are from Part Four of *Splendeurs et misères des courtisanes*, respectively in the chapters 'Les grands fanandels' and 'Essai philosophique, linguistique et littéraire sur l'argot, les filles et les voleurs'.

[17] 'He understood that there were two classes of men that society always kept at a distance – those who preyed upon it and those who protected it. He only had a choice between these two classes. At the same time he was upright, a man of regularity, probity and with a profound hatred for the race of gypsies from which he came. He joined the police'. Victor Hugo, *Les Misérables*, Part One, Book Five, Chapter 5.

Jean Valjean for a petty offence, the point was nevertheless made by Hugo that it took an expert to spot, and to deal with a dangerous criminal. After all, as Vidocq had explained to readers of *Les Voleurs*, criminals were a distinct class with their own language. Part Four, book seven of *Les Misérables*, following in the tradition of other novels of the period, provides a lengthy digression on *argot*: 'Quoi! comment! l'argot! Mais l'argot est affreux! mais c'est la langue des chiourmes, des bagnes, des prisons, de tout que la société a de plus abominable!'[18]

Understanding criminal *argot*, and recognising criminals were both things which professional policemen during the nineteenth century liked to emphasise as being among the skills of their *métier*. Balzac's discussion of criminal argot has already been noted; Vidocq's *Les Voleurs* contains similar references. It is also to be found in the memoirs of Louis Canler who himself served as chief of the *Sûreté*, and who considered that the occupant of this post,

> doit connaître la manière de vivre, de travailler, et les habitudes de ces êtres dangereux; il doit au besoin savoir parler leur langage (argot), soit pour inspirer confiance aux voleurs qu'il veut amener à lui faire des aveux ou des révélations, soit pour traduire les lettres saisies et écrits en jargon par les malfaiteurs, lettres qui très souvent fournissent des renseignements précieux.[19]

Canler's memoirs first appeared in an abbreviated form in the same year as *Les Misérables*. It is unclear why cuts were made in Canler's original manuscript, but it may have been to prevent any offence to his old superiors and to the current regime. Even so, the book still did not find favour with the authorities. Two months after the publication the book was seized and suppressed.[20] Yet Canler was no Vidocq and he insisted that the chief of the *sûreté* should be a man above reproach and above suspicion. He was highly critical of Vidocq and his men.

> Que devait-on attendre de tels hommes? Quelle estime pouvait-on avoir pour un service ainsi composé? Devait-on s'étonner de voir l'opinion publique assimiler au rang des malfaiteurs ceux qui les arrêtaient, et ce diction de Vidocq, dans son intérêt, s'était plu à accréditer: 'Pour pouvoir découvrir les voleurs, il faut l'avoir été soi-

---

[18] 'What? Pardon? Argot? But argot is frightful! It's the language of galley-slaves, of the penal colony, the prison, of everything that is most abominable for society'.

[19] '[He] must know the way of life, the work and the habits of these dangerous beings. He must know how to speak their language (*argot*) so as to inspire confidence in thieves that he is encouraging to make confessions or revelations, so as to translate letters and writings in the jargon that have been seized from offenders, letters that often furnish precious information'. Louis Canler, *Mémoires de Canler, ancien chef du service de sûreté*, edited and annotated by Jacques Brenner (Paris: Mercure de France, 1968) p. 152.

[20] See Brenner's introduction to Canler, *Mémoires*, pp. 11–12. The book appears to have provoked official condemnation for its candid account of the events surrounding the Orsini bomb plot.

même', était d'autant plus vrai, du moins apparence, que Vidocq s'attachait à choisir de préférence pour auxiliaires les practiciens qui lui paraissaient les plus hardis et les plus effrontés.[21]

A veteran of Napoleon's armies, Canler had joined the Paris police in 1820 and had served as an *inspecteur* in the *sûreté*. He became chief of the bureau in March 1849, as the Paris police was reconstituted in the wake of the Revolution of 1848. In his memoirs Canler stressed how, even when he had employed former convicts, they had remained at a distance from the honest, upright policeman. He had authorised the recruitment of a squad of informers (*indicateurs*) from recent convicts; these were, he maintained, strictly disciplined and given good pay to ensure that they stayed clear of their former criminal activity. The task of Canler's *cosaques irréguliers* was *faire le dépôt* and *faire le Saint-Jean*. The former involved accompanying the formal agents of the *sûreté* to the Prefecture every afternoon to see if they could identify any of the individuals arrested during the previous 24 hours. The latter involved the *indicateur* walking some 50 paces ahead of a patrol of *sûreté* agents and lifting his hat in a particular way if he saw a sought-after offender or an escaped convict. The intention was that an *indicateur* would never be identified as linked in any way with the proper policemen.

> Jamais, en aucune façon, mes cosaques irréguliers ne prêtèrent la main en quoi que ce fût, d'une manière active, à la police; jamais ils ne participèrent à une arrestation, ils ne furent même jamais appelés à faire nombre dans une opération quelconque, et ils ne furent jamais entre les mains de mes agents que des instruments passifs, agissant d'après les ordres qu'on leur donnait, comme le boeuf obéit à l'aiguillon, mais composant ainsi une surveillance étendue et surtout secrète, destinée à servir d'appendice à la police, et non pas à la représenter comme cela se pratiquait sous Vidocq et son successeur Coco-Lacour.[22]

Canler died in 1865, his book still banned. But within a decade there began to be a detectable shift in the literary image of the policeman and the individuals charged with the detection of crimes and the pursuit of their perpetrators. Already, in the

---

[21] 'What could be expected of such men? What esteem could be had for a service thus constituted? Public opinion quite naturally classed the offenders with those who arrested them, and Vidocq's words, 'set a thief to catch a thief', were true since he always chose his assistants from those who seemed the most bold and the most insolent'. Canler, *Mémoires*, p. 112.

[22] 'My irregular cossacks never took any initiative, they never participated in any arrest, nor were they ever called upon to make up numbers in any operation. They were never more than passive instruments in the hands of my officers, acting on the orders given them as the ox obeys the goad, but providing a broad surveillance that was, above all, secret. They were an auxiliary service for the police and did not represent the police as had been the case under Vidocq and his successor Coco-Lacour'. Canler, *Mémoires*, pp. 384–85.

1840s, Edgar Alan Poe had created the cerebral Auguste Dupin who advised the Prefecture in *The Murders in the Rue Morgue* (1841), *The Mystery of Marie Rogêt* (1842–43) and *The Purloined Letter* (1845). In France, however, the most notable figures in this new genre were the detectives in Emile Gaboriau's popular novels such as *L'affaire Lerouge* (1866), *Le crime d'Orcival* (1867), and *Monsieur Lecoq* (1869). These men had no personal or family links with the underworld; they carefully analysed clues, employed the marvels of modern science and carefully reasoned their way to the solution of crimes and the apprehension of offenders. Gaboriau's stories were full of the usual nineteenth-century clichés of children substituted at birth, of young women seduced, and of remarkable coincidences. Yet good always triumphed over evil, and while not yet the full-blown detective novels of the turn of the century – with characters such as, most famously, Sherlock Holmes – the books of Gaboriau and others contained detectives who were not only popular with the reading public, but who could also be seen as models for the *inspecteurs* of the *sûreté* themselves.[23]

In 1872 Achille Rabasse, an *inspecteur* in the Paris Police, prepared, apparently for his superiors, a lengthy manuscript on 'La Police municipale'. Lurking within society, Rabasse claimed, was *le monde obscur*:

> une autre société, si on peut l'appeler telle, qui est composé de Gens obscurs, des bandits qui sont la haine sans exception et font l'unique péril social. Ils sont paresseaux, menteurs, ivrognes, voleurs, meutriers et assassins. Ils attendent pour se montrer que le ciel soit noir, ils sortent le soir d'un trou, d'un bouge d'où ils en étaient entrés avant les faibles lueurs du jour.[24]

For such individuals, Rabasse claimed, brigandage and theft were a *métier*. They lived with prostitutes, had rank, guttural voices, and looked different from members of respectable society. Nevertheless, 'il faut un oeil bien exercé pour reconnaître un malfaiteur dangereux'.[25] The experienced, skilled policeman, it went without saying, had developed just such an eye.

---

[23] This point was made by the criminologist and police scientist Edmond Locard in *Policiers de roman et policiers de laboratoire* (Paris: Payot, 1924). For a brief discussion of Gaboriau, and others, see Dominique Kalifa, *L'encre et le sang. Récits de crimes et société à la Belle Epoque* (Paris: Fayard, 1995) pp. 30–31.

[24] 'An alternative society, if you wish to call it such, which is composed of lowly persons, bandits who, without exception, are filled with hatred and who consitute a singular social menace. They are idle, liars, drunks, thieves, murderers and assassins. They wait to appear when the sky darkens, in the evening they come out of their holes, their hovels into which they had withdrawn before the feeble glimmers of day'. Archives de la Préfecture de Police (hereafter APP), 398/3, Achille Rabasse, 'Police Municipale', 1872, p. 169.

[25] 'It needs a well-practiced eye to recognise a dangerous offender'. APP, 398/3, Rabasse, 'Police Municipale', p. 180.

The professionals

In the first half of the century in France it remained an uphill struggle to get away from the idea of the police detective as an ex-criminal, and the man that the average bourgeois gentleman, taking his cue from Prefect Pasquier, would not wish to invite across his threshold. Yet following Allard and then Canler all of the chiefs of the *sûreté*, and all of their detectives, were professional policemen. They were no longer from the criminal class but sought to appear as knowledgeable experts on the subject of that class. English suspicions remained, yet, as noted earlier, when in 1878, following a major fraud scandal, there was a need to reorganise the detective force of London's Metropolitan Police, the man chosen for the task was an energetic former soldier, war correspondent and lawyer, Howard Vincent, who had visited Paris with the express purpose of studying the detectives of the *sûreté*.

From the 1880s the men of the *sûreté* enjoyed a prestige that contrasted markedly with the generally poor reputation of the Paris police as a whole.[26] By the 1890s the bureau had 145 men: it was commanded by an *officier de paix*; there were four clerks, four *inspecteurs principaux*, six *brigadiers* (the nearest English equivalent being a sergeant), 177 *inspecteurs*, and seven auxiliaries. According to Maxime Du Camp, one of the authors to lionise the organisation, the *inspecteurs* were chosen with great care from among those NCOs leaving the army and seeking a job with the police. They were mainly married men, the fathers of families, and possessed of good morals and the rectitude necessary to avoid the temptations with which they were faced daily.[27] As with previous commentators on the organisation, Du Camp stressed the expertise of the *métier*.

> Ils doivent tout voir, tout entendre et ne jamais être remarqués; avoir fait une étude des moeurs particulières des voleurs, de façon à pouvoir trouver ceux-ci, les suivre et les arrêter. A cet égard, ils sont extraordinaires, et bien souvent sur le simple déclaration d'un vol, ils disent: C'est le fait d'un tel; nous le *pincerons* ce soir, à tel endroit: et ils le font comme ils l'ont dit.[28]

---

[26]   Berlière, *Le monde des polices*, p. 102.

[27]   Maxime du Camp, *Paris: ses organes, ses fonctions et sa vie dans la seconde moitié du XIXe siècle*, 6 vols (Paris: Hachette, 1883–98) iii, 85.

[28]   'They must see everything, hear everything and never be noticed; they must have studied the particular behaviour of thieves, the ways of finding them, following and apprehending them. In this respect they are extraordinary and often, on the simple report of a theft, they say: "That's the work of so-and-so; we'll nick him this evening at such-and-such a place". And they do as they have said'. du Camp, *Paris*, iii, 86.

The *métier* demanded courage, but it was satisfying to pursue and apprehend offenders, to pull off their masks and demolish their lies. Moreover, the detectives' experience meant that they could see through their quarry.

Une oscillation des traits du visage, une contraction involontaire des muscles de la bouche, un mouvement des yeux leur suffit parfois et leur indique sur quelle corde ils doivent specialement appuyer pour amener les criminels à se confesser.[29]

This, of course, was the kind of skill for which Vidocq and his men had been recruited; and some of the other old tricks of the trade were also noted as remaining in place, such as the use of disguise and the employment of *indicateurs*.

The professional expertise of the police detective, and also of the men who ran the commissariats and who continued to conduct some investigations, became a marketable commodity at the close of the nineteenth century in France. Several police detectives followed the route first taken by Vidocq and on retirement, resignation and even dismissal, they established themselves as private investigators carrying out discreet enquiries for anyone who could pay their fees. Paul Jaume had entered the police in the early 1870s after military service in which he had reached the rank of sergeant major. He rose rapidly, appears to have been highly regarded by his superiors and was periodically praised in the press for his exploits. It was a mark of pride that, in his long police career, he never carried a weapon. In the purge of the *sûreté* that followed the dismissal of Marie-François Goron in 1894, however, Jaume was also a casualty; it seems that he fell foul of the personal animosities and bureaucratic back-stabbing that went with the purge. Together with a colleague, who had also been dismissed, Jaume set himself up in a private detective agency. For several years there were concerns that Jaume would publish memoirs detrimental to the *sûreté*, and for several months his agency was kept under police surveillance. When the memoirs eventually appeared, 12 years after his dismissal, there was little to justify the anxieties. Jaume appears to have been a man of some integrity whose departure from the police was as a result of internal dissension. Louis Latapie was rather different. His police career began illustriously and he rose rapidly from being a *commissaire*'s secretary to *commissaire* in little more than a dozen years. But from then on his work and his behaviour began to cause alarm. He was noted as mixing with notorious men (*individus mal famés*) and undesirable women (*femmes légères*) and drinking heavily; his work became 'very mediocre' and in 1885, when he was still only 52 years old, the Prefecture

---

[29] 'A variation in facial features, an involuntary contraction of the muscles around the mouth, a movement of the eyes sometimes suffices for them and indicates what strings they need to pull to make a criminal confess'. du Camp, *Paris*, iii, 100.

decided to dispense with his services. Latapie promptly established a private detective agency in partnership with a former *inspecteur*.[30]

Of the nine men who followed Canler and who commanded the *sûreté* until just before the First World War two in particular appear to have stood out for their apparent probity and efficiency, though this may in part be the result of their having published colourful and lively memoirs – something that also contributed to the prestige of the organisation as a whole. Gustave-Placide Macé held the position from February 1879 to March 1884. It was during his tenure of office that the bureau moved adjacent to the Prefecture proper at 36 Quai des Orfèvres made famous by Georges Simeon's Maigret stories. Marie-François Goron commanded the bureau from November 1887 to July 1894.[31] Both Macé and Goron cultivated the image of the scientific expert. The former was responsible for encouraging the work of the Prefecture clerk Alphonse Bertillon and the development of the files, based on *anthropométrie*, which contained the measurements of certain physical features of arrested offenders, together with full-face and profile photographs. This, in itself, appeared a classic example of the detectives' harnessing of modern science for the surveillance of offenders. Goron led from the front, taking charge of several major cases and winning considerable praise from the press for his successes. In 1894 he left the *sûreté*; there were accusations of financial irregularity and of not having pursued politicians involved in the Panama Scandal with sufficient vigour. In the following year he followed the route already taken by Vidocq and established himself, in partnership with his son, as a private detective. Again, reminiscent of Vidocq, he published several crime novels loosely based on his police experience. Yet, in spite of the impression which both Macé and Goron sought to give of the cerebral detective solving crimes by careful thought, the analysis of 'clues', and the development and deployment of Bertillon's files, they also stressed the courage, probity and devotion to duty of their agents who were on

---

[30] Kalifa, *Naissance de la police privée*, pp. 166–73. Jaume's memoirs began to be published in *Le Matin* in August 1908.

[31] The nine chiefs of the *Sûreté* during this period were Antoine-François Claude (1858–1875), Etienne-Eugène-Léopold Jacob (1875–1879), Macé, Théophile-Jean Kuhn (1884–1885), Hippolyte-Ernest-August Taylor (1885–1887), Goron, Armand-Constant-Théophile Cochefert (1894–1902), Octave-Henri-Adéodat Hamard (1902–1912). Dossiers exist on all of these men, except for Kuhn, in the Archives de la Préfecture; see, in particular, APP EA/ 88 (Claude, and Cochefert), APP EA/89 (Goron, Hamard, Jacob, and Macé), EA/90 (Taylor). The relevant autobiographies are Marie-François Goron, *Les mémoires de M. Goron, ancien chef de la Sûreté*, 4 vols (Paris, 1897); Gustave Macé, *La police parisienne, aventuriers de génie* (Paris, 1884); idem, *La service de sûreté par son ancien chef* (3rd. edn. Paris, 1885). Antoine-François Claude, *Mémoires de M. Claude*, 10 vols (Paris, 1881), was not written by Claude. There is a brief biographical sketch of each of these chiefs in Benjamin F. Martin, *Crime under the Third Republic: The Shame of Marianne* (Baton Rouge, La.: Louisiana State University Press, 1990) pp. 53–61.

duty day and night, whatever the weather, whatever the danger. These men, declared Goron, specifically expressing his agreement with points made earlier by Macé, were

> la troupe d'élite qui protège la société contre le crime, [et ils] sont en réalité, les plus désintéressés des serviteurs de la patrie. Ces hommes, qui ne rechignent jamais quand ils s'agit de passer des nuits à la belle étoile, qui se disputent les missions dangeureuses, ne gagnent guère plus que les gardiens de la paix ... .
> Ce n'est pas donc l'intérêt qui les guide, et il y a parmi eux une probité professionelle telle, qu'on n'en jamais vu un seul consentir à accepter une grosse somme d'argent pour ne pas arrêter un coupable. C'est l'amour-propre seul qui les fait agir ...[32]

At the same time both Goron and Macé conceded that their agents continued to rely heavily on informers. Goron himself stressed the importance of not using professional *indicateurs*; he spoke out against the use of men who might be *provocateurs* or who gave evidence against former comrades so as to avoid prosecution themselves. As far as Goron was concerned the best informer was 'l'indicateur de hasard, l'indicateur qui, vivant dans les bourges fréquentés par les voleurs, entend parler d'un coup à faire et vient répéter à la Sûreté ce qu'il a surpris'.[33]

But, of course, what a police chief wrote in his memoirs for a respectable audience, and what went on between his subordinates and their 'narks' could be very different things. Moreover, from 1881 the opportunities for the *sûreté* in recruiting informers, or rather in pressurising prostitutes to act as informers, were increased when the *brigade des moeurs* – the squad responsible for the surveillance of prostitutes and the suppression of vice – was incorporated with the bureau, then under Macé. This incorporation was announced as a reform of the corrupt *brigade des moeurs* which had been heavily criticised.

The problem with the *police des moeurs* was that its agents could victimise and threaten young working-class women on the suspicion of them being prostitutes. Yet, while this was commonly condemned by reformers it was probably little

---

[32] '[They are] the elite band that protects society from crime, [and they] are in truth, the most selfless servants of the motherland. These men, who never make a fuss when it is a question of passing nights under the stars or quarrel over dangerous missions, earn hardly more than the uniformed police constable.... It isn't therefore personal interest that guides them, and there is among them such a professional proberty that you will never see one of them agreeing to accept a large sum of money in exchange for not arresting a guilty party. It is self-esteem alone that motivates them....' Goron, *Mémoires*, i, 215.

[33] ' ... the opportunist informant, the informant who, living in the districts frequented by thieves, hears word of an intended offence and comes to repeat what he has heard to the *Sûreté*'. Goron, *Mémoires*, iv, 107.

different from the way that the *inspecteurs* of the *sûreté* put pressure on young working-class men for information, especially those from stigmatised areas of the city or who were already known to have been in trouble with the police. Du Camp explained that the *inspecteurs* could identify an offender from the moment an offence was reported because they knew the way that different individual criminals worked. Louis Lépine argues in much the same way in his recollections of 14 years in command of the Prefecture de Police.[34] No doubt a few such recognisable offenders did exist but *le rafle*, by which the usual suspects were rounded up, followed by *la cuisine de la sûreté* or *le passage au tabac* – euphemisms respectively for a lengthy interrogation and a beating – or both, while they might yield confessions, as we now know from recent British detective scandals, might not yield genuine confessions.[35] Moreover, another century of criminological research has highlighted issues which do not appear to have troubled either those detectives who burst into print during the nineteenth and early twentieth centuries, or those who wrote approvingly of them – namely that a very high percentage of thefts appear to be opportunist, that only a few murders are committed by serial killers, and that where a crime is 'solved' it is common to have a suspect and, probably the perpetrator, identified by witnesses or by events from the outset.[36]

Conclusion

There continued to be commentators and critics with suspicions about the *sûreté* at the close of the nineteenth century. There were jealousies, frictions and demarcation disputes within the Prefecture that could not have helped the institution's efficiency, but which men like Goron and Macé sought to turn to their advantage in their memoirs.[37] Moreover, at the turn of the century there was a wave of concern about crime, notably street thugs, known as *apaches*, bandits and

---

[34] Louis Lépine, *Mes souvenirs* (Paris: Payot, 1929) pp. 150–51.

[35] One of the most striking recent examples was the case of Stephen Downing whose murder conviction, based on a confession secured after nine hours of questioning without a formal caution and without legal assistance or advice, was overturned on appeal after 27 years on 15 January 2002. At the time of his confession Dowling was 17 years old with the reading age of an 11-year-old. The matter was fully reported in every national newspaper in England on 16 January 2002 and, more recently, was the focus of a BBC TV docu-drama, *In Denial of Murder*, broadcast in two parts on 29 February and 7 March 2004.

[36] See, for example, Peter W. Greenwood, Jan M. Chaiken, Joan Greenwood, et al., *The Criminal Investigation Process* (Lexinton Mass.: D.C. Heath, 1977) and David Steer, *Uncovering Crime: The Police Role* (London: HMSO, 1980).

[37] Macé, for example, stressed the difficulties that he faced when he took charge, no telephone and having to use the telegraphic equipment of the head of the uniformed branch. *Le service de sûreté*, pp. 306–7.

vagabonds. It was these concerns that prompted the reorganisation of the *Police spéciale* into a dozen mobile brigades of between 13 and 18 men stationed in major cities and charged with assisting in the investigation of major crimes. But in general, and in Paris in particular, by the turn of the century the image of the French police detective had significantly altered and improved since the 1830s. Narratives, whether by policemen themselves, by novelists, even sometimes by social observers, were morality tales in which the good detective tracked down and apprehended the bad criminal. Police detectives still boasted the same skills as their ex-convict predecessors. They claimed to 'know' the offenders by their looks or their *modus operandi*. They employed disguise, but only when necessary. They used former offenders as informers; but they were no longer from the same milieu, the police detectives were now professional policemen rather than ex-professional criminals. Most important perhaps, the expertise of the police detective could be linked with the ideas of progress and modernisation. They claimed, and had it claimed on their behalf, that they employed reason and science to solve crimes; they were thus a part of the force of progress illuminating, and by illuminating undermining, the dark and sordid world of criminality. In publishing their books Canler, Goron and Macé followed in the tradition of Vidocq and sensational novelists like Sue. Their books were marketed much like the serialised, sensational novels which dealt with Parisian crime and low life earlier in the century. These detectives may have been honest and moral yet they were, like others who contributed to reformist literature during the nineteenth century, pandering to the fascination with crime and the sordid side of metropolitan life and teetering 'dangerously on the edge of voyeurism'.[38] But while the reader of Goron and Macé, like the reader of Gaboriau and others, could vicariously enjoy the criminal underworld, he or she could also rest assured that they were now protected by honest, professional, expert detectives supported by the powers of reason and science.

---

[38] Ann-Louise Shapiro, *Breaking the Codes: Female Criminality in Fin-de-Siècle Paris* (Stanford, Cal.: Stanford University Press, 1996) pp. 39–40.

Chapter Four

'Crime Does Not Pay': Thinking Again About Detectives in the First Century of the Metropolitan Police[1]

R.M. Morris

As a title, 'Crime does not pay' sounds familiar, even banal, enough. What follows, however, will seek to reveal a cryptic meaning which challenges some old, and offers ways in to some new, perspectives on detectives and how detective work developed in the Metropolitan police. It concentrates on perceptions of, and by, detectives rather than on the predominantly organisational and operational issues that have been dealt with elsewhere.[2]

In the beginning there were no detectives in the Metropolitan police. It was deliberately a preventive and not a detective force. All this was in stark contrast to the Bow Street Runners discussed above by John Beattie. Indeed, for the first ten years of its existence the Metropolitan Police existed alongside the forces established under stipendiary magistrates from 1792. The stipendiaries were situated in what were known as the Police Offices and each had their own force of constables. It was a situation in which the Bow Street officers happened to be the best known principally because they generally undertook the higher profile cases.

This dualism stimulated rivalry and dysfunctional jealousies which were only brought to an end by the Metropolitan Police Act of 1839. This act separated the judicial from the executive functions of the Police Office magistracy in London, abolished their forces, and thus left the Metropolitan Commissioners in sole charge

[1]   Earlier versions of this text were prepared respectively for a talk to the Metropolitan Police History Society on 6 March 2002, and a European Centre for the Study of Policing seminar at the Open University on 28 November 2003. I am very grateful for comments – and corrections – on both occasions.
[2]   For example, generally in Clive Emsley, *Crime and Society in England* (2nd edn London: Longmans, 1996); P.T. Smith, *Policing Victorian London* (Westport, Conn.: Greenwood, 1985); and Stefan Petrow, 'The Rise of the Detective in London, 1869–1914', *Criminal Justice History*, 14 (1993) pp. 91–108.

– except for the City of London – of policing in London. Whilst a number of the former magisterial officers then joined the Metropolitan force (as some had done earlier), that fact did not result in the creation of a detective cadre recognised as such.

Two cases changed this. The first was in 1840 and concerned the Mayfair murder of a septuagenarian peer (brother of the Duke of Bedford and an uncle of the Colonial – and former Home – Secretary, Lord John Russell) by his Swiss valet, François Courvoisier. Police efficiency was called into question because it took repeated searches of the butler's pantry to discover concealed items belonging to the victim.[3] A trial initially forced to proceed only on circumstantial evidence was dramatically altered by last minute appearance of fresh evidence. A witness prompted by press coverage of the affair was able conclusively to link the valet with the murder when she realised the significance of goods that he had passed to her for safe keeping.

The sensational case riveted Londoners, and the apparently adventitious character of aspects of the investigation demonstrated – without observers necessarily being able to put a name to it – a lack of professionalism. The *Times* was quick, too quick perhaps, to express alarm only two days after the murder:

> … it must not be considered that we are disposed to blame the metropolitan police. On the contrary, from its first foundation we have always approved of the system, and maintained that the public have derived great benefit from it. It is, however, impossible not to perceive that the excellence of the metropolitan police consists chiefly in the general protection it affords to the community and in its prevention of crime by the constant display of its power and vigilance. The semi-military nature of the regulations by which it is governed, the duties required of its members in continually patrolling their respective districts, render it almost incapable of engaging in such inquiries as can alone lead to the discovery of offenders. Whatever may have been the defects that formerly existed in our police establishments, the officers employed had acquired great experience, and were in every respect qualified for the discharge of the important duties entrusted to them. Neither their numbers nor their organisation were calculated to prevent crime, but as a detective police they seldom failed and we are satisfied that to ensure the apprehension of offenders recourse must be had to them.[4]

The other case concerned the Wandsworth murder in April 1842 of a young woman by Daniel Good. The identity of the murderer was never in doubt, and his

---

[3]   National Archives/Public Record Office, London (hereafter NA), MEPO 3/44, for Inspector Pearce's report of 9 June 1840, on a visit to the crime scene by Captain Lister (a relative by marriage of Lord John Russell) with a 'mechanic' to check whether a new search could discover more that had been overlooked by the police.

[4]   *Times*, 8 May 1840.

eventual arrest was a typical demonstration of how a disadvantage can be an unintended and unforeseeable benefit. At a time when officer turnover ran at well over 20 per cent a year, Good was arrested because a *former* Metropolitan officer, who had known Good, had, whilst working on a railway site in Tonbridge, recognised him. Another precipitating factor was the failed assassination attempt on 30 May in Constitution Hill when John Francis shot at the Queen.

The outcome was that the Home Secretary, Sir James Graham, authorised the establishment of a Detective Department at Scotland Yard. The rapidity with which the commissioners responded to the Home Secretary's remit by nominating two inspectors and six sergeants suggests that the Department already in practice existed in all but name.[5] The officers were directly answerable to the commissioners, and, in reply to an inquiry from the police commissioner of Madras in 1859, the Metropolitan Police Commissioner, Sir Richard Mayne, said: 'My practice is to see the Detective officers frequently shewing that I repose full confidence in them, while a strict control is maintained'.[6] In this, as in other matters as he got older and the force larger, Mayne almost certainly deluded himself.

Gradually, this group of officers began to attract a good deal of attention and some éclat. The *Times* in 1853, for example, ran a laudatory piece on Inspector Field relating his success in a west country case: 'Mr Field, it will be seen, arrived at a great result through very simple means; and we have no doubt that many persons will think, they could have done as well as he, now that they have been shown the way. The officer's skill lies in finding the way'.[7] In a long piece three years later, the *Quarterly Review* praised the calibre of the members of the Detective Department: 'From among the 6000 persons comprising the force a splendid field is provided for selecting good men; and Bow Street, great as was its fame, did not turn out more intelligent officers than we now possess'.[8]

There were, of course, some downs. The *Times,* having urged the resurrection of detectives in 1840, subsequently in 1845 attacked their resort to effective means. An Old Bailey trial had revealed that a coining gang had been caught by officers adopting plain clothes and assumed characters to get close to their quarry:

---

[5]   It is known that the commissioners used a select number of A or Whitehall Division officers – as necessary in plain clothes – to conduct the more difficult inquiries – see Belton Cobb, *The First Detectives* (London: Faber, 1957).

[6]   NA, MEPO 1/46, letter of 30 June 1859.

[7]   *Times,* 'A Detective in his vocation', 19 September 1853. The article also referred to Dickens' use of Field's experiences in the character of Inspector Bucket in *Bleak House,* and added that Dickens was understood to be engaged in writing Field's biography.

[8]   [Andrew Winter], 'The Police and the Thieves', *Quarterly Review,* XCIX (1856) pp. 160–200: at p. 175.

It is much to be regretted when any public body, abandoning the strict line of its legal functions, resorts to practices mischievous, or even suspicious, though for the purpose of attaining the legitimate objects of its original constitution. And in such a cast it is no valid excuse that these objects cannot be obtained by ordinary ways, for it is an indisputable proof of some radical defect in an institution, when it is unable to obtain good ends without the use of evil means. When such a defect appears the time is come for inquiry, or reorganization, and possibly even for total abandonment of the institution.[9]

In a later sensational case, Jonathan Whicher was accused of incompetence when he arrested the adolescent Constance Kent in Road, Somerset, for the murder of her half brother in 1860. He was later vindicated when Constance came forward to confess.[10] On the other hand, the first murder on a railway train led to a sensational transatlantic arrest and lifelong fame for Mueller's captor, Richard Tanner, whose retirement some years afterwards was noted in the *Times*.[11]

It was in this period that the Department attracted the favourable attention of Charles Dickens. In a famous series of articles in his periodical *Household Words* in the 1850s, Dickens gave a glowing portrait of the wisdom and competence of the Department's members, including Field. In particular, he contrasted them favourably with the officers of the old magisterial forces abolished in 1839 and whose reputations he comprehensively demolished:

> To say the truth, we think there was a vast amount of humbug about these worthies. Apart from many of them being men of very indifferent character, and far too much in the habit of consorting with thieves and the like, they never lost a public occasion of jobbing and trading in mystery and making the most of themselves. Continually puffed besides by incompetent magistrates anxious to conceal their own deficiencies, and hand in glove with the penny-a-liners of that time, they became a sort of superstition.[12]

John Moylan, the then Receiver, made a similar point in his centenary history of the Met in 1929:

---

[9]   *Times*, 2 December 1845. The leading article was enthusiastically seconded two days later by a letter asserting 'The whole "plain clothes system" opens such an avenue to fraud, connivance and corruption, that no discovery can compensate the deceit. It taints and vitiates whatever it crawls on – *delenda*'. *Times*, 4 December 1845, letter from Pall-mall [sic] signed 'P'.

[10]   The Metropolitan police website in November 2003 contained an inadequate and inaccurate account.

[11]   *Times*, 21 July 1869.

[12]   Charles Dickens, 'The Detective Police', in *Reprinted Pieces* (London: Odhams, n.d.) p.136.

The Bow Street Runners were more of a private detective agency than a public service ... The contrast between the Bow Street system and that of the new police was illustrated by the division of labour during the ten years (1829–1839) that the runners and the new police co-existed: the runners took the jewel robberies and left the murders to the Metropolitan police. All the murderers were discovered, but very few of the jewel thieves were brought to justice.[13]

The Victorian inquiries

The failure, however, to prevent the Fenian attack on Clerkenwell prison in December 1867, despite accurate intelligence from the Irish police, caused a serious crisis of public and parliamentary confidence. A great Fenian panic ensued. So serious was this Fenian crisis that the normally invisible Home Office came on the scene to deal with what *Punch* and others called the Defective Department. It did so again in the wake of the 1877 case of the Turf Frauds, where a resourceful confidence trickster suborned senior members of the central Detective Department, and the corrupt officers went forward to a sensational and protracted trial at the Old Bailey.

The Home Secretary did what Home Secretaries do in such circumstances – he set up inquiries. The 1868 inquiry recommended that, amongst other things, there should be a considerable strengthening of detectives by establishing detective officers in the Divisions as well as at the centre.[14] The Detective Department remained largely unchanged but without any authority over the divisional detectives who remained responsible to their divisional superintendents. Again, this arrangement seemed largely to ratify a process in the divisions where for some time there had been the growth of an informal specialisation where selected officers in plain clothes undertook inquiries not usefully undertaken by beat patrolmen.

Between 1877 and 1879 there were, in fact, three inquiries: the first specifically into the detective system, the second into every other policing function, and the last (the only one not to be completed) into relations between the commissioner and the Receiver, the Crown appointee responsible for the finance and supply of the force answerable to the Home Secretary direct. None of these inquiry reports was published, and nor was that of 1868–69.

Each report looked back, of course, to events leading up to the particular inquiry. One of the themes in the reports was the dearth of educated manpower, and the need to ensure an adequate supply of it for detective work. Throughout the

---

[13] John Moylan, *Scotland Yard* (London: Putnam, 1929) p. 150.
[14] NA, HO 347/1, *Report of the Departmental Committee on the Metropolitan Police*, 1868, Evidence, pp. 21–22.

Victorian period there was a great shortage of officers with educated skills sufficient to undertake the more demanding 'staff' and higher clerical work required in so large and varied an organisation. Looking back from 1912, Sir Edward Henry (Commissioner 1903–18) observed:

> A uniform Constable of more than ordinary intelligence and education can by obtaining employment in the clerical staff secure promotion more quickly than he could in the Criminal Investigation Department, and in fact nearly all the best men there who rise to the highest posts have at some time in their career held clerical posts.[15]

This situation was one of the reasons for the special status of the civilian clerks in the Commissioner's and Receiver's offices. At the same time, it was also true that educated men were not attracted to the police service if they could do better elsewhere. As the Superintendent of C Division memorably put it in 1868, 'in my whole experience [he had joined in 1835] I never knew a man of superior education join unless there was a screw loose somewhere'.[16]

Nonetheless, the Detective Department was at least partly successful in obtaining men of less ordinary stripe. Frederick Williamson, ultimately the first Chief Constable of the Criminal Investigation Department (CID), was the son of the first Superintendent of T Division. After a brief spell as a clerk in the Ordnance Department, he joined the Metropolitan force in 1850 and after only 20 months became a sergeant in the Detective Department. He was a comparatively well-educated man with some facility in French. Both Nathaniel Druscovitch, one of the guilty men in 1877, and James Thomson, who by then was the long-serving Superintendent of E Division, had polyglot backgrounds in the Eastern Mediterranean and, like Williamson, had, as well as language skills, better than average education. George Greenham, recruited direct in 1869, had a similar background, and had worked as a marine engineer's draftsman.

Those detectives who gave evidence to the 1868 and 1878 inquiries (each chaired by the then Home Office Parliamentary Under Secretary and held in private) fought the good fight for their corner. On his first appearance in the 1860s, Williamson maintained that the Department required a superior class of man – and

---

[15]　NA, HO 45/11000/223532, Henry to Home Office, 13 May 1912. Cavanagh's history exemplifies these processes – see Timothy Cavanagh, *Scotland Yard Past and Present* (London: Chatto, 1892). Joining in 1855 aged 19, he swiftly became assistant divisional clerk. Coming as a result to notice at headquarters, he was taken into the central Executive Department, becoming an inspector (at age 24) less than two years later, and chief inspector in the Public Carriage Office from 1865. Speaking of a colleague, Howes, who succeeded to higher things abroad, Cavanagh referred to him (p.72) as 'an educated man and in the days of which I am speaking we had very few of them in the Metropolitan Police'.

[16]　NA, HO 347/1, *1868 Committee*, Evidence, p. 269.

at a superior rate of pay. His reward was promotion from chief inspector to superintendent.[17]

Williamson maintained that it was best to recruit detectives early in their service before they acquired inappropriate habits, for example the gait and stance that came from long, long years on the beat. Invited to choose between whether for operational purposes he preferred 'traitors' to 'spies', Williamson plumped for the former: '... traitors I think are pretty honest to you because they are entirely in your hand'.[18] Yes, he acknowledged, gratuities were a welcome addition to pay, but they did not amount to much in fact. That detectives could look to rewards was well known, and when giving his evidence in the Courvoisier trial, the defence had sought to undermine Inspector Nicholas Pearce's credibility by getting him to admit his expectations in that regard.[19] There is evidence, too, that Mayne himself supported the gratuity culture.[20]

Gratuities featured prominently at the 1878 inquiry. Williamson defended them as apt to encourage zeal. Some others felt that, on the contrary, they should be abolished on the principle that every case should be treated alike regardless of anyone's ability to pay. The official rule was that all gratuities had to be declared so that the source was known before permission to retain was granted. The Commissioner, Edmund Henderson, said that in 12 months a total of £600 had been declared. The Chief Constable of Birmingham – where a similar rule applied – thought that in practice only the larger gratuities were declared.[21] Despite Williamson's protestations to the contrary, the Legal Adviser, James Davis, said 'I must say that in most cases I think that it [the gratuity] comes from a suggestion more or less direct from the men themselves'.[22]

---

[17] Superior is a relative term: John Byron, a retired inspector, asserted that on divisions a number of sergeants and even inspectors were of so low educational attainment that they struggled to take down simple dictation accurately. Ibid, Evidence, p. 418.

[18] Idem, p. 280.

[19] It is not clear exactly what sum Pearce received. However, if the recommendations of the prosecutor were upheld, Pearce would have received £100 from the £400 subscribed equally by the crown and the family. See NA, MEPO 3/44 for undated post-trial note by Hobler.

[20] See NA, MEPO 1/47 for letters of 18 June and 21 July 1862, where Mayne in the former accepted £10 gratuities from the Foreign Office for officers who had been attached to the Japanese Ambassador, and in the latter solicited gratuities from Claridges for officers attending another foreign visitor. See also NA, HO 45/7211 for Mayne's participation in the lengthy correspondence about what gratuities should be awarded to police and civilian staff who had undertaken extra work as a result of the 1862 Exhibition.

[21] NA, HO 347/1, *Report of the Departmental Commission to Inquire into the State, Discipline and Organisation of the Detective Force of the Metropolitan Police*, 1878, Evidence, q. 3273.

[22] Ibid, q. 5060.

But crucial evidence came from a former detective, Edwin Coathupe. One of the men recruited directly into the Detective Department, he served there during 1863–66. Unusually, he had a medical background and had spent periods in practice in Chippenham and at the Tredegar ironworks. He had also been a detective in Manchester and, at the time of giving evidence in 1878, was Chief Constable of Bristol where he remained until 1894. Speaking of his time in London in the 1860s, he recalled:

> ... not one of the officers of Scotland Yard would ever look at a case of picking up a thief in the streets; it was beneath them. "It does not pay" used to be the answer; "I can wait and get a case from Mr So-and-so, or Mr So-and-so's solicitor, which will bring me in £5 or £7 pounds". Those people would hang about the office for five or six days with the hope of getting a case of that kind. I never knew but one man who would go into the street to catch a thief.[23]

In other words – as in the title of this piece – crime does not pay.

Warned that abolishing gratuities would simply lead to officers taking them surreptitiously, the 1878 Committee nonetheless recommended their abolition. Their reasoning was very much linked to their thinking about improving detective pay to levels 'considerably in excess of the other [i.e. uniformed] branch of the service'. The Committee's scheme was that gratuities should invariably be paid into a fund administered by the Commissioner who would be empowered to allocate sums from it on the recommendation of the head of the detectives: '... should their suggestions as to increased pay and position for this branch of the force be adopted, they believe the future class of detectives will be so different, and the tone of the men so improved, that this objectionable system of gratuities may with safety be abolished'.[24]

Vincent's police code

In the event, gratuities were *not* abolished, and the system of declaration was retained. Whilst gratuities were only one of the topics that engaged the 1878 Committee whose recommendations led to the separation of the detective function from the uniformed hierarchy, gratuities were nonetheless significant in the concerns about *control* that ran through the Committee's deliberations. How were the senior officers responsible for the force to exercise effective control over a body largely autonomous in its operations, and which lay outside the strict hierarchical model of the uniformed force?

---

[23] Idem, q. 4663.
[24] NA, HO 347/1, *1878 Report*, pp. 52 and 53.

Evidence of this continuing concern may be found in the first edition of C.E. Howard Vincent's *Police Code* in 1881. Although designed principally to impart information accessibly to police officers of all kinds, the Code may also be seen as a conduct manual. What conduct manuals tend to do is surface the worst fears of their authors. Vincent, the 29-year-old appointed in 1879 as the Director of Criminal Investigations (that is, in charge of the unified detectives) devoted no less than 11 paragraphs to the gratuities problem insisting that there should be no solicitation, that declaration was compulsory and that 'Any failure to report a gratuity will, if its gift is discovered – as is very likely – entail severe punishment'.[25] Diplomatically, these fulminations were dropped from later editions, Vincent no doubt being convinced of the undesirability of washing dirty Yard linen in public. Another example of his own self-censorship was the deletion after 1881 of an introductory sentence in his 1881 Preface: 'The duties of a police officer are so varied, and depend to so great an extent upon surrounding circumstances, that much must necessarily be left to practical experience, and the exercise of individual tact'. This was true, but too impolitic to be retained in a manual with a quasi-official status.

But those were by no means the only emendations and changes of emphasis that occurred in the text of a Code that survived until its final – 17th – edition of 1931. Thus, for example, whereas in 1881 officers were advised that 'Detective officers should be especially guarded against the arrogation of individual credit...' the advice in 1912 became against 'the *improper* arrogation...'. Similarly, the advice about the handling of informants was changed. In 1881, Vincent wrote:

> Detectives must necessarily have informants, and be obliged to meet them when and where they can. But it is very desirable that the public house should be avoided as much as possible. Tap room information is rarely worth much. Occasionally, perhaps, refreshment must be given to an informant, but when possible it is best to give money.

However, this was considerably altered in the 15th edition of 1912, the first to appear after Vincent's death and the first to be wholly in the hands of the Yard to which he had willed the copyright. The last two sentences were replaced with a single sentence on a wholly fresh point about respecting promises of confidence.

A final example of senior officer concern about control is to be found in the Code's treatment of police/press relations. In 1881 these were defined in four paragraphs of very decided language. The first paragraph stated the general rule:

---

[25] C.E.H. Vincent, *A Police Code and Manual of Criminal Law* (London: Cassell, 1881) pp. 170–71. See also 15th edn, Butterworth, 1912; and 17th edn, Butterworth, 1931.

> Police must not on any account give any information whatever to gentlemen connected with the press relative to matters within police knowledge, or relative to the duties to be performed or orders received, or communicate in any manner, either directly or indirectly, with editors, or reporters of newspapers, on any matter connected with the public service, without express and special authority.

The second paragraph spelled out the consequences of breach of the first:

> The slightest deviation from this rule may completely frustrate the ends of justice, and defeat the endeavour of superior officers to advance the welfare of the public service. Individual merit will be invariably recognised in due course, but officers who without authority give publicity to discoveries, or the progress of a case, tending to produce sensation and alarm, show themselves wholly unworthy of their posts.

The final paragraphs asserted the sole right of the Commissioner and the Director of Criminal Investigations to direct relations with press, and – to encourage compliance – explained in minatory terms that the Executive Branch Chief Inspector examined all newspapers daily and 'submits all extracts bearing upon the duties of the police, or the conduct of any individual in the service'. The final two paragraphs did not survive beyond the first edition. Although a sentence was added to the effect that the press could also be helpful in certain circumstances, the first two paragraphs survived otherwise up to and including the 1931 edition.

What changed and what stayed the same

This concern about gratuities, informants and press relations has an inescapable sense of *déjà vu*. What was it the famous author said about the old pre-1839 detectives? – '... there was a vast amount of humbug about these worthies ... far too much in the habit of consorting with thieves and the like, they never lost a public occasion of jobbing and trading in mystery and making the most of themselves ... hand in glove with the penny-a-liners of that time'. If the cap fits...

Of course, none of this is to deny that the more exacting inquiries did require superior abilities, or at least abilities superior to those of the divisional detectives established in 1869 and less than ten years later described as 'the least educated and the least intelligent men in the force'.[26] But the evidence of the persistence of practices that existed *before* the force was established shows how slowly the older world evolved into one with a recognisable public service ethic where the ideal was that pay should be regarded as the sole source of remuneration, and the whole

---

[26]   NA, HO 347/1, *1878 Report*, p. 45.

of an officer's time should be devoted to the service's work. Also shown was how conscious senior officers were of their powerlessness to insist that their standards be observed in all circumstances.

Now that these standards are taken for granted, it may seem surprising that the public response to the 1877 scandal was not unsympathetic. One paper noted that one of the convicted officers had fallen into temptation in order to clear a debt of just £60. The *Standard* in August 1877 pointed out how low the officers' salaries were: 'A question will naturally arise, how can the intellectual capacity, the linguistic knowledge, the acumen, the experience of the world that are called into play in the investigation of crime be subsidised for such salaries as these?'[27] Whilst this perhaps exaggerated the difficulty of the general run of criminal cases where, the Commissioner said, 'in 99 out of every 100 cases of crime, the detection is most humdrum work, and it only requires just ordinary care and intelligence. You do not want a high class mind to do it at all',[28] it also clearly spoke a truth. In a leader after the trials, the *Police Service Advertiser* observed:

> ... it was pleasing to find the daily press of the country dealing with the case in a careful and moderate spirit, and not including the entire service in one sweeping condemnation, but rather pointing out the difficulties and temptations to which many officers had been subjected, and to find, if possible, a remedy.[29]

In other words, the root of the problem in some ways was the very fact that, in the Coathupe sense, crime did not pay. What the Victorians struggled with was how, perversely, to make it pay and in ways consonant with a changed ethic of public service.

Professionalising detection

Williamson and Vincent discussed the problem of how to recruit and retain the right sort of officer. Williamson had earlier offered views on recruitment to the central detective department on the appointment of Henderson as Commissioner in 1869:

---

[27] Quoted in *Police Service Advertiser*, 31 August 1877.

[28] *1878 Committee*, Evidence, q. 5251. In his autobiography, Robert Anderson sought to belittle Henderson's views: 'He never took to the details of police work, and least of all to thief catching'. See Robert Anderson, *The Lighter Side of My Official Life* (London: Hodder, 1910) p. 124. Modern social scientists would probably side with Henderson. See, for example, Dick Hobbs, *Doing the Business* (Oxford University Press, 1989) p. 186.

[29] *Police Service Advertiser*, 28 December 1877.

The number of superior officers would appear to be large for so small a force. But I submit that it desirable to attract to the Detective department as intelligent and trustworthy men as can be found in the Service, and when once attached to it, they should be induced to remain, as men in time become valuable, and a depository of 'information'. This end can only be attained by holding out such inducements as regards pay and promotion, as might be hoped for if they remained at the ordinary police duties. Men qualified to be Detective Officers would if their conduct was good have a fair prospect of rising to superior ranks in the Service and would not come into the Detective Department unless the advantages were equal to those of the other branches of the service.[30]

Williamson's views had not changed by 1880. He excoriated 'the old plain clothes man'. He repeated that disparities in promotion opportunities discouraged recruitment of the best qualified. He added that conditions of service were a disincentive, particularly the uncertainty and irregularity of the duties 'which are no doubt in many cases very distasteful and repugnant to the better class of men in the service, as their duties constantly bring them into contact with the lowest classes, frequently cause unnecessary drinking, and compel them at times to resort to trickery [sic] practices which they dislike'.[31]

Vincent forwarded Williamson's views with his own. The burden of his argument was that he was simply not getting the best men. There had been no applications for well-paid inspector posts even though financially attractive. Vincent put the cause down entirely to the loss of the avenue of promotion to superintendent. In all other respects he concurred in Williamson's arguments whilst offering two remedies of his own. These were that every officer on promotion should spend 12 months as a detective, and that there should be a detective allowance. In the margin of the latter proposal someone – perhaps Henderson himself – had written 'to buy the incompetent!'[32]

Nothing came of these proposals. The fact was perhaps that, apart from the degree of specialisation entailed in detective work at that time, it could not be maintained that it involved a degree of expertise, still less merited separate professional status, different from and superior to that of the rest of the service. Indeed, there was resentment from the uniformed branch in a situation where, despite their corruption, the detectives were seen to have been rewarded with promotion and enhanced pay. As one disgruntled Superintendent of 25 years service put it: '... the general feeling is that the department which brought scandal

---

[30]   NA, MEPO 2/37, Williamson to Commissioner, 20 February 1869.

[31]   NA, MEPO 2/37, memorandum of 22 October 1880.

[32]   NA, MEPO 2/39, 'Confidential memorandum on the Detective Force of the Metropolitan police' signed by Vincent and dated October 1880.

and disgrace upon the police has been met with rewards all round, whereas the others have been left out in the cold'.[33]

Moreover, both the senior officers of the force and the police authority continued for some time to appoint to the leadership of the CID men whose detective experience was, initially at least, negligible. At 29, Vincent was a complete tyro, a shot in the dark with only some small military and legal experience. His successor, James Monro, with considerable police experience in India was an exception. But Monro himself recommended the appointment of his friend Melville Macnaghten first as Williamson's deputy and then as his successor in 1890. Macnaghten had no police background whatsoever but, as an old Etonian of parts, his personal qualities were alone thought sufficient to recommend him. Monro's successor as Assistant Commissioner was Robert Anderson, formerly Secretary to the Prison Commission, who had at least some experience in Fenian counter-intelligence and was, though not practising, a barrister. Anderson was succeeded first – but only briefly – by Henry who had solid police experience and was the inventor of the first workable system of classifying fingerprints. In turn, he was succeeded by Macnaghten, and the latter by Basil Thomson in 1913.

Thomson, like Anderson, Secretary to the Prison Commission, had governed a number of prisons, had been admitted to – though never practised at – the Bar in 1896, but had no detective or police experience. However, Thomson's appointment did not go without remark. John Kempster, the police journalist and editor of the *Police Review*, wrote to the Home Secretary in very direct language: '... previous experience in the difficult work of criminal detection ought to be an essential qualification...; the imposition of an outsider at the very head of a department necessitating so much technical skill and experience is a disparagement to the entire Criminal Detection Profession...'[34]

Kempster's was a large claim: he purported to speak for what he called a 'Criminal Detection Profession'. No one, not even Williamson or Vincent, had made such a claim before. Was it simply journalistic hyperbole, an editor using the g ft of the gab to butter up his readers and help to promote their self-interest? Whilst there was some of that, it would have been difficult to argue even in 1913 that the claim was entirely without foundation.

The reasons for this were, however, less to do with any marked change in detective personnel or method than in organisational changes which affected public perceptions of detective work. Fingerprinting, even if widely misunderstood as a means of detecting criminals rather than simply identifying them, was seen to give

---

[33] NA, HO 347/1, *Report of the Commission to inquire into the State, Discipline, and Organisation of the Metropolitan Police Force other than the Criminal Investigation Department*, 1879, Evidence, q. 315.

[34] NA, HO 144/21176/163976, letter of 3 July 1913.

an infallible, scientific support to detection procedure. No longer did finding the belongings of Lord Russell in Courvoisier's pantry fail to give more than circumstantial proof of the valet's guilt. In future, Courvoisier's prints could be expected to be found on the Waterloo medal. In addition, Scotland Yard was seen to have developed systems of registration and classification in support of detective operations. Crime was apparently declining, and street behaviour, and public manners generally, were thought to have improved.

The emphasis here is on perception. The fact is that little is known about actual detective behaviour beyond what emerged in court and what, in an increasing stream of memoirs, mainly Metropolitan detectives chose to reveal. Much of the apparent agonising about the use of informants has perhaps been taken too seriously. Vincent's 1881 Code and all its successors accepted that the use of informants was axiomatic: the problem was not whether they should be used but how they should be controlled. Even in 1868 Mayne had made no bones about using them: 'I think it prudish and weak not to take advantage of the vices of men for the prevention and detection of crime as well as their good qualities'.[35]

It has also to be borne in mind that detectives had to operate within a criminal law which remained in many ways inchoate so far as their own operations were concerned. The 1880 Titley case – where a chemist selling abortifacients was convicted at the Old Bailey as the result of a police 'sting' operation – led to much parliamentary alarm about 'espionage' and an undertaking from the Home Secretary that such operations would not be undertaken without his express authority. Such concerns could still easily be raised by adroit defence counsel, and press sympathy quickly engaged. The Home Secretary's undertaking did not extend to agreeing that such operations should never recur. Indeed, he made it clear that the trial judge had been involved in a similar case ten years before when he had consulted his brethren and allowed the trial to proceed.[36]

Throughout the nineteenth century there was no authoritative guidance to the police on how interrogations of suspects should be conducted. From 1882, Vincent's Code attempted to remedy this lack by including a wordy, hortatory piece by Sir Henry Hawkins, a celebrated puisne judge. Authoritative Judges Rules were not promulgated until 1912. And the truth is that despite the 1929 Royal Commission much of the relevant law and procedure relating to the investigation and prosecution of crime was not settled until the Police and Criminal Evidence Act 1984.

---

[35]   NA, HO 347/1, *1868 Committee*, Evidence, p. 96.
[36]   Hansard, Commons, 11 January 1881, cols 442–44.

Rewarding detectives

By the Edwardian period the CID was clearly an established and accepted fact. Its co-existence with the much larger uniformed branch meant that the commissioner had always to keep an eye on their relative positions. Although no formal representative machinery was instituted until 1919, CID officers had their spokesman in the Assistant Commissioner (Crime) who was zealous in addressing both the questions of pay and, equally important, promotion prospects. This meant that detectives had an advocate their uniformed colleagues lacked since no one senior officer was similarly responsible for their interests. Thus, for example, when arguing for an increased detective establishment in 1908 to keep abreast of population increase, the Assistant Commissioner (Macnaghten) successfully proposed a distribution of the additional numbers by rank specifically 'for the purpose of ensuring a steady flow of promotion in the future'.[37]

The Commissioner, Henry, returned to the charge in 1912. In a long and carefully considered letter, he asked the Home Office for a further augmentation but cast in a way designed also to improve lower rank promotion and pay. What was wanted was an improvement in the conditions of service, and better opportunities for the man of exceptional aptitude and ability to rise to the higher ranks. The language he used illustrates not only the priority he accorded detective work but in some measure also how the CID had come to be regarded at large:

> The work of this Department is in many ways the most important and is certainly the most difficult, which falls upon the Metropolitan Police... The importance of this work being adequately done can scarcely be over-rated. The public judges of the efficiency of the Police generally largely on its detective work, and as far as the judicial investigation of crime is concerned, it is not too much to say that the proper presentation of the case, both for and against the accused, depends almost entirely on the Police enquiry being thoroughly, intelligently, and honestly performed.[38]

When invited by the Home Office to comment on the proposals, the Receiver George Tripp was not unsympathetic. Including pension costs, the proposals amounted to only an extra £6,000 a year. On the other hand, he pointed out that the CID was not as disadvantaged as the Commissioner implied. Promotion was substantially better in the CID than in the uniformed branch: whereas in the latter the proportion in the ranks of inspector, sergeant and constable were respectively 3 per cent, 12 per cent and 85 per cent, in the CID they were 11 per cent, 48 per cent and 41 per cent. Moreover, the average pay of the two higher ranks was about 20 per cent higher in the CID. In addition, CID men received a plain-clothes

---

[37] NA, MEPO 2/1148, memorandum of 28 January 1908.
[38] NA, HO 45/11000/223532/1, Henry to Home Office, 13 May 1912.

allowance, had more freedom of action, had better opportunities of obtaining gratuities, were free from patrolling and night duty, had access to travelling and subsistence allowances which 'must not infrequently yield some profit', and were more sought after for further employment when pensioned.[39] The Home Secretary, Reginald McKenna, discussed the proposals with Henry and then authorised the changes to take effect over a three-year period.

Henry did not, it seems, merely see himself as promoting detectives' interests: there is evidence that he also sought simultaneously to improve control. An inquiry he initiated throughout the force about gratuities in 1905 seemed to show unspectacular levels in most divisions, and resulted in a revised General Order in 1907 which emphasised the reporting rule and that 'Any infringement ... will be dealt with as a serious offence'. A Police Order of 20 December 1904 spelled out the procedures for detective diaries, emphasising that local inspectors had to examine diaries not less than twice a week.[40]

An attempt by Henry's successor, General Sir Nevil Macready, in 1919 to further improve the position of detective sergeants did not succeed. The new Receiver, Moylan, was sceptical: 'I attach a note which puts the "grievance" of the CID Sergeants in a different light. No CID sergeant would wish to change places with a uniform Sergeant. I do not therefore think that there is any real grievance which requires remedying'.[41] Tactfully, the Commissioner was invited to await the outcome of the Desborough Committee then sitting, and to whom the sergeants had put similar claims.

What these exchanges showed was that detectives had over time been very successful in drawing ahead of their uniformed colleagues. The latter sometimes felt this keenly: 'It is common talk that the Commissioner is looking after his pet department at the expense of the Uniform Branch, and that a large reduction in the CID would not reduce its efficiency'.[42]

---

[39]   Ibid, minute of 20 June 1912.

[40]   NA, MEPO 2/842 and 2/1760 for gratuities; NA, MEPO 2/741 for diaries. The 1905 gratuities inquiry did not include central detectives, and the extent of their officially acknowledged benefits as well as those taken surreptitiously are alike unknowable. It is possible that, as detective remuneration increased and more democratic forms of exchange asserted themselves, the gratuity culture declined. Another factor may well have been the displacement of 'private' inquiries into the private inquiry agent sector, itself liberally peopled by former officers. These processes do not yet, however, appear to have been examined.

[41]   NA, HO 45/11000/223532/17, Macready to Home Office 22 March 1919, and Moylan's minute of 27 March 1919.

[42]   *Police Review*, 13 March 1914, 'Metro Criminal Investigation Department' by 'Progressive'.

Macnaghten acknowledged, even celebrated, the fact. When comparing the London CID with their Paris equivalents: 'At no time, however, do I honestly consider that it was superior to our detective force. Certainly, taking man for man, we never had anything to fear from a comparison of the officers. We pay our men better, and we get a more educated and, therefore, superior article'.[43]

Having examined the experience of Metropolitan officers over the period 1829–1914, one of Haia Shpayer-Makov's conclusions was 'Many officers continued to view their work in purely instrumental terms, as a means of survival, but a growing proportion, primarily among detectives and those who rose to a privileged position in the force, developed an intrinsic affinity for their work, deriving great satisfaction from it'.[44]

Detective perceptions

There has been much interesting discussion about public perceptions of detective activity. Some of it has focused on the way in which detective activity became incorporated in literary representation, first as an element in novel plots and, secondly, as a separate genre. The Sherlock Holmes stories of Conan Doyle are usually regarded as representative of the full-blown detective story/novel, though typically of its kind featuring a detective who was not a police officer. On the contrary, his greater intellect and scientific ability made him superior to the plodding representatives of the Yard.

Paul Lawrence has illuminatingly compared and contextualised French and English police memoirs.[45] In the following chapter Haia Shpayer-Makov shows how determined police memoirists were to counter these elegant and condescending fictions. She points out that these memoirs may be understood in a number of different ways, for example as narratives of self-improvement, as work histories, or as apologias in relation to an unusual but prideful occupation. The purely personal details of background and work history are usually swiftly covered as a prelude to anecdotes designed sometimes to glamorise and usually to emphasise the skill of detective work and the assiduity of its practitioners.

---

[43] M. Macnaghten, *Days of My Years* (London: Arnold, 1914) p. 225.

[44] Haia Shpayer-Makov, *The Making of a Policeman: A Social History of a Labour Force in Metropolitan London, 1829–1914* (Aldershot: Ashgate, 2003) p. 266.

[45] Paul Lawrence, ' "Scoundrels and scallywags, and some honest men..." Memoirs and the self-image of French and English policemen, c. 1870–1939', in Barry Godfrey, Clive Emsley and Graeme Dunstall, eds, *Comparative Histories of Crime* (Cullompton: Willan, 2003).

There are further, alternative possible readings of these texts. First, to take them at face value, they declare the great worth to the writers of the relative autonomy that detective work, especially in the central branches, conferred. It has to be borne in mind that most police work in the then existing uniformed branches was iterative and routine requiring a shackled, grinding care of detail in often adverse circumstances. The detective was a freer agent. In addition, as already shown, the promotion position changed over time as the CID and its attendant bureaucracy grew. Especially with the creation of the four Area Superintendent posts – glamorised as the 'Big Four' – it was difficult to maintain that detectives' promotion opportunities even at the most senior levels were less favourable than those for other officers.

Secondly, since it is possible that many of the memoirs (except perhaps those appearing initially in instalments) were at least partly composed by ghost writers, it is necessary to be very sceptical about relying too much on the content – or inferring the levels of literary attainment of their supposed authors. Their very structure – commonly, personal details at the front end and anecdotes for the rest – suggests how the works were compiled. Their purpose was to entertain with stories of 'real life', sometimes with mild social or sexual titillation. They were not designed to place the apparent authors in a poor light, so conventional moralising was the order of the day. Attacking the writers of detective fiction was not only to inject some safe controversy but helped to underline the essential seriousness of the authors' occupation. Throw in 'pride of regiment', some admiring stories of real, if usually dead, former colleagues, and a few unremarkable reflections on the state of crime, and the formula was complete. These elements remained the typical mix of a genre that started at the end of the nineteenth century and whose decline in the next seems associated with the decline and extinction of capital punishment. Current police narratives are no longer dominated by detective reminiscence: they are as often representative of managerial or political memoir.

Paul Lawrence and Haia Shpayer-Makov confine their analyses mostly to superintendent level memoir and below. However, some senior Metropolitan officers also published memoirs, three of the four immediate successors of Monro for instance. None could be described as a professional detective, though all had been Assistant Commissioners in charge of the CID. The memoirs differ not only from the 'ranker' detectives but also from each other.

Robert Anderson, head of the CID between 1888 and 1901, had had a varied career where the common thread was his involvement in Irish counter-intelligence from 1867. His memoirs,[46] trailed first as articles in *Blackwood's Magazine*, caused a sensation in Irish political circles because he revealed that he had, whilst an official, not only assisted with but had actually composed some of the articles

---

[46] Anderson, *The Lighter Side of My Official Life*.

that appeared in the series of articles 'Parnellism and Crime' published by the *Times* in 1887. In the ensuing full dress debate on 21 April 1910, whilst the government carried the day, Anderson did not escape censure with the Home Secretary commenting on the *Blackwood*'s articles' 'spirit of gross boastfulness' and their offensive and pointless observations' about well-respected individuals.[47]

Anderson's comments on detective work in his autobiography did not rise above the conventional or vainglorious. His main views on crime control were contained in an earlier work published in 1907. There he argued that preventive detention could clear a great deal of crime from the streets, and admitted to disregarding the law.[48] In addition, in his autobiography, Anderson confirmed his entirely cavalier attitude to dealing with the press.[49]

The memoirs of Macnaghten, Assistant Commissioner 1904–13, were a more urbane and relaxed account of his life and career devoid of any impulsion to pay off old scores. Macnaghten said much about detective activities but little about detective methods.

Thomson produced a number of volumes about his experiences in the prison service as well as at Scotland Yard. His line was always to praise the quality of the teamwork that supported him as Assistant Commissioner 1913–21. Though indulging in it himself, he took the conventional line noted by Haia Shpayer-Makov about detective fiction:

> Real life is quite unlike detective fiction; in fact, in detective work fiction is stranger than truth. Mr Sherlock Holmes ... worked by induction, but not, so far as I am able to judge, by the only method which gets home, namely, organisation and hard work.[50]

Police/press relations

It would not be enough to rely on detective memoir as the sole source of police attempts to influence how they were seen. Another important nexus was the police's relationship with the press. Although police press/media relations departments are mostly the creation of the second half of the last century, the Metropolitan Police like other forces was involved directly with the press from the beginning. In fact, of course, crime reportage has been a staple of all newspapers throughout time.

---

[47] Hansard, Commons, 21 April 1910, cols 2335–436.
[48] Robert Anderson, *Criminals and Crime* (London: Nisbet, 1907) especially p. 82.
[49] Anderson, *The Lighter Side of My Official Life*, p. 201–2.
[50] Basil Thomson, *Queer People* (London: Hodder, 1922) p. 1.

From the beginning, Rowan and Mayne followed up newspaper reports alleging police wrongdoing, and required superintendents to investigate and report. Wherever possible, false reports were corrected or redress afforded where misconduct was proved. Mayne made no bones about approaching the editor of *The Times* direct.[51]

With the general rise in literacy during the nineteenth century, newspapers became an increasingly powerful medium influencing perceptions of policing. The growth in the number of newspapers was necessarily accompanied by a growth in the number of journalists. Something like a symbiotic relationship appears to have developed between detectives and journalists. Each needed the other: the detective required the journalist to broadcast details that might assist identification or even capture; and the journalist wanted as many details as exclusively as possible – with perhaps casting 'individual credit' as a lure. Confidences had to be traded for responsible reticence. As one journalist put it when invited to produce a series of articles for the *Evening News* critical of the police: 'I was careful not to abuse the confidence of men with whom I have been for many years associated in a most friendly spirit, the police'.[52]

Of course, the relationship did not always correspond to such neat reciprocity. In the end, no journalist was going to be persuaded out of a good story. One example of where the attempt was made was related by Aaron Watson. When writing for the *Pall Mall Gazette*, he was tasked in the early 1880s to follow up stories of 'fighting gangs' whose existence was denied by the police. He claimed to have found evidence that they did indeed exist and the story duly appeared in the *Gazette*, a well regarded journal with a potentially influential readership.

Watson found himself invited by Howard Vincent to an interview with the Commissioner, Henderson, and himself. According to Watson's account, Henderson pressed him for his evidence:

> This was an uncomfortable interview in the large long room of Old Scotland Yard, with the feeling on my part that I was being subjected to an examination in the French fashion, with the object of drawing from me some admission which might be communicated to my editor to my disadvantage, and with the consequence of the destruction of his belief in my credibility. However, the questioning that I underwent was gentle enough in its manner. It was, indeed, almost felinely polite.

---

[51] NA, MEPO 1/47, for example, letters of 13 October 1862, 4 May 1863 and 31 January 1865.

[52] R.P. Watson, *Memoirs of Robert Patrick Watson: A Journalist's Experience of Mixed Society* (Smith, Ainslie, 1899) p. 306.

Although pressed, Watson claims he refused to pass any further information he received first to Scotland Yard. He told Henderson 'I was not a detective...and I could not consent to be a spy'.[53]

In his memoirs, Macnaghten expressed himself warmly about his relations with the press:

> At certain times pressmen did hamper one, but in nine cases out of ten they have been of the greatest use to me, and on occasions rendered yeoman service in the successful investigation of crime. The old idea used to be that detectives best served the interests of justice by keeping journalists at a distance, with the natural result that pressmen, being under the necessity of reporting something, used to string together unreliable stories, and to set about investigations themselves in a manner very maddening and handicapping to the detective officers who had the handling of the case.[54]

However, G.R. Sims – a well-known journalist in his day – showed in his memoirs that Macnaghten was not just a passive recipient of press support, he positively cultivated it. Macnaghten, whom Sims claimed as a friend, customarily gave 'Corinthian' dinners on Monday nights at his Warwick Square home as a prelude to visits to the boxing at the National Sporting Club. Sims testified that 'In my investigations...I always received the generous assistance of my friends the officers and officials of the Metropolitan Police'.[55]

The conduct of relations at the Macnaghten level was one thing, but the reality of what happened further down was another matter altogether. Not only was the improper arrogation of individual credit involved, there was also an unregulated cash nexus. Macready moved to control the situation and in 1919 successfully invited the Home Office to authorise his instituting a press bureau to short circuit a situation where the press spent money to procure 'often inaccurate' information:

> A great deal of the money spent has, no doubt, found its way directly or indirectly into the pockets of Police officers in spite of General Orders issued on the subject. From experience in my present appointment, and in others I have held, I am of

---

[53] A. Watson, *A Newspaperman's Memories* (London: Hutchinson, 1923) Chapter 11, 'An adventure with Scotland Yard', pp. 103–10.

[54] Macnaghten, *Days of My Years*, p. 64.

[55] G.R. Sims, *My Life: Sixty Years' Recollection of Bohemian London* (London: Eveleigh Nash, 1917) pp. 176–77 and 323. It was Sims who, as a result his own investigation, established in the *Daily Telegraph* that Mme D'Angely's claims of innocence in 1906 – one of the claims precipitating the Royal Commission of 1906–8 – were untrue. Sims also wrote detective novels, was active over the Beck case, and was a member of a dining club with lawyers, medical men and writers (including Conan Doyle and H.B. Irving) who discussed crime together – see G. Turner, *Unorthodox Reminiscences* (London: Murray, 1931). Turner, a surgeon at St George's, named no police officers as members.

opinion that an effort should be made to enlist the co-operation of the Press in the work of the Police, and to so direct its energies that instead of, at present, hampering the work, the Press should become an active and intelligent assistant.[56]

Detective popularisation

Whilst healthy press relations were indispensable for operational purposes, it would be wrong to overlook other sources of detective representation as contributing to creating/reflecting a favourable and supportive climate. The contribution of detective fiction is, of course, well known.[57] In addition, however, favourable perceptions of the police were projected by what can be described as professional volunteers, writers who saw a market for broadcasting, sometimes in popularised form, information about how Scotland Yard or the police service more generally worked.

An early example was Clarkson and Richardson's *Police!*, published in 1889 and extending to the City force as well as the Metropolitan. Written by a retired policeman and a journalist, the book was a thorough description of the latter force at the time. Adopting a knowing/stoical style, it did not gloss over failures or concentrate especially on detectives. Its declared object was to 'rivet the bonds between the public and the police'.[58]

Arthur Griffiths, a former prison governor, was early to concentrate on detectives with his *Mysteries of Police and Crime* published in 1898. Largely anecdotal in form, it went out of its way to contrast the attainments of the contemporary detectives with their predecessors, and treated a number as if they were celebrities. In his later autobiography, he described his membership of the Committee on the Identification of Habitual Criminals, the development of fingerprinting, and reflected on visits to the French police in ways contributing to the good reputation of both Parisian and London detectives.[59] The stress,

---

[56] NA, HO 45/24442/390493/1, Macready to Home Office, 27 September 1919. In his memoirs, Macready claimed: 'One well-known man in newspaper circles told me that this source of information cost him £1,000 a year. From the police point of view it was all wrong that officers should take money, or its equivalent, on any pretence whatever, as, while the information given was at times harmless enough, the principle was vicious and might at any moment lead to public scandal'. C.F.N. Macready, *Annals of an Active Life*, 2 vols (London: Hutchinson, 1924) ii, 416.

[57] J. Symons, *Bloody Murder* (London: Pan, 1992) gives a celebrated and accessible account.

[58] C.T. Clarkson and J.H. Richardson, *Police!* (London: Field and Tuer, 1889) p. 370.

[59] Arthur Griffiths, *Mysteries of Police and Crime* (London: Cassell, 1898); idem, *Fifty Years of Public Service* (London: Cassell, 1904); idem, *Tales of a Government Official* (London: F.V. White, 1902).

unemphasised but constant, was on contemporary forensic and professional expertise. *Tales of a Government Official* in 1902 traded on his prisons and police knowledge to give authenticity to the anecdotes.

The several works of H.L. Adam and George Dilnot fall into the same category. Published in the period from just before the First World War up to the Second World War they were both informative and celebratory in tone. Adam's *Police Work from Within* of 1914 was a fully facilitated account of detective work at Scotland Yard by a writer/journalist who had been publishing on 'real' crime subjects since 1908: 'The primary purpose of this volume is enlighten in an entertaining manner the uninformed and the ill-informed as to how our police force is constituted and how it works in the prevention and detection of crime'. His *Police Encyclopaedia* of 1920 ran to eight volumes, Volume V containing photographs of all the senior detective officers at Scotland Yard, a positive iconography of contemporary officers verging on the hagiographic.[60]

Dilnot's oeuvre[61] was similar, though his *Scotland Yard* published for the centenary in 1929 was more an historical chronicle than any of Adam's or his own other works. These concentrated on detectives with such titles as *Triumphs of Detection, The Real Detective, Great Detectives and Their Methods*. In addition, Dilnot was the General Editor of the *Famous Trials* series published by Geoffrey Bles, and the *Trial of the Detectives* was one of his contributions to that series. Adam contributed to the parallel Hodge series, *Notable British Trials*, with a study of Lamson, the poisoner.

These texts helped to consolidate the concept of detection as a profession. Readers were flattered by being put in the know by sharing the author's intimate knowledge of the personalities and their characteristics – in some cases even to the point of detailing their office furniture. The photographs that accompanied the expository works emphasised modernity and forensic excellence. A classic of this kind was Teignmouth Shore's two-volume *Crime and its Detection* of 1931.[62] This described contemporary forces, discussed forensic methodologies at some length, and devoted the second volume to accounts of cases.

Fed no doubt partly by the vogue for detective fiction, such works supplemented the fictional diet with the stronger meat of plausible realism. Indeed, the two streams evidently fed off each other: Dilnot dedicated his *Great Detectives*

---

[60] H.L. Adam, *Police Work From Within* (London: Holden and Hardingham, 1914) and *Police Encyclopaedia* (London: Waverley, 1920); his *CID: Behind the Scenes at Scotland Yard* (London: Sampson Low, 1931) returned to former subjects during the Byng regime.

[61] George Dilnot, *Scotland Yard* (London: Bles, 1929): idem, *Triumphs of Detection* (London: Bles (n.d.)); idem, *Great Detectives and Their Methods* (New York: Houghton Mifflin, 1928); idem, *Trial of the Detectives* (London: Bles, 1928); and idem, *The Real Detective* (London: Bles, 1933). Dilnot also published detective novels.

[62] W. Teignmouth Shore, *Crime and its Detection* (London: Gresham, 1931).

and Their Methods to Edgar Wallace. As Moylan observed in 1929, 'this change in public opinion has been helped by the enormous vogue of the detective story, which has cast a halo of romance and adventure round an occupation which used to be regarded, at its best, as that of a Paul Pry'.[63]

Conclusion

Looking back over this first century of the new police, can it be said whether crime paid? For the new classes of professional detective and journalist/writer there cannot be much doubt that it did. Both rose with crime, as it were. As people felt more secure, detective methods became less controversial. And as the detective hierarchies consolidated, older means of enhancing remuneration faded away, though not – recurrent scandals reminded – to the point of extinction. On the one hand, detectives had to come to terms with new, more insistent and more popular/populist forms of journalism; whilst, on the other hand, these could be enlisted to support the detective function. Matters became more, though by no means absolutely, transparent: by 1906 private Home Office inquiries into alleged police misdemeanours had become unthinkable and there was a Royal Commission instead.

Although detective officers sought to distance themselves from their fictional counterparts, both were part of a similar cultural narrative. That is they stood for confronting and overcoming the chaos of uncontrolled human action. The fictions sought to reassure their readers that order was at the end restored, and the memoirs explained how it was *really* done.

---

[63]   Moylan, *Scotland Yard*, p. 193.

Chapter Five

Explaining the Rise and Success of Detective Memoirs in Britain[1]

Haia Shpayer-Makov

An exploration of working-class autobiographies and memoirs of the late nineteenth century and the first few decades of the twentieth century in Britain reveals that, relative to other occupational groups, detectives were more inclined to write and, moreover, managed to publish accounts of their working lives. Some of these life stories appeared as articles or series of articles in journals and newspapers.[2] Even more remarkably, dozens of memoirs by detectives were issued as books. Given that most detectives in this period originated from working-class homes and were themselves ordinary workers before joining the police, and that publishers were not prone to publish memoirs by working people, the impetus behind both the detectives' and the publishers' atypical course of action merits exploration.[3] Other workers felt a need to put pen to paper and recount their life experiences, but only a few saw these accounts in print.[4] Moreover, a large

---

[1] An earlier draft of this essay was presented to the European Social Science History Conference (The Hague, The Netherlands, 2 March 2002) entitled 'The Work Histories and Self-Image of British Detectives during the Late Nineteenth and Early Twentieth Centuries: A Study of their Memoirs'.

[2] By way of example, Detective Chief Inspector Charles Arrow first published several of his reminiscences in the London *Evening News*; Charles Arrow, *Rogues and Others* (London: Duckworth, 1926) p. 9. Also see Inspector Moser (Recorded by Charles F. Rideal), *Stories from Scotland Yard* (London: George Routledge and Sons, 1890) and Timothy A. Cavanagh, *Scotland Yard. Past and Present* (London: Chatto & Windus, 1893) Preface. Some memoirs appeared solely in newspapers and never reached the book market, such as that by Patrick McIntyre in *Reynolds's Newspaper*, published during February–May 1895.

[3] The detectives whose memoirs are mentioned here all joined the police before the First World War, when the vast majority of recruits belonged to the working classes.

[4] A small market for autobiographies of the lower classes developed during the nineteenth and early twentieth centuries, but it remained limited. John Burnett, ed, *Useful Toil* (London: Allen Lane, 1976. First published 1974) pp. 11–12.

proportion of the detectives' memoirs was published by the most distinguished publishers in Britain, including Hutchinson, Duckworth, Chatto & Windus and George Routledge & Sons. The questions that arise are why so many detectives felt impelled to reveal their life histories to the wider public, and what made their memoirs attractive to well-established publishing firms.

All official detectives in Britain at the time started at the bottom of the police hierarchy as uniformed policemen and slowly made their way to the detective department, where they generally spent most of their working life. Coming from a manual background in nearly all cases, and having shared a common work environment, they displayed a distinctive approach to their work experience, as reflected in their memoirs. Further, the memoirs reveal a unique self-image that these writers shared. The essay argues that this special approach and image, perceptible in the memoirs, offers additional evidence of the motivation of their authors to produce memoirs and the attractiveness of such literature to publishers. The first part of the essay explores relevant aspects of the cultural environment in Britain, the special circumstances of the memoirists and the work context of detectives, while the second part analyses additional factors in the shared sentiments and values expressed in the memoirs. Significantly, most of the published memoirs were written by detectives who served in the Metropolitan Police of London, i.e., by men working in the Criminal Investigation Department (CID).[5] Because of their profusion and the recurrent themes incorporated in them, memoirs by London detectives are the focus of this chapter.[6]

The emergence of a literary form

Remarkably, the detectives whose memoirs were published in book form seem to have adopted a professional approach to their writing. Although they produced a single, or at best two books, they appear to have been keenly aware of the rules of the publishing industry (even if in some cases the books were edited or ghosted). Their rhetoric indicates that, like professional writers, they understood the necessity of catering to public taste and tailored the material in their books for commercial consumption.[7] Confident that their occupational life had the potential

---

[5]   The department acquired this specific title in 1878, but it had existed since 1842 and was simply called the detective department or the detective police.

[6]   Detectives serving in the City Police of London also published memoirs, see, for example, Ernest Nicholls, *Crime Within the Square Mile* (London: John Long, 1935), but their number was small as was the size of the force.

[7]   Edwin T. Woodhall, *Detective and Secret Service Days* (London: Mellifont, 1929) p. 5.

to be highly appealing to 'the general reading public', they sensed, nevertheless, that the 'routine duties' and 'commonplaces of a detective's experience' could be 'of little interest to the average reader'.[8] Rather, their guiding rule seemed to be the wish to entertain, and towards this end they carefully selected only the stories that would engross the public. Typically, Detective Chief Inspector John Littlechild, conscious of the need to concede to public taste, made special efforts 'to avoid repetition, for necessarily much of the experience which I have gained presents features of similarity'.[9] His aim was 'to select cases in which the criminal has hit upon some new idea, or original plan, which, in turn, has demanded exceptional skill on the part of the detective to bring the crime home to its perpetrator'.

A priori, however, and in contrast to most other persons of working-class origin, detectives had the good fortune to engage in a vocation that captured the imagination of both publishers and readers. They were mainly concerned with the pursuit of criminals and guarding of members of the political elite, and as such their working lives were filled with suspenseful incidents and episodes that for them may have been part of a demanding work routine but for the general public was the stuff of a good read. This widespread interest in accounts about crime was far from new and could be traced far back into history. With the growing production of printed material generally, the demand for such texts accelerated. In the latter decades of the seventeenth century, and increasingly during the eighteenth century, genres such as the crime report, the anatomy of roguery, providence books, the criminal biography, gallows speeches, and trial reports gained a position of cultural centrality.[10] In the course of the nineteenth century, the subject of criminality became steadily more topical both in the press and in literature.[11]

More significantly, with the creation of a detective unit at Scotland Yard in 1842, crime investigation, in particular, attracted growing public attention, and the detective replaced the criminal as the focus of literary interest. The figure of the detective, both private and official, had in fact surfaced in the printed media well before this date and even predated the establishment of the Metropolitan Police (in 1829) – the first modern police force in the country, which later incorporated the

---

[8] Percy J. Smith, *Crooks in Clover* (Philadelphia: J.B. Lippincott, 1938) pp. 40, 136 (In England the book appeared under the title *Con Man*, published by Jenkins in 1938); Andrew Lansdowne, *A Life's Reminiscences of Scotland Yard* (London: Leadenhall Press, 1890) p. 5.

[9] John George Littlechild, *The Reminiscences of Chief-Inspector Littlechild* (London: Leadenhall Press, 1894) p. 7.

[10] Hal Gladfelder, *Criminality and Narrative in Eighteenth-Century England* (Baltimore: Johns Hopkins University Press, 2001) p. 5.

[11] Peter D. McDonald, *British Literary Culture and Publishing Practice, 1880–1914* (Cambridge University Press, 1997) p. 160, quoting the *Westminster Review* for April 1897.

detective department at Scotland Yard. One of the earliest detective figures in English fiction was Caleb Williams, the protagonist of a book titled *Things as They Are or, the Adventures of Caleb Williams* by William Godwin (1794), which many critics view as the first 'sustained detective narrative'.[12] Novels set in the British colonies, such as *Confessions of a Thug* by Philip Meadows Taylor (1839), also included crime investigators.[13]

However, only with the consolidation of detection as a distinctive occupation within the British public service during the middle decades of the Victorian era did detectives appear more regularly in British literature. Initially, imported fiction, whether translated (mainly from the French) or written in English (by Edgar Allan Poe, for example), showed more of a tendency to incorporate detectives in the narrative, but native writers, too, gradually became more interested in the figure of the detective.[14] Although fictional private detectives outnumbered the official variety, a growing number of police detectives, particularly those who belonged to Scotland Yard, surfaced in indigenous literary works and also on the stage. The most famous writer to show a keen interest in police detectives was Charles Dickens, who not only included them in several of his novels and stories, but also made an effort to meet real-life police detectives and thereafter reported positively about them in a series of articles published in the early 1850s in his journal *Household Words*.[15] Wilkie Collins was another popular novelist who wove characters of police detectives into the plots of more than one novel, the most famous of whom was Sergeant Cuff in *Moonstone* (published in 1868).[16] It is

---

[12]   Caroline Warren Reitz, 'The Necessary Detective: Police, Empire and Victorian National Identity', PhD, Brown University, 1999, pp. 14, 47. The book was later simply known as *Caleb Williams*. There is no consensus as to when detective fiction made its entry in English. While some critics consider Godwin's *Caleb Williams* to be the first text of this genre, others view 'The Murders in the Rue Morgue' by the American writer Edgar Allan Poe as 'the founding document', and still others refer to the essential contributions of Charles Dickens and Wilkie Collins as stepping stones to the emergence of the detective narrative. Martin A. Kayman, *From Bow Street to Baker Street* (London: Macmillan, 1992) p. 137; Reitz, pp. 145–46. Many accounts, including Martin A. Kayman's, identify Sherlock Holmes as 'the patriarchal source' of detective fiction (p. 135). According to Kayman, the appearance of a detective character in literary texts does not make these texts detective fiction (p. 130). For Kayman's discussion of the definition of 'detective fiction', see ibid., pp. 3–5, and chapter 5. For a variety of views on the lineage of the genre, see T.J. Binyon, *'Murder Will Out'* (Oxford University Press, 1989) chapter 1.

[13]   The novel is discussed at length in Reitz, 'The Necessary Detective', chapter 3.

[14]   'Detective Fiction', *Saturday Review*, 4 December 1886, p. 749.

[15]   For details about the detective figures contained in Dickens' novels, stories and articles, see Peter Haining, ed, *Hunted Down* (London: Peter Owen, 1996) pp. 7–21.

[16]   For details see A.E. Murch, *The Development of the Detective Novel* (London: Peter Owen, 1968. First published 1958) pp.107–114.

important to note, however, that neither in Dickens' or Collins' works did a police detective constitute the central figure.

The last two decades of the nineteenth century saw a dramatic rise in the presence of detectives, whether amateur or professional, in novels, stories and articles, a development which was largely the result of changes unrelated to the world of crime. The period witnessed the expansion of formal education among working people following the passage of the Elementary Education Act of 1870. At the same time, leisure activities proliferated in all sectors of society, including in the upper stratum of the working class, where income rose. Reading became habitual in all classes. These trends prompted book and magazine publishers to augment their output and make it accessible to a broader population. New sensationalist newspapers appeared, filling their columns with such popular topics as crime, criminal trials and law enforcement, and attaining circulations of hundreds of thousands of readers. New publishing firms were established as well, in response to the growing demand for reading material. Attentive to market conditions, they, too, 'constantly tested the waters in order to maintain an up-to-date and interesting product in a competitive market'.[17] Their primary aim 'was the greatest return on investment', and towards this end they developed a mass market in both popular fiction and non-fiction.[18] Printed matter about law enforcement was so much in demand that even the *Police Code* written by the founder and director of the CID, Howard Vincent, and consisting of instructions for police officers, became popular reading as soon as it was published in 1881, and ran through several editions during the next few years.[19] In an age that witnessed the decline of religious faith and was torn between a belief in scientific discovery and social and economic progress on the one hand and doubt and pessimism in the direction in which society was going on the other, the detective as a secular figure who pursues the truth and solves riddles and mysteries had a special appeal. No doubt, the appearance in 1887 and popularity of the captivating private detective figure Sherlock Holmes, was a result of these developments. His fame, and the towering sales of the works in which he was the protagonist, attested to the inclination and taste of the reading public. In turn, these stories boosted interest in crime investigation, *inter alia* in investigations conducted by detectives who were not private gentlemen, as he was, but ordinary employees of the police.

Authentic memoirs by publicly employed crime fighters were not a new phenomenon, but they began to mount in numbers at this propitious junction, when

---

[17]   Joseph McAleer, *Popular Reading and Publishing in Britain 1914–1950* (Oxford: Clarendon Press, 1992) p. 9.

[18]   Ibid, pp. 23 and 13.

[19]   S.H. Jeyes and F.D. How, *The Life of Sir Howard Vincent* (London: George Allen, 1912) p. 83.

the figure of Sherlock Holmes began to fire public imagination. Beforehand, there were only a few retired police detectives, and they had neither the literate skills nor access to the publishing world that would enable them to record their experiences in print. Even so, the potential attraction of memoirs by real detectives had become apparent during the time of the precursors of the detective unit at Scotland Yard – the renowned Bow Street Runners.[20] The Runners, formed in London in 1749, continued to function after the establishment of the Metropolitan Police in 1829 until they were abolished in 1839. Given the limited educational background of these early detectives and the small size of the force – starting with half a dozen men and expanding by only a few more in the course of their existence – it is not surprising that none published memoirs at that time. However, Henry Goddard, who served in this force between 1834 and 1839, did write his life story in the 1870s, bequeathing it to his descendants after his death in 1883.[21] It was published only in 1956. Interestingly, King William IV, when still Duke of Clarence, recognised the intrinsic appeal of memoirs by Runners. He suggested to John Townsend, the most famous Bow Street Runner and a bodyguard for the royalty, to undertake the task.[22] Townsend considered his advice but never implemented the project.

While the Runners themselves did not reveal the inner workings of their lives to the reading public in the first half of the nineteenth century, elements outside the world of detection did try to exploit the Runners' reputation. In 1827 a book was published in London entitled *Richmond: Scenes in the Life of a Bow Street Runner*, but the anonymous author was most probably not a Runner himself, and the book in any event did not prove a great success.[23] The Bow Street Runners did appear as minor characters in several contemporary novels, the most famous of which was Charles Dickens' *Oliver Twist* (1837). Essentially, however, the exploits of the Runners, during the existence of the organisation, became known mainly through police-court reports published in contemporary newspapers. By contrast, the more

---

[20] The Bow Street Runners, founded by the novelist Henry Fielding, are usually considered the first organised detective force in England. Combining both official and private functions, they lived on wages and allowances as well as private rewards – which were actually the principal source of their income. For details see John Beattie's chapter at the beginning of this volume; also, Anthony Babington, *A House in Bow Street* (Chichester: Barry Rose Law Publishers, 1999) pp. 186–96 and 233–35.

[21] For the life of Goddard, see Introduction to Henry Goddard, *Memoirs of a Bow Street Runner* by Patrick Pringle (London: Museum Press, 1956) pp. xxii–xxix.

[22] Charles Tempest Clarkson and J. Hall Richardson, *Police!* (New York: Garland Publishing, 1984. First published 1889) p. 50. Apparently, another Bow Street Runner, George Ruthven, had written a history of his life, but never published it (p. 54).

[23] See the introduction of E.F. Bleiler to *Richmond: Scenes in the Life of a Bow Street Runner* (New York: Dover Publications, 1976) p. x.

enterprising founder and chief of the French Sûreté, the ex-convict Eugène François Vidocq, published his memoirs in France during 1828–1829, which were translated and circulated in England soon after.[24] These memoirs had an immediate appeal among English readers, as did the later memoirs of the founder of the American Pinkerton agency, Allan Pinkerton, during the 1870s.[25]

So obvious was the attraction of detectives' life stories to certain perceptive writers during the mid-nineteenth century, that although they themselves had no detective experience, they nonetheless wrote fictional recollections in growing numbers as if written by real-life detectives. A prominent example was a series of stories, each with its own title, though under the general heading *Recollections of a Police-Officer*, published in *Chambers's Journal* between 1849 and 1853. The writer was anonymous, but the protagonist, who speaks in the first person, is called Waters. In 1856 the stories were compiled in book form and published by J. and C. Brown under the title of the series.[26] The name of the author appeared as 'Waters', the pseudonym for journalist William Russell. The book was an immediate succedss both in England and abroad and served as a model for other writers of pseudo-factual memoirs.[27] From the 1860s onwards, some of these books featured lady detectives, such as Mrs. Paschal in *The Experiences of a Lady Detective* by W.S. Hayward (1861).[28] No doubt, the establishment of the detective unit at Scotland Yard in 1842 inspired these writers' efforts.

Gradually, though, men who served as detectives in the police force in Britain also began to write their memoirs, although few saw print before Sherlock Holmes made his appearance in the latter 1880s.[29] It was only at the end of the century that

---

[24] For details see Murch, *Development*, pp. 41–48.

[25] The novels by the French author Emile Gaboriau were also highly popular. His detective-hero M. Lecoq was a fictitious figure but modeled on the chief of the Sûreté M. Claude (*Saturday Review*, 5 May 1883, p. 558). For details see Clive Emsley's chapter, p. 71. Also see illustration 5.1.

[26] In his introduction to the 1972 edition of *Recollections of a Detective Police-Officer*, Eric Osborne mentions a pirated issue of the book in 1852. Eric Osborne, introduction to *Recollections of a Detective Police-Officer* by 'Waters' (London: Covent Garden Press, 1972) p. 4. This text is reproduced from the first collected edition of 1875. See Osborne's introduction for the publication history of *Recollections*. In 1859 another volume appeared in England under the same title and included some more stories. Thereafter the *Recollections* were published in various other editions under different titles both in England and abroad.

[27] Osborne, *Recollections*, p. 1.

[28] Kayman, *From Bow Street*, pp. 122–29.

[29] See, for example, James McLevy, *Curiosities of Crime in Edinburgh during the last thirty years* (Edinburgh: William P. Nimmo, 1861); Thomas P. McNaught, *The Recollections of a Glasgow detective officer* (London?: Simpkin, 1887); P. Alexander Clark, *Reminiscences of a Police Officer in the Granite City* (Aberdeen: Lewis Smith, 1873).

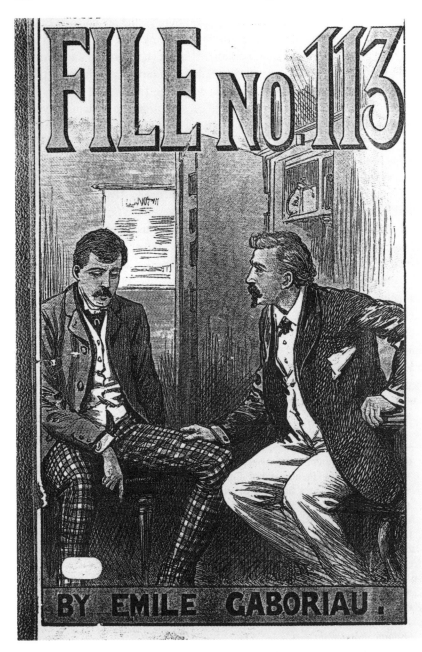

**Illustration 5.1 The cover of the English translation of Emile Gaboriau's
detective novel *File No. 113* (1887). Originally published in
French (1867).**

a trend – almost a fashion – became observable among detectives, especially in London, to record their working lives, and in a particular style, as will be shown later.[30] This proclivity continued at the early twentieth century and, after a break during the First World War and immediately thereafter, resumed in the inter-war period, resulting in the creation of a substantial body of police memoirs united by common themes and certain literary conventions.[31] While the memoirists could certainly draw on scattered precedents of successful published materials centred on criminality and law enforcement, the period beginning at the close of the nineteenth century constituted particularly fertile soil for the convergence of interests, desires and abilities of both detectives and publishers. Encouraged by market demand in a society that was becoming progressively better educated, and possibly feeling more confident about their own literary proficiency at the end of careers which increasingly required them to read and write reports, police detectives ventured into the publishing world more frequently and encountered a responsive public. Not only did their tales of dramatic law breaking and the clever pursuit of criminals evoke suspense and constitute a popular source of entertainment, the fact that they were based on unequivocal real-life experience added to their popularity, even if readers were aware of certain gaps between the lived experience and the written record. Publishers alert to the possibilities of this non-fictional literary form could not but welcome the reminiscences of retired police officers.

Why the men wrote

While detective memoirs clearly served the publishers' purpose, the overlapping of interests between the writers and the publishers does not fully account for the rise of detectives as memoirists. The questions of how a significant number of men

---

[30] See, for example, Moser, *Stories from Scotland Yard* (1890); Lansdowne, *A Life's Reminiscences of Scotland Yard* (1890); Cavanagh, *Scotland Yard. Past and Present* (1893); Littlechild, *The Reminiscences of Chief-Inspector Littlechild* (1894).

[31] Police detectives, of course, continued to publish memoirs after the Second World War, but by that time a large number of these officers originated from social groups more prone to writing, and, therefore, the phenomenon investigated in this article is less relevant. Moreover, the post-war memoirs no longer adhered consistently to the cultural conventions discussed here. For a bibliography of British police officers' memoirs and biographies, see Martin Stallion, *A Life of Crime* (Leigh-on-Sea: M.R. Stallion, 1998); For a graph describing the number of police memoirs published in England and France between 1861 and 1939, see Paul Lawrence, '"Scoundrels and scallywags, and some honest men..." Memoirs and the self-image of French and English policemen, c. 1870–1939', in Barry Godfrey, Clive Emsley and Graeme Dunstall, eds, *Comparative Histories of Crime* (Willan: Cullompton, 2003) p. 127.

from a working-class background succeeded in entering the publishing world, and what impelled them to write their memoirs, still require study.

Significantly, nearly all the detectives who published memoirs were men who had managed to advance up through the ranks and became senior officers: most were inspectors and chief inspectors, and some were even superintendents. Only a few memoirs were written by sergeants (one rank above constable, the lowest in the force).[32] By the time their memoirs were published, they were no longer ordinary workers, and their memoirs, therefore, do not reflect the lives of working people locked in a struggle to make ends meet. Indeed, publishers may have been motivated to publish these memoirs not only because they revolved around a topic attractive to the public, but also because they represented success stories – stories of people who advanced themselves in the British public service. Detectives became administrators and authority figures, and as such were objects of public interest. Their status and the upward social route they took, may well have constituted an additional reason to publish their literary output. This, however, still does not yet account for the impulse behind the detectives' determination to see their memoirs in print and their success in fulfilling this ambition.

Another clue may be found in the occupational culture of detectives. Although most detectives came from a socio-economic background that generally did not promote the values of education or a literary career, their books are marked by a relatively high quality of writing, which cannot be attributed solely to editorial assistance. Admittedly, most of the memoirists had benefited from the Elementary Education Act of 1870 and had had several years of formal schooling, and, in addition, they may have constituted a self-selected group with a natural talent for writing. Nonetheless, their work environment provided a fertile ground for the nurturing of literary talent. Policing generally, and crime investigation in particular, were amongst the few working-class occupations that not only required literacy as a condition of acceptance, but also incorporated this skill in the daily work routine and thereby improved it. Every uniformed policeman was obliged to report to his superiors in writing about his activities. Policemen also practiced writing when preparing their evidence in court. Writing requirements were even greater for detectives who, in addition to reporting to their superiors and preparing cases for prosecution, had to take notes when interviewing people. They were also expected to answer letters from members of the public who provided them with information.[33] Equally important was their duty to produce dockets containing the

---

[32] Most of the few positions above the level of superintendent were filled by nominees from an upper- or upper-middle-class background, and their memoirs, therefore, are not relevant to this study.

[33] *Departmental Committee of 1889 upon Metropolitan Police Superannuation*, P[arliamentary] P[apers], 1890, vol. 56, p. 436.

'bare facts' of every case. According to Detective Inspector Andrew Lansdowne, following an initial report, the detective committed 'everything to writing as he goes, so that, if the investigation be at all complicated, and there are several officers engaged in the matter, the bundle of papers grows hour by hour until it forms a complete history of the proceedings taken in connection with the unravelling of a mystery or the tracking home of a crime'.[34]

Detectives also acquired the habit of editing. In order to present reports in 'good form', they copied them from pencil to ink, put them 'in a grammatical form' and rewrote them.[35] It may be no exaggeration to speculate that the writing skills they developed were quite unique among persons who came from a lower-class background.

Although senior officers repeatedly complained about the low level of the men's reports and were critical of their deficient writing ability, the general atmosphere and the requirements of the job could not but enrich their language and refine their literary skills.[36] Moreover, since most of the memoirs were not written by detectives at the lower level, but by those who had managed to rise up through the ranks, the authors may have been better skilled at writing than detectives who had not been as successful. The higher up they reached in the CID hierarchy, the more extensive the obligation to submit written materials. Promoted detectives were also more likely to have had better education in their youth than those who remained at the bottom of the police scale. In short, the writers of memoirs within the CID were especially prone to master the art of reporting. Given that their occupational duties forced them to chronicle the cases in which they were engaged and narrate a series of events, they developed an expertise in writing precisely the kind of narratives on which their memoirs were based. Sometimes they had to serve as witnesses in criminal trials, and not infrequently the cases they handled were reported in the press. It could not have been too difficult for some detectives to reconstruct the details of their cases yet again, if they were so inclined. Trained specifically, if unwittingly, in a literary style that was to become popular to the public, they were in fact good at it. Their books were readable and well written and therefore publishable.

Most of the detectives whose personal reminiscences saw the light of day wrote them after their retirement from the police. Generally recruited in their early twenties, and serving from 26 to 40 years, they were usually in their late forties or fifties when they set about documenting their working lives. Although working class by origin, they were not poor by then, and had earned the privilege of

---

[34] Lansdowne, *A Life's Reminiscences*, pp. 1–2.
[35] *Royal Commission upon the Duties of the Metropolitan Police*, PP, 1908, vol. 51, p. 169.
[36] Ibid, p. 382.

financial independence, provided by a pension that rose with rank. Thus they lived in relative comfort with the leisure time to engage in writing. Some supplemented their pension with work as private detective agents, whether as employees or self-employed. Most other workers of humble background did not enjoy such circumstances. Moreover, although several detectives made a point of reiterating that while writing their memoirs they drew on memory only and not on written materials, they, unlike most other kinds of workers, did have access to documents which allowed them to reconstruct events in their past, such as the notes they had taken on the job, or press cuttings which many detectives were in the habit of keeping.[37] Clearly, such aids made it possible for them to present vivid details of exciting cases, enhancing the quality of their narrative.

Additional explanations for the impulse underlying the detectives' determination to record their life stories may be found in some of the common themes and sentiments expressed in the texts. An analysis of the texts reveals the use of a certain joint formula, namely, a generally short introductory section, in which the author reveals personal details, followed by a much longer section describing his work experience.[38] Specifically, the books almost always begin with biographical details which also include the author's *raison d'etre* for writing. Thereafter, the text barely alludes to his personal life outside work. Unlike the fictional detective, or the middle-class autobiographer, little is revealed about family circumstances, leisure activities or views about issues other than law enforcement. Nor is space devoted for self-analysis or self-reflection. The bulk of the book is taken up by various episodes and cases which occupied the author on the job. This consistent formula may suggest that the retired detectives were aware of memoirs by other detectives, which they imitated. Or, the adoption of this formula may have reflected a commercial decision to concentrate on what interested the public most, which probably did not include depictions of the daily life of detectives outside their work or of the drudgery many of them experienced before joining the police. However, a careful reading of the texts points to the supreme significance of their work for the narrators. If for many ordinary workers during the nineteenth and early twentieth centuries work was 'not a central life-interest' but was taken as a given, detectives appear to have derived a deep sense of fulfillment and satisfaction from it, even if their pronouncements about their feelings should be taken with some skepticism.[39] The occupational self clearly

---

[37] Lansdowne, *A Life's Reminiscences*, pp. 2 and 4; Cavanagh, *Scotland Yard*, p. 171; John Sweeney, *At Scotland Yard* (London: Grant Richards, 1904) pp. v–vi; Tom Divall, *Scoundrels and Scallywags* (London: Ernest Benn, 1929) p. 177; Benjamin Leeson, *Lost London* (London: Stanley Paul, 1934) p. 7.

[38] In some cases the personal details appeared at the end of the memoirs or not at all.

[39] Burnett, ed, *Useful Toil*, pp. 15 and 17.

predominates in these autobiographical works. In presenting their life stories retrospectively, the retired detectives used a selective approach that underlined the importance of work for them.[40] The narrative sequence itself is determined by their work life: once they retired, the book came to an end. Having left police (or private detective) service, there was no sense in continuing the life story. This intense identification with their vocation constitutes another key factor in explaining why detectives wrote memoirs. It also leads to an understanding of the meaning of work for these men and the kind of message they wanted to transmit to the intended audience.

Almost invariably, the writers of detective memoirs felt a need to explain their motivation in approaching this task, an apologia that may have indicated a certain unease at venturing into a domain outside their natural habitat.[41] Detective memoirists were not alone in availing themselves of this practice. Other autobiographers, primarily those who were also unconnected to the literary world, frequently felt compelled to explain what led them to unveil their lives to unfamiliar audiences.[42] A common thread that unified the detectives and certain other memoirists was their insistence that they had no literary aspirations, but that other people, notably friends and acquaintances, had pressed them to write about themselves.[43] This admission may have been another literary convention that the detectives knew and followed, yet, consistently implicit in the texts is the authors' sense of a self-imposed task. Clearly, it was not only outside pressure that prompted detectives to embark on publishing their recollections. The texts are uniformly invested with a sense of vocation and a resolve to communicate an important message to a wide audience. Furthermore, in this mission the memoirists represented not only themselves, but the police force as a whole.

---

[40] This was also true of autobiographies of soldiers and sailors during the nineteenth century, see Clive Emsley, *British Society and the French Wars 1793–1815* (London: Macmillan, 1979) pp. 172–73 and David Vincent, *Bread, Knowledge and Freedom* (London: Methuen, 1981) pp. 2–3.

[41] In contrast, a few detectives, such as James Berret, were unhappy with this style. From the outset he exclaimed: 'I need offer no apology for the publication of my reminiscences. Whether they are of interest or not is a matter for the reader to decide for himself, but I, myself, know that people are interested in the cases which a detective officer handles'. James Berrett, *When I was at Scotland Yard* (London: Sampson Low, Marston & Co., 1932) p. v.

[42] See, for example, reference to the personal narratives of politically active women during the late Victorian period, in Pauline Polkey, 'Reading History through Autobiography: politically active women of late nineteenth-century Britain and their personal narratives', *Women's History Review*, 9 (2000), 3, pp. 488–89. See also reference to William Lovett's autobiography in Vincent, *Bread, Knowledge and Freedom*, p. 28.

[43] Cavanagh, *Scotland Yard*, preface; Lansdowne, *A Life's Reminiscences*, p. 2; Divall, *Scoundrels and Scallywags*, p. 9; Leeson, *Lost London*, p. 7.

The institutional element

Undeniably, the texts can be viewed as success stories of individuals and as accounts of personal triumphs. Besides being exposés of crime detection, the memoirs are also implicitly records of men who were born to humble circumstances and ended their work life in positions of command, having transcended class boundaries and the limitations of low social and economic status. Although the memoirists tell the readers little of their private lives, it is impossible to disregard their achievements as self-made men. Their life course is structured along a line of social ascendancy both within the police and in society at large. Each detective narrative projects a sense of forward movement and a belief in progress. In this sense they can be classified as narratives of improvement.

Yet, the memoirs are not only tales of individual achievement. The detective was not only an agent propelled by his own inner drives, but part of an institution, and the voice of the institution is integral in the books. True, the 'I' of the narrator is dominant throughout. The disparate anecdotes of crime investigation on which each of the books is based are connected into a narrative with a beginning and end. His life as a detective and his voice as a narrator provide a unifying structure to the book. Moreover, the investigations usually come to a successful end owing to the enterprising spirit and good judgement of the narrator. The role of the individual author is therefore highly important in these texts. However, as pervasive in the texts is the sense that the detective speaks on behalf of a collective entity; that he represents much more than his personal self and his accomplishments. It is not always clear whether he represents the police as a whole or the detective constituency specifically, but he is always an advocate of the work of the police. Detective Inspector Lansdowne conveys this sense most succinctly. 'Why should I write a book? What is my title to speak for Scotland Yard?', he asks, answering: 'Well, without egotism, I suppose I may say that, having spent twenty years of my life there, and having, for six years prior to that, served in almost all grades of the metropolitan police, I have some claim to talk of the system as it existed during the whole period of my acquaintance with it'.[44]

Indeed, the narratives in no way constitute life histories of detectives, for they do not usually describe the private experiences of their authors outside the context of criminal investigation. Essentially, the books are work histories under a very specific employer. In contrast to most other workers of the time,[45] detectives spent nearly the entire length of their adult life in one workplace. Since this practice was not common to people of their class, they must have had a special affinity to their employer. Indeed, such an affinity is readily discernible in the way they depict the

---

[44]   Lansdowne, *A Life's Reminiscences*, p. 2.
[45]   Peter N. Stearns, *Lives of Labour* (London: Croom Helm, 1975) p. 242.

CID and in the titles of the memoirs themselves which usually refer either to Scotland Yard or to the authors' occupational identity. Their affiliation with Scotland Yard provides the *raison d'être* for their activities and for the books as a whole. The authors function more as representatives of the law than as individuals with distinct characteristics. It is this affiliation that allows them to engage in the pursuits of criminals and become all-powerful investigators and that legitimises their actions and decisions. They owe a great deal to this affiliation. Each detective-author is one of many, and his story is theirs as well. Detective Chief Inspector James Berrett aptly reflects this feeling: 'For the purposes of these reminiscences the word "I" must often be used', but 'that "I" represents not only myself but the many assistants…who joined with me as part of the organisation to solve the problem before us'.[46] Writing as the organisation's representative, each memoirist took upon himself the task of promoting a positive image of the body to which they all belonged.

Some of the texts read almost as advertisements for an attractive place of employment. Chief Inspector Charles Arrow expresses this intention explicitly:

> It has been suggested to me that a more detailed account of some of my experiences with criminals might be of interest, not only to the general public but particularly to a new generation of police, and might serve as a guide to young men of to-day in search of a useful and interesting career, such as I claim the police service to be.[47]

Having in mind 'the young man at the threshold of a career in search of a profession', he candidly acknowledges that 'if anything I have written should influence him to follow my example and join the police as a candidate for the Criminal Investigation Department, I shall have my reward'.[48]

However, more than any other motive for the positive portrayal of their workplace, the memoirists were impelled by an underlying urge to correct the impression that many people had of the police. Their books are permeated by a crusading tone aimed at eradicating extant misconceptions and illuminating what they insisted was the true work of a police detective.

Criticism of the detective force of the Metropolitan Police had been levelled at the department from its very inception in 1842. While the uniformed Metropolitan Police had been established in 1829 (also against much criticism), the notion of plain-clothes policing, associated in the public mind with spying and the notorious French secret police, was even more widely opposed, and it took another 13 years before a small detective unit was set up.[49] The slow development of the detective

---

[46] Berrett, *When I was*, p. vi.
[47] Arrow, *Rogues and Others*, p. 9.
[48] Ibid, p. 12.
[49] Phillip Thurmond Smith, *Policing Victorian London* (Westport, Conn: Greenwood

force – from a unit of eight at Metropolitan Police headquarters in 1842 to a force of approximately 300 with a presence in all the divisions by 1889 – was accompanied by censorious public discourse.[50] During the course of the century, the public gradually came to accept the necessity of a police force in each locality, and this acceptance slowly extended to detectives as well, but because of the lingering suspicion of plain-clothes policing, the work of the police and their detective units was constantly subject to closer public scrutiny. Revelations about corruption among detectives (especially in 1877),[51] and the inability of detectives to eradicate crime and find the perpetrators in a number of celebrated cases (notably those connected with Jack the Ripper in the late 1880s), perpetuated this negative image. Although occasional articles praised the London detectives, many found fault with them. It was only towards the end of the century that the reputation of CID detectives began to change significantly for the better, but the change was gradual and the feeling among members of the police organisation was that a great deal still needed to be done to refute the prejudices harboured by the public. Granted a unique opportunity to appeal to the public directly through their published memoirs, many detectives took upon themselves the task of improving the image of their occupation, thereby enhancing their own social status as well.

The blatant device used by detective-authors to rectify their impaired image was unabashed praise of their organisation and its men. Detective Chief Inspector Tom Divall had no qualms about asserting: 'The Metropolitan Police are the admiration of the world, and one constantly reads of high officers of the Police-forces of other nations paying visits to England in order to gain practical hints and information respecting the reason for this wonderful efficiency and discipline'.[52] Detective Chief Inspector James Berrett considered it 'a great privilege to have been a member of the Criminal Investigation Department', calling it 'a wonderful institution', and Detective Superintendent Percy Savage declared the Metropolitan Police to be 'the finest police force in the world'.[53] The CID workforce is described as efficient, vigilant, kind, helpful, honest, clever, capable, intelligent and

---

Press, 1985) pp. 61–62.

[50] James Monro to Under Secretary of State, 11 November 1889, National Archives/Public Record Office, London, HO 45/10002/A49,463/13.

[51] For details see George Dilnot, ed, *The Trial of the Detectives* (New York: Charles Scribner's Sons, 1928).

[52] Divall, *Scoundrels and Scallywags*, pp. 9–10.

[53] Berrett, *When I was*, p.xii; Percy Savage, *Savage of Scotland Yard* (London: Hutchinson, 1934) p. 15. Also see Arthur Fowler Neil, *Man-Hunters of Scotland Yard* (New York: Doubleday, Doran & Co., 1933) p. 2 (In England the memoirs were published by Jarrolds in 1932 under the title *Forty Years of Man-Hunting*).

perceptive, as 'cogs in a machine, the workings of which are felt in continents other than ours and across other seas'.[54]

The message that CID detectives were highly talented in their vocation was enhanced by the occasional presentation of the criminal as 'a formidable enemy to defeat'.[55] In Berret's view 'criminals are certainly not beaten men'.[56] Detective Inspector Percy J. Smith found 'the elite of Crookdom' to be 'men of intelligence, fascinating, indeed charming', squandering 'their easy-made fortunes at casinos, race-courses, and the Continental playgrounds of the rich and fashionable'.[57] Con men, said Smith, were 'audacious, ingenious, tenacious'.[58] Yet, however formidable the struggle was between the detective and the criminal, the former almost always won. Each was a specialist in his own way, but the detectives were perfectly in control and proved the greater tricksters.[59]

The distorted fictional image

If the criminal was presented as the arch enemy of the detective, the fictional detective was an enemy of a different kind. Running through all the memoirs is an underlying assumption that the distorted image of police detectives was the product of the way they were depicted in fiction. This portrayal was considered the source of most of the misconceptions about the police as a whole and about police detectives in particular. Indeed, detectives had good reason to feel this way. Long after the establishment of the detective unit at Scotland Yard, translated and English popular literary works that incorporated police detectives as characters in their plots were in the habit of portraying them as unimpressive and generally not highly competent. A few literary texts did include laudable police detectives, for example Emile Gaboriau's French detective M. Lecoq.[60] Charles Dickens portrayed both his fictional detectives (the most famous of whom was Inspector Bucket in *Bleak House*) and real members of the detective unit in Scotland Yard as

---

[54] Littlechild, *Reminiscences*, pp. 8–10; Sweeney, *At Scotland Yard*, pp. 18–19. Also see Robert A. Fuller, *Recollections of a Detective* (London: John Long, 1912) p. 28. See illustration 5.2

[55] Berrett, *When I was*, p. vi.

[56] Ibid, p. 55.

[57] Percy J. Smith, *Crooks in Clover*, p. 8.

[58] Ibid, p. 9.

[59] Ibid, pp. 39–40.

[60] See note 25 above.

Illustration 5.2 The cover of Robert A. Fuller's memoirs, entitled
Recollections of a Detective **(1912).**

able, honest, respectable, impartial and proud of their profession, but his admiration was not generally shared in the literary world.[61] The image of ineptness (sometimes combined with cunning) was echoed in Edgar Allen Poe's tales (published in England during the 1840s and 1850s), which were highly popular from the 1870s onwards. Poe's brilliant amateur detective Dupin had typically low regard for police officers. Such fictional tales helped create a tradition that posited police detectives as inferior to amateur detectives.

The persistent literary need for the private eye to further investigations was solid proof that the legal system could not operate effectively without him. In Arthur Conan Doyle's very first detective narrative, *A Study in Scarlet* (1887), Holmes proudly declares that when government (and private) detectives 'are at fault they come to me, and I manage to put them on the right scent'.[62] Doyle did not present a uniform picture of police officers, and he even portrayed some of them in positive terms. Still, it was mostly their courage, energy or honesty that he commended, while consistently representing them, even when successful in their investigations, as conventional and unimaginative bureaucrats devoid of the mental acuity that characterised Sherlock Holmes. The many detective novels of the first decades of the twentieth century, which stereotyped police officers as 'conspicuously lacking in intelligence', perpetuated this tradition.[63] Even when the literary arena both before the First World War and in the inter-war period increasingly contained police detectives who were not figures of fun and were far from inefficient, the number of private detectives in fictional works far exceeded that of police agents and their portrayal outshone that of their official counterparts. The message implicit in Doyle's tales that the private detective was so much more impressive – both in his ability and performance – continued to dominate the genre. Holmes persisted as an influential figure well after the death of Conan Doyle in 1930, and much of the pre-war literature that depicted the police officer in unflattering terms maintained its popularity. This had the ongoing effect of galvanising the detective-memoirists into action, mounting a counter-offensive against detective fiction. Repeated disparaging references to this literature in their memoirs gave their books a kind of crusading aura in battling the misrepresentation of police detectives.

---

[61] Ronald R. Thomas, *Detective Fiction and the Rise of Forensic Science* (Cambridge University Press, 1999) p. 147. *Bleak House* first appeared as serialised stories in *Household Words* during 1852–53. In 1853 *Bleak House* came out as a single volume.

[62] Arthur Conan Doyle, *A Study in Scarlet* (New York: Readers' League of America, 1930) p. 17.

[63] Murch, *Development*, p. 211.

Correcting the image

Convinced that most people acquired 'their conception of the detective from the works of writers like Sir Arthur Conan Doyle', in which it appeared that 'we at Scotland Yard were a crowd of inept blunderers', they set out to answer a question they believed all readers were keen to know: 'Are the methods used by the real-life detective at all like those of the detective of fiction?'[64] Replying, the author-detectives attempted repeatedly to differentiate between themselves and fictional detectives by stressing that while works of fiction were 'unreal', their related experiences 'are true' and factual.[65] Detective Chief Inspector George H. Greenham vouched that he gave 'simply the bare facts of the cases'.[66] Detective Inspector John Sweeney assured readers that 'I have in no way romanced', and affirmed he only writes 'facts'.[67] Presenting themselves as experts in sifting out fact from fiction in their professional life, this expertise, by implication, was to be viewed as carrying over into their writing as well.

Detective fiction, they asserted, was not to be taken seriously. Conan Doyle's novels and stories, in particular, were singled out as false. James Berrett called upon the reader to 'disabuse his mind of any idea of Sherlock Holmes and he will understand Scotland Yard better, and see it in its real light'.[68] The retired officers of Scotland Yard were determined to uproot any confusion between fictional sleuths and real ones, whether such misimpressions concerned the official representative of the law or the private detective. They had a strong interest in presenting both misimpressions as false, and their own accounts as true. Imbued with this missionary zeal to set the record right, Detective Inspector Lansdowne wrote:

> This idea of a modern detective is purely fictitious. It is as absurd as that other notion which, I believe, owed its first suggestion to a romancer, and its continued existence to the exaggerations of sensational writers – I mean the popular fallacy that a detective must necessarily be a man of mystery, an astute actor, an

---

[64] Francis Carlin, *Reminiscences of an Ex-Detective* (London: Hutchinson, 1920) p. 215; Neil, *Man-Hunters of Scotland Yard*, p. 204.

[65] Harold Brust, *In Plain Clothes* (London: Stanley Paul, 1937) pp. 10–15; Lansdowne, *A Life's Reminiscences*, p. 1.

[66] G.H. Greenham, *Scotland Yard Experiences* (London: George Routledge & Sons, 1904) p. 6.

[67] Sweeney, *At Scotland Yard*, p. vi. Also see Carlin, *Reminiscences*, p. 13; G.W. Cornish, *Cornish of Scotland Yard* (New York: Macmillan, 1935) p. ix (In England the book was published by Bodley Head under the title *Cornish of the Yard*).

[68] Berrett, *When I was*, p. 231.

accomplished comedian with a wardrobe of an extensive kind, and as difficult to 'corner' as a lively eel.[69]

This was all wrong, they informed their readers. Detectives were entirely different from the characters who were the figment of their creators' imagination. Detective Superintendent Percy Savage affirmed: 'There are no super-detectives in real life ... no man, however brilliant his record may be, is infallible'.[70] In contrast to detective literature, the memoirists portrayed detectives as 'professional men with human virtues – and vices', who sometimes 'find the work tiresome' and sometimes 'get annoyed and jealous'.[71] 'When they do their work well, when success attends their efforts, they know a feeling of satisfaction. They laugh and joke, take an occasional drink with each other, and now and again use bad language', recounted Detective Chief Inspector James Berrett, emphasising the mundane side of detective life in the police, while simultaneously implying that the job was prosaic for private detectives as well.[72]

Proceeding to illustrate how imaginary detective fiction was, the memoirists described 'how it's [really] done'.[73] While fictional detectives were likely to engage in solving murder cases, in reality, Berrett attested, 'murder cases are exceptional'.[74] Furthermore, the police detective was not concerned 'with master criminals, great swindlers, cracksmen of the fictional type, and forgers who aim to wreck Governments, but with pickpockets, housebreakers, snatch thieves, car stealers, and the like'.[75] Indeed, Berrett had never actually met a master criminal, a type who, by contrast, frequently inhabited crime fiction.[76] He had 'known one or two receivers, a few organisers, half-a-dozen gentlemen known as "putters-up", because they "put up" jobs for braver men to carry out, but no single individual who could approach his peer of fiction in either ability or ruthlessness'.[77] Much of the detective's time was occupied by petty crime, Berrett asserted.[78]

Time and again the memoirists argued that the methods used by the fictitious detectives could not have produced results. Similarly, the successful resolution of a case was not the only possible outcome. Detective Superintendent Francis Carlin

---

[69] Lansdowne, *A Life's Reminiscences*, p. 3. Also see Fuller, *Recollections*, pp. 213–14.
[70] Savage, *Savage of Scotland Yard*, p. 162.
[71] Berrett, *When I was*, p. v.
[72] Ibid, pp. v–vi.
[73] Lansdowne, *A Life's Reminiscences*, p. 3.
[74] Berrett, *When I was*, p. 231.
[75] Ibid, pp. 231–32.
[76] Ibid, p. 125. Also see Cecil Bishop, *From Information Received* (London: Hutchinson, 1932) p. 35.
[77] Berrett, *When I was*, p. 125.
[78] Ibid, p. 232.

cynically observed: 'The sleuth in fiction always gets his man, of course. But he is usually allowed three hundred and fifty to four hundred pages of the novel to do so...the Scotland Yard officer has to get his man quickly or not at all in the majority of cases'.[79] The Yard may have worked 'with less brilliance' than the Parisian police, Carlin conceded, but the English police detective was more careful than his French counterpart and operated strictly according to the law.[80] His integrity, according to Carlin, was unblemished and his performance commendable. 'He obtains his clues; establishes reasonably that they are clues; and then *deduces* the inferences from them. Only when those inferences are obvious enough from the legal point of view can the English C.I.D. man safely "take his man inside"'. The English police agent did not make pre-judgements but rather conducted exhaustive inquiries.[81] Alluding to the lax ways with which fictional detectives discovered the truth behind crimes, Savage explained that 'in real life the detective must confine himself to whatever facts he can glean, and however meagre they may be, he must not allow his imagination to interfere in the slightest degree with a careful and unbiased analysis of the evidence'.[82] 'Only from evidence can deductions be formed', he insisted.

In another attempt to disabuse the public of the notions embedded in detective tales, Lansdowne clarified: 'Detectives are neither remarkable for their big feet, nor for their histrionic capabilities and changes of dress'.[83] Since it was precisely the fear of invisible surveillance and policing which accounted for the widespread resistance to the establishment of the police as a whole and of the detective unit in particular, many memoirists made a point of emphasising how little, if at all, they had resorted to this questionable method of attaining results, unlike Sherlock Holmes, for example, who often disguised himself in his attempts to unravel mysteries.[84] To Detective Cecil Bishop, the greatest point of difference between the Scotland Yard of fact and the Scotland Yard of fiction was that '"narks" and informants rarely appear in fiction, whereas in real life they are of the greatest importance in the solution of almost every crime'.[85]

Confident about the attraction of their world and occupation, the memoirists did not hesitate to document their life's 'rough way'.[86] Detective Inspector Robert A. Fuller wrote:

---

[79]　Carlin, *Reminiscences*, pp. 215–16.
[80]　Ibid, p. 225.
[81]　Ibid, p. 98.
[82]　Savage, *Savage of the Yard*, p. 54.
[83]　Lansdowne, *A Life's Reminiscences*, p. 3.
[84]　Carlin, *Reminiscences*, pp. 220–21; Littlechild, *Reminiscences*, p. 76; Fuller, *Recollections*, pp. 213–14.
[85]　Bishop, *From Information*, p. 39.
[86]　Fuller, *Recollections*, pp. 7 and 16.

[Ostensibly, the detective] sees life at its various angles. Certainly he is oftener in its darkest places than other men are, and, like the rain, he goes among the just and unjust. He is from time to time in close personal contact with the duke and the beggar, the cardinal and the criminal; in fact, every sort and condition of man, woman, and child is encountered, and not merely in the glare of Courts of Law and other public places, or in the presence of others, where words are often few and carefully chosen, but alone, in the quiet of the people's own surroundings, where no restraint is imposed or necessary.[87]

Police agents were ordinary men, though they were, like the fictional detectives, highly intelligent, perceptive, enterprising, courageous and possessed with exceptional powers of observation. While detectives did employ scientific means such as fingerprinting, anthropometric methods, photography and the Habitual Criminals Registry held at Scotland Yard, theirs was a different kind of professionalism from that attributed to Sherlock Holmes, portrayed as a scientific expert (see illustration 5.3). As Chief Constable Frederick Porter Wensley explained: 'There have been all kinds of successful [police] detectives, but they haven't got anywhere near the top by making flashing deductions from the scratches on a watch and enmeshing a criminal by the exercise of pure reason'.[88] Their professionalism was, rather, anchored in hard work, which involved spending hours in surveilling or tracking suspects, sometimes in different parts of the country or even abroad, unlike the private middle-class detective who often solved puzzling crimes while sitting in his armchair and using scientific deduction.[89] In James Berrett's view: 'If a man is a real detective, long hours mean nothing to him. He is naturally industrious and naturally observant. He possesses a wide knowledge and applies it with intelligence'.[90] John Sweeney recalled: 'At any hour of the twenty-four I might be on some errand, nor could I even go away on furlough without feeling that at any moment I might through some pressing need be prematurely summoned back to headquarters'.[91] Echoing this message, Percy J. Smith writes:

---

[87] Ibid, p. 16.

[88] Frederick Porter Wensley, *Forty Years of Scotland Yard* (New York: Doubleday, Doran & Co., 1933) p. 68 (In England the book was published by Cassell in 1930 under the title *Detective Days*).

[89] Sweeney, *At Scotland Yard*, pp. 18–20; Littlechild, *Reminiscences*, p. 3; Charles E. Leach, *On Top of the Underworld* (London: Sampson Low, Marston & Co., 1933) p. 22.

[90] Berrett, *When I was*, p. 102.

[91] Sweeney, *At Scotland Yard*, pp. 19–20.

" HOLMES WAS WORKING HARD OVER A CHEMICAL INVESTIGATION."

Illustration 5.3   Sherlock Holmes as illustrated by Sidney Paget in 'The Adventure of the Naval Treaty' (1893).

Investigating crime is a hard and exacting task, demanding a man's every energy and making him a not unwilling slave of his job. There are no such things as fixed hours or regular mealtimes for a detective; and while engaged on a case his home-life practically ceases to exist. His assignment must come before everything else.[92]

Conceivably, the silence of the memoirists about their family life was meant to suggest their total and undivided dedication to their work.

Night work, in particular, entailed a variety of hardships, including the difficulty to stay awake and harsh weather. Describing an unforgettable night time incident, John Littlechild recalls that his blood froze when he frightened a flock of hundreds of sparrows who made a rushing noise that filled him with terror.[93] Such descriptions were a far cry from the comfortable life led by many fictional detectives. They conveyed hard physical tasks akin to the toil of manual workers. Yet, the message emanating from the memoirists' discourse is that the methods they used, even if not based principally on pure reasoning or encyclopaedic knowledge of the individual investigator, were in no way less efficient or effective than the fictitious ones attributed to detectives in novels and stories.

Assimilated into these descriptions of hard work were revelations about the risks involved. Lansdowne pointed out that 'an account of the life of a police detective would be incomplete without some reference to the dangers of death which beset the calling, and which every detective in the service must be prepared to run'.[94] In a similar fashion, Berrett commented that 'officers took big risks in those days. Not infrequent were the attempts made to injure, even indeed, to murder them'.[95] Some criminals operated alone and others were organised in dangerous gangs. According to Detective Sergeant Benjamin Leeson, the criminals involved in the Sidney Street siege in January 1911 were not 'the ordinary burglar type', but a 'sinister organisation which was causing me and my colleagues so many sleepless nights'.[96] Leeson, who was wounded during the siege, had to be discharged from service as a result and live 'on a sum much below the wages of a constable'.[97]

The memoirs of Special Branch officers, in particular, are replete with incidents involving dangerous Fenians, nihilists, anarchists and Bolsheviks, which heightened the sense of danger under which detectives operated but at the same

---

[92] Percy J. Smith, *Crooks in Clover*, pp. 167–68. Also see Fuller, *Recollections*, p. 18.

[93] Littlechild, *Reminiscences*, pp. 3–5.

[94] Lansdowne, *A Life's Reminiscences*, p. 184. Also see Cornish, *Cornish of Scotland Yard*, p. 31.

[95] Berrett, *When I was*, p. 85. For examples, see ibid., pp. 81–82.

[96] Leeson, *Lost London*, p. 208.

[97] Ibid, p. 278.

time glamorised their work.[98] The first task of the Special Branch, when it was established in the early 1880s, was to fight the rising tide of Fenian terrorism. Littlechild 'shudder[ed] to think of the consequences if these emissaries had been successful in all their operations', as 'the public does not realise the peril in which it was placed'.[99] He used the opportunity to make the point that 'evil-doers rarely give Scotland Yard credit for efficient policing'. Another public enemy – the anarchists – was depicted as no less ruthless. Of all the political refugees who found asylum in Britain, they were considered the most dangerous, 'an ever-present menace to the peace of Europe', in the words of Detective Inspector Harold Brust.[100] There was 'always a chance that their antagonism might extend to British institutions ... [so] the authorities dared not take a chance', Detective Inspector W.H. Thompson explained.[101] The Special Branch was on the alert as the 'relentless enemy of anarchists', constantly keeping aware of their whereabouts and meeting places.[102] Even senior officers took part in apprehending anarchists.

Intent on gaining support for the police organisation, the memoirists not only attacked the stock figures and descriptions in detective literature as untrue, but also adopted a rhetorical strategy that highlighted the positive aspects of the work life of police agents. However arduous detective life was, the memoirs do not leave the reader with the impression that police work was unattractive. If for most working people, especially during the Victorian and Edwardian periods, work was 'to be endured rather than enjoyed', for detectives, at least in their reminiscences, work was the main source of enjoyment in life.[103] With all the hardships, investigative policing was celebrated as an interesting, rewarding and highly satisfying job.[104] At the start of his book, Berrett stated: 'In spite of all the hardships and inconveniences I have endured as a consequence of the duties I had to perform, I can say sincerely that I have enjoyed every day of every year'.[105] Later on in the book he wrote: 'I worked hard because I loved my job ... if sometimes the hours were very long and wearisome, I found fresh interest every new day'.[106] Indeed,

---

[98] See, for example, Sweeney, *At Scotland Yard*, pp. 20–33; Littlechild, *Reminiscences*, p. 12; W.H. Thompson, *Guard from the Yard* (London: Jarrolds, 1938) pp. 25–36; Brust, *In Plain Clothes*, pp. 64–65. The Special Branch was engaged mainly in surveillance of local radicals and political refugees and in guarding the royal family and political leaders.

[99] Littlechild, *Reminiscences*, p. 12.

[100] Brust, *In Plain Clothes*, p. 64.

[101] Thompson, *Guard from the Yard*, p. 32.

[102] Baroness Orczy, 'Forward', in Herbert T. Fitch, *Memoirs of a Royal Detective* (London: Hurst & Blackett, 1935) p. vii; Brust, *In Plain Clothes*, pp. 64–65; Bishop, *From Information*, p. 170.

[103] Burnett, ed, *Useful Toil*, p. 15.

[104] Fuller, *Recollections*, p. 18; Sweeney, *At Scotland Yard*, p. 348.

[105] Berrett, *When I was*, p. 3.

[106] Ibid, p. 69.

the interest and excitement the job generated were particularly emphasised. Detective Inspector Sweeney maintained: 'There are to-day few walks of life likely to surpass that of the detective' in terms of the interest it involved, while Detective Inspector Edwin T. Woodhall (both of the Special Branch) acknowledged that detective service was 'the most interesting and instructive, and, indeed, exciting part of my life'.[107] The stories recounted by the writers stressed the thrill of pursuing and capturing criminals and the sense of power they gained thereby.[108] After thirty-five years of active work as a detective, Francis Carlin could 'still feel the thrill'.[109] Time and again the authors highlighted the richness and variety of their work.[110] Littlechild pointed to 'the ever-varying changes in the daily duty, in scene and incident, the uncertainty of movement and lack of monotony that necessarily attaches to the career, and the excitement that must be present with even the coldest and most unimaginative of natures'.[111] The detective's duties could take him 'from end to end of the United Kingdom', and even abroad.[112]

No less impressive was the feeling of solidarity highlighted in the memoirs. 'We were all quite happy and always ready to joke', Berrett recalls.[113] Detective Superintendent Percy Savage refers to himself 'as a member of a hard-working team of good fellows with only one object in view – the subjugation of crime'.[114] The sense of comradeship, togetherness and team work created an image of the CID as not only an efficient and compelling organisation, but also an agreeable and satisfying place of employment.[115] This solidarity extended beyond the Metropolitan Police and even national boundaries and encompassed detectives worldwide.[116] What emerges from the narratives, therefore, is not only pride in the institution to which they belonged, but also in their profession.

---

[107] Sweeney, *At Scotland Yard*, p. 348; Woodhall, *Dectective*, p. 5.

[108] That some of these pronouncements intended to hide a more intricate reality is indicated, for example, by the gap between testimony by John Littlechild in a public inquiry and the content of his memoirs. While during the inquiry he acknowledged how difficult it was for him to serve in the Special Branch, declaring: 'I can simply say that I have no desire to go through my career again', in his memoirs he announced: 'I have certainly been fortunate, and have always congratulated myself on the fact that the life of a detective was suited to me in every way'. *Departmental Committee of 1889 upon Metropolitan Police Superannuation*, PP, 1890, vol. 56, p. 436; Littlechild, *Reminiscences*, p. 2.

[109] Carlin, *Reminiscences*, p. 13.

[110] Arrow, *Rogues and Others*, p. 43; Sweeney, *At Scotland Yard*, p. 19.

[111] Littlechild, *Reminiscences*, pp. 2–3.

[112] Sweeney, *At Scotland Yard*, p. 19. Also see Fuller, *Recollections*, p. 186.

[113] Berrett, *When I was*, p. 85.

[114] Savage, *Savage of the Yard*, p. 157.

[115] Arrow, *Rogues and Others*, p. 38.

[116] Fuller, *Recollections*, p. 186.

Apart from the sense of belonging, detective work also offered material and social compensations, which the memoirists did not fail to mention. They themselves were living proof that promotion up to and including the rank of superintendent was possible within this work organisation, which allowed detectives to enjoy the kind of social mobility denied to most other workers in society prior to the First World War. Every step up entailed small but valued social and economic rewards, with the ranks of chief inspector and superintendent opening the door to a life of relative affluence and standing in the community. Several of the authors explicitly referred to this opportunity.[117] Furthermore, detectives, more than ordinary policemen, were likely to gain both monetary and other awards beyond routine wages and benefits. Special Branch officers were particularly privileged in this respect. In gratitude for their services, they were liable to receive gifts, awards and decorations from local celebrities and foreign royalty.[118] Some of the rewards were substantial, for example, the award to Detective Inspector Herbert T. Fitch of the famous order of Officer of the Red Eagle of Prussia – a jewelled decoration – from the German Kaiser.[119] Beyond material benefits, the proximity to kings and rulers in itself was a reward. Fitch boasted that sometimes he 'was able to make suggestions which, the royal guests later assured me, added to their enjoyment of England'.[120] Some detectives, therefore, not only protected the public interest but also promoted their country's image.

Indeed, Scotland Yard was depicted as a benevolent organisation, profiting the whole of society. Not only were police detectives world experts in their field, but they were also, unlike the fictional detective, public servants in the true sense of the word, offering invaluable and disinterested service in the legal domain as well as helping people in their daily life. Significantly, law-abiding citizens were not the only persons to benefit by the service ethos of the detective force. Detective Chief Inspector Divall went so far as to describe Scotland Yard as a philanthropic agency. Rebutting accusations of police brutality, he argued that the police in fact did 'their utmost to prevent exposing offenders and expired convicts', tried 'to help them to obtain an honest living' and even assisted them financially.[121] Detective Superintendent Carlin joined Divall in refuting the allegation that Scotland Yard officers were lacking 'in all forms of human sympathy' and showed that they

---

[117] Sweeney, *At Scotland Yard*, p. 7.

[118] For example, Bishop, *From Information*, p. 173; F.S. Stuart, 'Preface', in Fitch, *Memoirs of a Royal Detective*, p. v; Neil, *Man Hunters*, p. 2.

[119] Herbert T. Fitch, *Traitors within* (London: Hurst & Blackett, 1933) p. 113.

[120] Fitch, *Memoirs of a Royal Detective*, p. 24.

[121] Divall, *Scoundrels and Scallywags*, p. 89.

helped convicts to resettle and treated them justly and fairly, if also firmly.[122] 'Dozens of detectives in London to-day have assisted people of both sexes to get a fresh start in life', he contended. Police officers, in short, contributed to society by way of rehabilitating offenders. Detective Inspector Fuller proudly stated that 'the public have a right to nothing short of [the] ... best services' from these public servants.[123]

The authors also appealed to the patriotic sentiment of the readers, describing detectives as the trusted guardians of their kings and queens and boasting that 'since the formation of the Special Branch no royal person has ever been hurt in Britain'.[124] Royal visitors were also well protected. As Cecil Bishop pointed out to readers, 'it was the efficiency of the British Special Branch that prevented any harm coming to King Alfonso' of Spain in his visit to London.[125]

Such depictions reinforced the conviction of a contemporary writer, Joseph Gollomb, that 'the story of the real Scotland Yard needs no colouring to give it richer glamour than fiction does'.[126] Insistent though the memoirists were that real detective work was unromantic and grueling, they also conveyed the impression that it was heroic, distinctive and even glamorous. Lansdowne had no difficulty in recounting 'incidents and scenes which would appear to me to be fiction, if I did not know them to have been real'.[127] This tension between the portrayal of detective life as at once ordinary and glamorous undoubtedly appealed to wide audiences, projecting an image of what it was like to be a detective while also colouring it with an alluring brush. The very need for those engaged in secret operations in the Special Branch to keep silent about some of their adventures must have stimulated the readers' curiosity and enhanced the appeal of detective work.[128]

Conclusion

The memoirists had various incentives to venture into the literary world. They knew that their recollections were of the kind sought by publishers and the general reader. Conscious of literary conventions, equipped with source material that they could use, and trained in the habit of writing while at work, it was no wonder that

---

[122] Carlin, *Reminiscences*, pp. 61–62.

[123] Fuller, *Recollections*, p. 17.

[124] Fitch, *Memoirs of a Royal Detective*, p. 19.

[125] Bishop, *From Information*, p. 170.

[126] Joseph Gollomb, *Scotland Yard* (London: Hutchinson, 1929) p. 7.

[127] Lansdowne, *A Life's Reminiscences*, p. 3.

[128] Harold Brust, *I Guarded Kings* (New York: Hillman-Curl, 1936) p. 44 (In England the memoirs were published in 1935 by Stanley Paul); Fuller, *Recollections*, p. 51.

they decided to reconstruct their life course in writing. Surely, a commercial incentive and an impulse for self-expression were not absent either. Yet, over and above these motives and favourable circumstances, the urge to rectify the adverse image of the police underlay the entire range of police memoirs. It is evident in the discursive style they used, intricately arguing against literary texts.

To garner public sympathy, the narrators projected an appealing picture of the CID. The memoirs show that police detectives were privileged neither by birth, class or education, as were many fictional detectives. They did, however, possess the ability and the natural gift to match their 'brains against the cunning and foresight of some of the most astute people in the world'.[129] So efficient was Scotland Yard that it was approached by other governments to help them deal with criminal investigations.[130] Moreover, Scotland Yard contributed to society in domains other than law enforcement.

By the outbreak of the First World War, 'those glamorous initials – CID – were ... as romantic and adventurous as the call of the East'.[131] Gradually, and more consistently after the war, the English police detective became identified with skillful observation, the detection of truth and internationally acknowledged authoritative methods of criminal investigation, despite the continuing popularity of fictional tales which depicted police detectives in less than glowing terms. While no cause-and-effect connection between police autobiographies and the redress of the image of the police can be proven, it is likely that they played a role in this process. As the authors repeatedly asserted, the glamour of their vocation was not the invention of a literary mind but rooted in reality. The awareness that the tales of the retired police officers were authentic, even if coloured, and that their descriptions presented an overall picture of detective life, including its less illustrious sides, must have persuaded at least some readers that the authors' observations should be taken seriously. These readers were likely to believe Chief Inspector Greenham's claim that the police detective needed 'to master every technique in Law, to be subtle of instinct, patient of endeavour, quick in emergency, and always ready to journey to the end of the earth at a moment's notice',[132] or Detective Inspector Fuller's assertion that the detective was 'superlatively zealous in his undertakings'.[133] Most probably the popularity of the fictional detective was unaffected by the memoirists' counter-offensive, but the memoirs served to diminish the uncomplimentary impressions conveyed by detective fiction and a portion of the press and elevate the institutional image of

---

[129] Carlin, *Reminiscences*, p. 143.

[130] Arrow, *Rogues and Others*, p. 193.

[131] Percy J. Smith, *Crooks in Clover*, p. 17.

[132] Greenham, *Scotland Yard Experiences*, p. 9.

[133] Fuller, *Recollections*, p. 16.

Scotland Yard. The reiterated messages embedded in the memoirs must have persuaded some readers to be less censorious of detectives and more receptive to positive evaluations. Further, the fact that these memoirs spoke with authority, and that their presentations corroborated one another, must have strengthened their case. Ultimately, the sheer number of memoirs that respectable publishers decided to print in itself may have legitimised the message in them for large sectors of the public.

Chapter Six

From Sleuths to Technicians? Changing Images of the Detective in Victoria

Dean Wilson and Mark Finnane

The image of the detective was transformed over the course of the nineteenth and early twentieth century from the concept of detection as a practice of individual prowess and cunning to a bureaucratically embedded notion of the detective as depersonalised technician applying procedure and forensic technique to criminal investigation. The transformations in detective policing in colonial and early twentieth-century Victoria capture this change. Shaping the change was the sharp criticism of the older style detective practice and organisation that helped make the Victorian police objects of derision in their failure to capture Ned Kelly's gang.

The notion of the detective as individual sleuth was personified in the self-promoting career of John Christie, whose use of disguises and unorthodox procedures to solve cases captured the imagination of the Melbourne public. Christie's high-profile cases popularised conceptions of the 'gentlemen detective' working beyond the constraints of routine police work. Christie's widely publicised exploits contrasted sharply with emergent conceptions of detection evident in the 1920s and 1930s. Increasingly detectives were represented as anonymous functionaries of the police bureaucracy applying scientific technique and bureaucratic procedure in criminal investigation. The imagery of detective work was thus partially severed from earlier notions of individual cunning and intelligence and fused with bureaucratic notions of a modern, scientific and efficient police force. Nevertheless, the image of the detective as cunning sleuth persisted, coexisting uneasily with emerging conceptions of the detective as procedural technician.

The birth of the detectives

It is frequently noted that in England, despite the formation of a small detective force in 1842, detectives were regarded with ambivalence if not outright contempt.

Detective methods were seen as 'un-English' and evoking images of espionage and agent provocateurs that offended English sensibilities.[1] In colonial Victoria, despite a similar emphasis upon prevention rather than detection in the policing of cities and towns[2], the birth of detective policing was less problematic. This owed much to the convict origins of the Australian colonies, and the widely held perception that they possessed a 'criminal class' of significantly greater dimensions than England.

The initial formation of a detective force in the 1840s had been justified by the belief that a nascent 'criminal class' was forming in the backlanes and alleys of Melbourne. In 1844, a small detective force consisting of four constables and a sergeant was formed.[3] This force consisted primarily of emancipists – convicts who had been granted a conditional or absolute pardon before the term of their sentence had expired. An abiding theme in detective work justified the employment of ex-convicts, namely the importance of familiarity with the subjects of one's attention. The principal duty of the detective force was to monitor arrivals from the southern penal colony of Van Diemen's Land, and it was reasoned that 'they are better acquainted with the style and character of the arrivals from Van Diemen's Land than any emigrants would be'.[4] Fears of an expanding criminal class were exacerbated when gold was discovered in the colony in 1851 and the colony's population rapidly expanded. In the three years from 1851 to 1854 Victoria's population grew from 77,000 to 237,000 and all but doubled again in the following three years. With one of the Empire's main convict outposts (Van Diemen's Land) on its doorstep, the fear of convicts and their purported taint of criminality were so prevalent that a *Convicts Prevention Act* was passed in 1852 to prevent those holding conditional pardons from entering the colony of Victoria.[5] By 1852, the detectives still only numbered four men and a sergeant. In the changed conditions of a goldrush colony however there were many who advocated the utility of a detective force and recommended its augmentation. The founder of the detective force, William Sugden, recommended before a Select Committee in

---

[1]   Stefan Petrow, *Policing Morals: The Metropolitan Police and the Home Office 1870–1914* (Oxford: Clarendon Press, 1994) p. 54.

[2]   Dean Wilson, 'On the Beat: Police Work in Melbourne 1853–1923', PhD, Monash University, 2000, pp. 71–79.

[3]   Robert Haldane, *The People's Force: A History of the Victoria Police* (Melbourne: Melbourne University Press, 1986) p. 17.

[4]   *Report from the Select Committee on the Police*, 1852, *Votes and Proceedings of the Legislative Council (Colony of Victoria)*, vol. 3, 1852–53, p. 8.

[5]   Geoffrey Serle, *The Golden Age: A history of the colony of Victoria 1851–1861* (Melbourne: Melbourne University Press, 1963) p. 127.

1852 that the number of detectives be increased to twelve men, paid more than ordinary police 'considering the danger and risk they run'.[6]

The expansion of the detective force was subsequently justified by the widely held belief that the Australian colonies possessed a far larger criminal class than England due to the continuing influence of the 'convict stain'. Such reasoning was evident in the remarks of Charles Hope Nicolson, Inspector of Detectives, in 1862. Nicolson claimed the criminal class in Victoria was much greater in proportion to the population than was the case in England, as they were 'more demoralized, owing to the convict element with which they come into contact'.[7] For both serious crime and more trivial offences Nicolson estimated that the numbers of the criminal class were 'at least double' those of England. Nicolson suggested that in Melbourne alone there were at least 1000 'thieves, prostitutes and persons who get their living by breaking laws'. There were also, Nicolson testified, a further 3000 to 4000 'questionable persons' whom the detectives 'would have an eye upon'.[8] Amongst the questionable persons were employees living beyond their means or of 'dissipated reckless habits', bankrupts, embezzlers, ex-prisoners, oyster sellers and fish hawkers.[9] The potency of this image of a criminal class shaped the normative world in which the detectives operated. In 1877 the *Police Regulations* suggested the attention of detectives should be 'principally directed to the detection of crime, and to a special surveillance of the criminal class'.[10]

Goldrush fears of a highly mobile population and an expanding criminal class justified the expansion of the Detective Branch in the 1860s. With the centralisation of policing in Victoria in 1853, a detective branch was formed covering the entire colony. The Detective Branch remained autonomous from the general body of police, having its own rank structure and recruiting civilians directly. By 1862, the Branch had expanded to 41 detectives distributed across the colony in detective districts, where one, two or three detectives were stationed.[11] The 1856 *Manual of Police Regulations* described detectives as 'a distinct body of the force, their duties being to detect rather than prevent crime'.[12] The separation of

---

[6]   *Report from the Select Committee on the Police*, 1852, p. 55.

[7]   *Report from the Select Committee on the Police Force*, 1863, *Votes and Proceedings of the Legislative Assembly of Victoria*, vol. 2, 1862–63, Appendix G, Minutes of Evidence, p. 104.

[8]   *Select Committee on the Police Force*, 1863, p. 106.

[9]   *Select Committee on the Police Force*, 1863, p. 125.

[10]   Police Department Colony of Victoria, *Regulations for the Guidance of the Constabulary of Victoria* (Melbourne: John Ferres Government Printer, 1877) p. 30.

[11]   *Select Committee on the Police Force*, 1863, p. 105.

[12]   Police Department Colony of Victoria, *Manual of Police Regulations for the Guidance of the Colony of Victoria* (Melbourne: John Ferres Government Printer, 1856) p. 39.

detectives from the general body of police was emphasised by their allegiance, no matter where stationed, to the Inspector of Detectives based in Melbourne. In theory detectives operated under a dual system of authority, being under the supervision of the superintendent of the district where they were stationed while ultimately answerable to the Inspector of Detectives. The autonomous character of the detective branch was underpinned by different policies of recruitment, rank and training. The 1856 *Manual* stipulated the detective force was to be formed 'by selecting from preventative police such as may be considered suitable for detective duty'. However, provision was also made for direct entry into the detective force for candidates 'who from previous habits, experience, or other reasons may be particularly adapted for detective duties'.[13] In the 1860s the Superintendent of Detectives claimed he would prefer to take on men from the uniformed police, except they were seldom 'as intelligent as the others'.[14] Recruits were therefore mainly civilians without prior policing experience.

While the general body of police became subject to ever more detailed and minute regulation, it remained difficult for police administrators to provide any clear definitions of what constituted detective work. Indeed, the 1856 *Manual* merely noted the administrative structure of the Detective Force, going on to remark that 'no further detail of detective work is here given, as the members of that branch of the service will from time to time receive such instructions as are necessary for their guidance from the officer in charge'.[15] For Charles Nicolson, the duties of the detective remained concentrated on the criminal class. Crime, Nicolson reasoned, was best reduced by close observation of the criminal class: 'studying and watching their movements, defeating their combinations and plans to escape discovery'.[16] Detectives received no training, but rather received a rudimentary instruction from a serving detective. After presenting themselves for a three-day trial, suitable applicants were then placed on a list. If later called upon they would then serve for one month on probation and if successful, the applicant would be sworn in as a third class detective.[17] Detectives, it seems, were born and not made.

Fiz-Gigs, bribes and the 'Nursery of Crime'

If the initiation of detectives in Victoria was relatively uncontroversial, the

---

[13] *Manual of Police Regulations*, 1856, p. 40.

[14] *Select Committee on the Police Force*, 1863, p. 105.

[15] *Manual of Police Regulations*, 1856, p. 40.

[16] *Royal Commission on Police, The Proceedings of the Commission, minutes of evidence, appendices, etc., Victorian Parliamentary Papers*, vol. 2, 1883, p. 193.

[17] *Select Committee on the Police Force*, 1863, p. 105.

detectives were nevertheless the subject of periodic scandals in the mid-nineteenth century. In the late 1840s Melbourne's small detective force enjoyed a positive reputation. In 1849 a group of Melbourne shopkeepers initiated a subscription to reward the Detective Police 'for their exertions in clearing the city of the bad characters who formerly infested the place'.[18] However, by the time gold was discovered in Victoria in the early 1850s the scent of corruption already clouded the image of the detective force. Before a Royal Commission into the organisation of policing in Victoria in 1852, William Kerr, Town Clerk of Melbourne, noted that several detective officers had displayed 'a most suspicious suddenness in getting rich', while William Sugden, the initiator of the detective force, remarked it was common knowledge that Melbourne detectives accepted bribes.[19] Scandal also surrounded disclosures in 1852 that detectives accepted bribes from the keepers of 'houses of ill-fame', who regularly paid money to officers in order to carry on their business unmolested.[20]

In this shadowy world there were those who sought to make detective work into an art form in which creativity and artifice would be deployed in the constant attempt to outwit the wiles of the criminal classes. Since the prime object was always to catch the crook, or at the very least, to bring their activities into a zone of semi-formal regulation, the not infrequent eruptions of scandal and allegation became part of the working life of the detective. In the detective career of the colourful John Christie, champion athlete, thief catcher, customs detective and latter day advertiser of his own exploits, we see a particular style of police entrepreneurship. Adept at avoiding judicial scrutiny of their activities, these practitioners of the art of detection played dangerously on the borderlines of legality. The self-confidence of these police in the fundamental integrity of their work is a feature of the popular journalism in which some of them dabbled – Christie being a prominent example. First writing up his exploits in the Melbourne press of the 1890s, Christie authorised in 1913 their collection and reworking as *The Reminiscences of Detective-Inspector Christie*.[21] Some examination of Christie's account of his career highlights these dimensions of nineteenth-century detective work.

---

[18]   *Argus*, 2 May 1849, p. 4.

[19]   *Select Committee on the Police*, 1852, p. 56.

[20]   *Argus*, 18 December 1852, p. 5.

[21]   J.B. Castieau, *The Reminiscences of Detective-Inspector Christie, related by J.B. Castieau* (Melbourne: Geo Robertson and Co., 1913). These memoirs together with Christie's newspaper articles archived at the La Trobe Library, Melbourne form the basis of a recent popular biography of 'Australia's Sherlock Holmes'. See John Lahey, *Damn You, John Christie! The Public Life of Australia's Sherlock Holmes* (Melbourne: State Library of Victoria, 1993). For photos of 'Australia's Sherlock Holmes', see http://www.museum.vic.gov.au/customshouse/stories/customs_detective.asp.

While some of the early detectives had come out of the ranks of convicts, Christie's background was typical of the recruitment of the officer class of colonial armed forces and police. His Scottish father, he tells us, was a major serving in Canada where he married the daughter of an Irish officer in the French Army, before later serving in India, where Christie's brother, another James, also served at the capture of Lucknow. Though Christie was intended for army service, colonial opportunity beckoned through an invitation from his mother's brother, a mining prospector, to travel to Victoria. There his fortunes were shaped by the random opportunities of colonial society. Physical strength, embodied in his boxing skills, combined with a good degree of native inventiveness to secure his recommendation for private detective inquiries in the service of a large employer. The nature of the task is not described but in order to obtain the information required we are told that Christie joined a railway survey party 'as an axeman', the disguise enabling him to obtain necessary information from another member of the party. His success in this endeavour gave him the reference necessary to his future employment in the Victorian Detective Police, as a man said to be 'good with head and hands'.[22]

Christie was a self-proclaimed master of disguise, a technique described at length in print and photograph in both his newspaper articles and reminiscences. After an initial period of fumbling in which he confesses to be more often taken in by spielers and crooks his career develops, so we are told, into that of a master detective viewed 'with awe' by offenders. Being 'good with head and hands' his methods were 'more and more cultivated, until in him detection assumed almost the dignity of an art'. At the same time his 'velvet glove always covered an iron hand'. Disguise takes the form not only of subterfuge in the course of obtaining information. As recounted in one story, Christie is joined by two prize fighters, including the famous Jem Mace (an English and colonial boxing champion), to help break up a 'larrikin push' disturbing the peace in the streets of Melbourne:

> The three pretended to be drunk, and were thus considered fair game for the gang of roughs, who commenced to jostle the seeming roisterers. But suddenly a startling sobriety took the place of staggering drunkenness. The trio, standing back to back in a triangle, dealt out blow after blow with lightning rapidity, felling their aggressors like ninepins... That push never foregathered again.[23]

---

[22] Castieau, *Reminiscences*, pp. 14–15.

[23] Castieau, *Reminiscences*, p. 22. This story must date from some time after 1877, when Jem Mace (the 'Father of Modern Boxing') moved to Australasia after his English career and was involved in regular exhibition bouts, especially with Christie: see entries on Mace in http://www.cyberboxingzone.com/boxing/mace-j.htm and http://www.geocities.com/kiwiboxing/mace.htm

In the cultivation of popular images of the detective police, such stories highlighted the twin values of a noble cause and the element of surprise seen to be at the heart of successful detection. Whether using hands or head the object was the same – to catch by surprise the criminal in the course of his act. The challenging problem of corroborating evidence in court would be best addressed through the accumulation of direct observations. Hence the highlights of Christie's book are those episodes where surveillance and entrapment are joined – above all in his exploits of the 1870s where repeatedly he takes on the organised burglary gangs of Melbourne and wins (see illustration 6.1).

Against conniving burglars who make fun of Constable Plod on his regular beat, taking advantage of the intervals between patrols to turn over a warehouse or a home, Christie employs the art of disguise – a swagman, a milko, an old labourer, a gardener, a tinker. Visiting a hotel in the disguise of a bushman he calls for a glass of rum, 'which by the way, he threw into the fire when the landlady's back was turned and, speaking with a strong Irish brogue, invited the lady to have a nip also' – and so it goes on with the lady becoming more 'agreeable' to disclose information after a second glass, doubtless with the artful Christie disposing of his in the well stoked fire.

More important than disguise however may have been Christie's cultivation of informers and collaborators in the service of crime detection. Here was the most dangerous path of all to tread. Detectives seeking information through such collaboration faced at least the challenge of being compromised in their work, or at worst might become ensnared in the very underworlds against which they were employed to act. The attractions of these modes of gathering evidence were obvious – even where challenged by the crooks in court the police could more often than not rely on the good opinion of the magistrate or judge or jury in any truth contest. At the same time the frequency in Australia of royal commissions of investigation into police corruption and inefficiency in the later nineteenth century suggests the failure of the courts to exercise an adequate authority in testing the veracity of police cases against those charged.[24] The presumption of innocence was usually exercised in favour of police against any convicted person who sought to query the integrity of a police case. Where we find such a challenge to police authority we also find insights into the mechanisms of police detection as the art of which Christie (or his amanuensis) spoke. This was an art in which the boundaries of the field of crime were negotiated between police and criminal, and by those congregated around the boundaries, such as the pawnbrokers who could be used by each side in its own cause.

---

[24] Mark Finnane, *Police and Government: Histories of Policing in Australia* (Melbourne: Oxford University Press, 1994) chapter 4.

Illustration 6.1 The detective in disguise: Christie watching a suspected dwelling.

In Christie's case one finds evidence of these negotiations less in his self-promoting memoirs than in the forgotten pages of the city's newspapers and the private diaries of the city's principal gaoler. In the summer of December 1871–72 Christie twice faced challenges from prisoners arrested and charged for burglary offences. In each case the prisoners alleged that Christie had been himself involved in the burglary business – and in each case their stories were plausible enough to warrant further investigation. Their credibility was given some weight by one who had good experience in hearing such stories, the governor of Melbourne Gaol, where prisoners were held while on remand or short sentence. An inveterate diary-keeper, John Buckley Castieau (the father of Christie's later amanuensis) had served in the Victorian prison service since his arrival in Victoria in 1852.[25] His diary entry for Saturday 16 December 1871 captured one of his more interesting days:

> Got up this morning at half past five & took Sissy & Dotty [two of his six children] to the market where we bought strawberries, Gooseberries & flowers. Got home at a little after seven o'clock. Was busy in the Gaol till after eleven o'clock, then I went into the Court & asked the Sheriff to attend an Enquiry at the Gaol with regard to a statement made by a prisoner concerning the conduct of Detective Christie. Went into town & called for Mr Sturt [the Sheriff]. Got him & brought him up in a cab with me. The Enquiry was gone into & the Detective was accused of what is called putting up robberies & conniving at others, in fact he was made out to be an infernal villain & a thorough faced scoundrel.

The allegations were serious enough to prompt further inquiry, in which Castieau himself turned detective for an hour.

> The prisoner 'Williams' who made the statement said Christie had given him some skeleton keys which he must have taken out of the Detective Office. Williams said these keys were now lying at the top of his house & could be identified by some of the detectives if they were got. After the Enquiry was over I took a cab & went with Turnkey [Buck?] to the place described & sure enough there was a bunch of skeleton keys. The statement of Williams is a most determined one & given with a fair show of frankness, still it is only a statement & it would be very unfair to judge Christie upon it without some substantial corroboration.

The following Monday the gaol governor was required again to corroborate a statement of Williams that Christie had given him a stolen watch to pawn. After consulting with the Sheriff and a senior police officer Inspector Nicolson (who had employed Christie in the first place), Castieau and Nicolson then visited a

---

[25] See Mark Finnane, ed, *'The difficulties of my position': the diaries of John Buckley Castieau 1855–1884* (Canberra: National Library of Australia, 2004).

pawnbroker's named by Williams and found the stolen watch which had been pledged. Two weeks later, this time with the prisoner and another police officer in tow, Castieau and Nicolson visited another pawnbroker's where they discovered a pair of stolen ear-rings allegedly given by Christie to the prisoner's wife. [26]

While such inquiries were sub-judicial and 'private', the nineteenth-century press coverage of internal gaol affairs was comprehensive. As gaol governor, Castieau was a regular source of information for the Melbourne press and these allegations were soon enough aired there. In January 1872 the newspapers reported the holding at the gaol of a 'private inquiry' by the Sheriff into allegations made not just by Williams but by another prisoner, George Holden, recently sentenced to two and a half years hard labour for receiving stolen jewellery. This time the inquiry involved the sheriff and a magistrate, along with the attendance of two senior police. Castieau was impressed with the prisoner's detailed allegations of the planting of evidence by the celebrated Christie.

> Some of the remarks made by a prisoner named Holden were very remarkable. He stated that Christie had given him stolen jewellery to take to a certain house so that Christie & his mates might search the house, find the 'Stuff' & convict the inmates of Feloniously Receiving. Holden stated he took the jewellery but instead of carrying out Christie's instructions stuck to it & made a bolt for Adelaide.

If there was anything to Holden's credit in this account then it was understandable why Christie might have done his best to put away somebody who had double-crossed him in this way. But Holden, a street-wise criminal of evidently numerous convictions and variously described as of 60 or 70 years of age, had more to tell. In Castieau's account:

> While Holden was making his statement he said, 'I had promised Christie a job that was coming off & I apologised to him for not having kept my word, stating that the men who were to crack the crib had gone up to Ballarat on another little job but that as soon as they came back it would be all right & the Melbourne affair would be sure to come off'.

Christie was thus accused not only of planting evidence but of conniving in robberies, and planning the dispersal of proceeds.

> Holden further said, 'Says Mr Christie to me, there's a job coming off, it might be this week, or next & perhaps not till the week after, if I get the stuff will you put it on "Barney Lane?" Holden then said, I will try & at another meeting told Christie,

---

[26] Diaries of J.B. Castieau, National Library of Australia, Mss. 2218, 16 December 1871, 18 December 1871, 28 December 1871.

"Barney will stand for the lot if it is good, but he wont have any silver mixed up with it"".

Was Christie so corrupt? Or was his alleged behaviour the product of an elaborate game in which the detective police attempted to stay one step ahead of the crooks by inserting themselves into the network of organised theft and its circulation back into the community through pawnshops and less open fencing operations? Whatever the case, George Holden's account of an underworld negotiation had enough credibility to impress the prison governor – and perhaps some of Christie's colleagues. Winding up his attempt to put Christie away,

> Holden described a visit from a detective to him in the Lock Up, says [Detective] Williams to me, this is a bad job George, says I well it is'ent a very good one. Can we do anything for you George, was the next remark of the Detective, in the way of getting you a light sentence you know. Says I, I have nothing to do with it, then says he 'Where the Hell did you get this from.' Says I, 'I got it from Christie.' Did you George, says he, 'then I wont ask you another word'.[27]

Without independent corroboration the possibility of a convicted criminal persuading an administrative inquiry that the detective putting him away was so intimately involved with the criminal underworld was remote – and there is little surprise in seeing a report that Christie was finally 'exonerated'.[28] It would take a different kind of challenge to unsettle the certainties that enabled this kind of policing to continue. That challenge was found in the activities of the Kelly Gang of bushrangers. Their exploits in the late 1870s divided the Victorian population and created an enormous disruption in the settled order of policing as crime management rather than crime eradication.[29]

In the aftermath of the Kelly 'Outbreak', with its bloody end at the siege of Glenrowan and the later execution of Ned, a Royal Commission was appointed to inquire into the organisation of the Victoria police, including the Detective Force. Its extended hearings of evidence were less inclined to apotheosise the detectives in the manner of Christie's later autobiography than to call to memory the less noble stories of George Holden.

---

[27] Diaries of J.B. Castieau, 8 January 1872. Holden was described as 'about 60' (18 December 1871), an 'old man' (27 December 1871), and 'about 70' (11 January 1872) by *The Argus*.

[28] *Argus*, 11 January 1872, p. 5.

[29] There is a vast Kelly literature, including the recent novel by Peter Carey, *True history of the Kelly gang* (St Lucia: University of Queensland Press, 2001), but see especially John McQuilton, *The Kelly Outbreak* (Carlton: Melbourne University Press, 1979); John Molony, *I am Ned Kelly* (Carlton: Melbourne University Press, 1980); Ian Jones, *Ned Kelly: a short life* (Melbourne: Lothian Books, 1995).

The report of the Royal Commission highlighted detective methods which had already been a matter of scandal. The most controversial method was the use of informers, known as 'fiz-gigs'. But the scope of criticism went further, to the heart of a system which had failed to respect the proper boundaries between policing and its object. The Detective Branch was roundly condemned by the commission which considered the branch 'a standing menace to the community' and little more than 'a nursery of crime'.[30] Indeed, the Royal Commission concluded that any limited success achieved by detectives could be attributed to:

> the employment of criminals to entrap their associates under circumstances repugnant to every principle of justice, and in order that individual detectives might achieve a spurious reputation for ability, obtain the reward given for the recovery of stolen property, and lull the public into a sense of false security.[31]

While Christie was long since gone, to duties in the customs service, these very phrases can be read in retrospect as a critique of the self-adulatory style of the gentleman detective: indeed, a repeated feature of Christie's stories is their boasting of the handsome rewards paid to successful detectives.[32] The proceedings of the Royal Commission suggested detectives were heavily reliant on a system of paid informers, and without the aids of these 'questionable auxiliaries' were comparatively helpless at solving even the most simple cases. By themselves they were seen as 'almost powerless to trace offenders':

> They are mainly dependent upon informers, 'fiz-gigs', and pawnbrokers; and in order to fully benefit by the co-operation of the first mentioned it is necessary to employ the second, a proceeding that comprehends something closely approximating to the subornation of crime.[33]

Under an extended analysis of the practice of 'employing criminals', the Royal Commission described a system that appears to explain in every detail the elements of George Holden's story about Detective Christie. George would seem to fit the very type of a 'fiz-gig', 'paid to start the prey which the expectant detective captures without a trouble or inconvenience'. Being paid meant not only getting a share of a reward but a right to negotiate future charges: hence George's account of the failed negotiation with Detective Williams. George Holden was, it may appear, a casualty in a failed operation. Things had not worked out as they should in this

---

[30] *Royal Commission on Police, Special Report on the Detective Branch, Victorian Parliamentary Papers*, vol. 2, 1883, pp. i–ii.

[31] *Special Report on the Detective Branch*, 1883, p. ii.

[32] Castieau, *Reminiscences*, pp. 53, 61, 69.

[33] *Special Report on the Detective Branch*, 1883, p. vii.

system where, as the Royal Commission summarised the arrangements ten years later, such a person 'is supposed to receive not only a subsidy from the detectives who employ him, but a share in the reward, and a certain immunity from arrest for offences with which he may be chargeable'.[34]

In this way the failings evident in Victorian policing under pressure from a bushranging outbreak far from Melbourne became the occasion for a sustained reflection on policing and detective work as systems to address serious crime. The Royal Commission was perturbed by the 'temptation to push the system to an extreme, and to use criminal agents as decoys'.[35] While the Royal Commission accepted that at times it was inevitable that criminals should assist the authorities, such practices in a badly run organisation could too readily evolve into a system that was 'manifestly un-English and opposed to every principle of honour and fair play'. Not that the English had always done it so well: in fact the Commission heard evidence from Inspector Dowdell of the Scotland Yard Detective Force on the dangers of using criminals in detection, and the Commission report went on to cite Howard Vincent's code and the Irish Constabulary instructions to sustain the case for a highly regulated management of relations between criminals and police. The 'fiz-gig' system in which unscrupulous detectives acted in concert with 'confirmed criminals' was one thought to result in 'infinite mischief' for the community.[36]

The sustained criticism by this Commission resulted in the early adoption of its main remedy – abolition of the detective force and creation of a criminal investigation branch within the general police. The CIB was to be a plain-clothes force, but entry was through the ranks of the constabulary.[37] However, this reorganisation offered only a partial solution to controlling detective work, and rumours of questionable methods and corruption persisted. By 1906, a further Royal Commission into policing noted some of the shortcomings of the CIB. While the Commissioners considered the CIB was not the 'corruption and dead men's bones' one Member of Parliament claimed it to be, it nevertheless lacked discipline and there were sufficient 'irregularities' to warrant concern.[38] The individualism of the Christie style would not disappear from detective work, nor would the temptations to corruption, noble cause or otherwise.

---

[34] *Special Report on the Detective Branch*, 1883, p. ix.
[35] *Special Report on the Detective Branch*, 1883, p. ix.
[36] *Special Report on the Detective Branch*, 1883, p. x.
[37] Haldane, *People's Force*, p. 98.
[38] *Royal Commission on the Victorian Police Force*, 1906, *Victorian Parliamentary Papers*, vol. 3, 1906, p. xv.

Science and the detectives

While Christie's individualistic style of criminal investigation persisted as a reference point for detective work, in the early decades of the twentieth century new conceptions of effective criminal investigation began to emerge. In this period methodologies of detection were subjected to more systematic regulation and in time embraced a variety of new technologies including fingerprinting and ballistics. These technologies were instrumental in shaping a new symbolism of detective work diametrically opposed to the individualistic and extra-legal image embodied by nineteenth-century detectives such as Christie. The technology of fingerprinting, in particular, was intimately aligned with emergent notions of criminal investigation as procedural, regulated and guided by the tools of science rather than chance, wile and human agents.

By the first years of the twentieth century, fingerprinting had become the official means of identification in Argentina, the United States, England and Australia.[39] A meeting of the State commissioners of police held in Melbourne in 1903 agreed on the establishment of a uniform system of fingerprint identification, and on the importance of the exchange of fingerprint data.[40] Victorian police were followers rather than leaders in their adaptation of fingerprinting, but it was significant that the police force was seen to embrace new methods – new methods seen to place them on a par with major metropolitan police forces in Britain and the United States.

Fingerprinting was warmly embraced by the Melbourne media which deployed arguments already familiar in England to hail the new technology as a modern and scientific advance in criminal detection. Fingerprinting was promoted as offering a potentially omnipotent police archive, facilitating the rapid detection of offenders. Police administrators and journalists became positively giddy with the potential of fingerprint technology. In 1912 a feature article in the *Argus* newspaper informed readers:

> The system is in fact a very much more delicate and accurate application of the clumsy Bertillon plan, which relied upon certain physical measurements in relation to others ... . The fingerprint expert relies upon certain coincident formations in relation to the central ridges. These formations never alter. The ridges formed upon the fingers before birth persist until the individual dies.[41]

---

[39]   Anne Joseph and Alison Winter, 'Making the Match: Human Traces, Forensic Experts and the Public Imagination', in Francis Spufford and Jenny Uglow, eds, *Cultural Babbage: Technology, Time and Invention* (London: Faber & Faber, 1996) p. 196.

[40]   Finnane, *Police and Government*, p. 80.

[41]   *Argus*, 14 March 1912, p. 6

Considering the potential applications of fingerprint technology for the future the writer became even more excited:

> It is not difficult, indeed to foresee the day when some state or nation, desiring a ready means of identification of any citizen at a moment's notice, may take a census of finger-tip impressions. In such an event no citizen could die unknown, the kidnapping and substitution of millionaire's babies would become a lost industry, and crime would become a very dangerous profession indeed, even for the beginner. Not the least extraordinary thing about such a fancy is its absolute ease of realisation.[42]

Fingerprinting imbued policing with the infallibility and precision of science, reinventing the detective as an expert in the field of criminal investigation. One commentator remarked of fingerprinting that 'to talk of it as a "fad" is as absurd as a similar definition of wireless telegraphy or aeroplanes ... it is a serious and scientific department of criminal investigation'. Examples of criminals brought to justice by way of their fingerprints proliferated in the press, usefully projecting an image of detective work as an exact and scientific enterprise. The following hypothetical – that of housebreaker William Sykes – was one of many such stories published in Melbourne's daily press to illustrate the utility of the new technology and the skill of its practitioners.

> William Sykes breaks into a house at Malvern. His prints have been taken when he was in gaol in New South Wales for assault and robbery. He is not progressive, and does not wear gloves. Upon the lid of a steel cash box which he prises open he leaves a varied assortment of faint finger prints. Some of these are smudged as he moved his fingers when they were made. But some are not. Detective Potter comes to the house, and brushes a fine powder over the prints. He picks out those he wants, photographs them, and enlarges them at the detective office. He looks through his records, and does not find the print. But the copy sent to New South Wales receives its answer. Inspector Childs has such a print and sends the duplicate down. Then comes minute examination. The inner line of the 'loop' nucleus is broken in a certain place. Just level with this the next line out 'forks'. The third line, at a point opposite these aberrations, breaks, continues as a dot, breaks again, and then runs on unbroken. The fourth line is perfect, and the fifth forks at a certain point. These minutiae are faithfully reproduced on one of the prints upon the cash box. Detective Potter goes further, until he has about 20 points of resemblance and Sykes is traced and arrested.[43]

Intertwined with this celebration of fingerprinting was a new conception of detective work as a highly professionalised occupation involving the mastery of

---

[42] *Argus*, 14 March 1912, p. 6.
[43] *Argus*, 16 January 1913, p. 12.

complex technology. Criminal investigation was reconceptualised as an expert system routinely applied, rather than the random outcome of individual cunning. Detective Potter, hunched over enlarged images of whorls, arches, and loops in the police darkroom is reminiscent of a pathologist gazing into the microscope to trace the origins of some as yet unknown disease. The symbolic power of such an image resided in its implicit suggestion that law enforcement might claim an ultimate victory over crime through the careful application of innovative modern techniques. As the *Argus* phrased it 'the identification of any print would be as easy to the expert as the finding of a word in a well-ordered dictionary'.[44]

The symbolism of fingerprints reinforced emergent notions of detective work as the systematic application of scientific method. At the same time, the image of detective work as the application of routinised scientific knowledge co-existed with entrenched suspicion of detectives, and scepticism prompted by those celebrated cases that seemed to indicate limitations rather than advances in criminal detection. In 1912, when fingerprints were projecting an image of modernisation, there was public disgruntlement that 'in many instances arrests have not been effected', while the detective force was subjected to 'a good deal of adverse criticism'. In newspaper columns there was discussion of the small number of detectives for the size of the state (in 1912 a superintendent, an inspector, three clerks and twenty size clerks). It was claimed that detectives were hampered in serious investigation by being burdened with 'trivial' matters such as wife and child desertion, unlawful assault and window breaking.[45] One ex-detective claimed publicly that despite protestations by senior administrators that the Criminal Investigation Branch was 'a happy family' he had known nothing but 'seething discontent and bitterness'. 'Ex-detective' suggested that poor remuneration and long hours of work led detectives to grow 'quite hard and indifferent in their performance of their duties; while the public suffer and wonder why'.[46]

Tentative reorganisation of the Criminal Investigation Branch in 1919 attempted to reconcile the image of scientific and modernised criminal investigation with the less than satisfactory reality of routine detective work. Chief Commissioner George Steward introduced a system of case management and training. Included in Steward's reforms was the establishment of a separate Fingerprint Branch, which would compile and archive records, train officers in the use of fingerprint technology and deal with the exchange of records both with other Australian States and internationally.[47] However, Steward's modernisation of

---

[44] *Argus*, 14 March 1912, p. 6.
[45] *Argus*, 1 May 1912, p. 13.
[46] *Argus*, 8 June 1912, p. 22.
[47] Victoria Public Record Series 807/698 File No: A6842 'Reorganization of CIB', 9 July 1919.

detective work largely lapsed following his death in 1920. The limitations of Victorian detectives and their methods of criminal investigation appeared to be thrown into sharp relief in 1922 during the investigation of the Gun Alley Murder case.

In 1922 the strangled body of a twelve-year-old girl named Alma Tirtschke was discovered in Gun Alley, a laneway in central Melbourne. The case aroused unprecedented interest and occupied the public imagination for four months as newspapers covered every detail of the case.[48] Amidst the frenzied media coverage however, the work of detectives itself became the locus of considerable criticism for their failure to quickly apprehend the murderer.

Contemporary studies of detective work reveal that most homicide investigations are cleared up as a result of the offender confessing soon after the commission of the offence.[49] Nevertheless, public expectations, no doubt heightened by the imagery of scientific infallibility accompanying the introduction of fingerprinting, were that detectives would seamlessly trace clues leading to the capture of the offender. In this context the reliance on information brought forward by members of the public was itself taken as an indication of ineffectual criminal investigation. The Detective Office remonstrated in the daily press for members of the public to desist from sending letters that were 'unfairly critical' and in some case abusive.[50] One angry letter to the editor encapsulated the tenor of public criticism:

> [W]e are given to understand that the detectives have been working night and day, with scarcely time to eat. They are experts, specialists in the detection of crime. We have seen photographs of some of them published in some of the papers. May I ask to what end? If I employ a specialist to build a house, or watch, or engine, or a theory, it is naturally expected that they would be able to do it, or go out of business.[51]

Despite an offender eventually being tried for the Gun Alley Murder, convicted and sentenced to death, the investigation had revealed the haphazard nature of

---

[48] Victoria Police Historical Unit File, 'Gun Alley Murder'; see also Deborah Tyler, 'The Case of Irene Tuckerman: understanding sexual violence and the protection of women and girls, Victoria 1890–1925', *History of Education Review*, 2 (1986), pp. 52–67. Since the writing of this chapter a new book on the Gun Alley Murder has provided a convincing evidence against the police case which convicted Colin Edward Ross for this murder, leading to his later execution, see Kevin Morgan, *Gun Alley: Murder, Falsehood and Failure of Justice* (Sydney: Simon and Schuster, 2005).

[49] Mark Findlay, *Introducing Policing: Challenges for Police and Australian Communities* (Melbourne: Oxford University Press, 2004) p. 51.

[50] *Argus*, 10 June 1922, p. 7.

[51] *Argus*, 10 June 1922, p. 7.

homicide investigations and their reliance on public information and a good deal of luck. Detective work, it appeared, was little more than hoping someone would come forward to provide a lucky break.

The ineffectiveness of methods of criminal investigation was not the only smear on the reputation of the Criminal Investigation Branch in the early twentieth century. Several scandals in the 1930s suggested endemic corruption within the Criminal Investigation Branch and raised longstanding concerns over the relationship between detectives and criminals. In 1933 serious allegations surfaced that detectives were working in collusion with motorcar thieves to obtain rewards for recovered vehicles from insurance companies and motor vehicle owners. Equally damaging allegations appeared implicating detectives in the trafficking of cocaine.[52] A subsequent Board of Inquiry failed to prove many of the allegations but nevertheless noted significant irregularities in the payment of rewards to detectives.[53] Scandal again descended on the Criminal Investigation Branch in 1936 when the head of the Branch, Superintendent Brophy, was shot in the arm in a chauffeur driven car with two female companions. The two women had accompanied Brophy on a journey to meet an informer. What was regarded as more scandalous however were subsequent efforts by the Chief Commissioner Thomas Blamey to conceal the incident from the public. A subsequent Royal Commission roundly condemned the Superintendent of Detectives for taking the two women to meet an informer, in addition to condemning the Chief Commissioner of Police for attempting to cover up the incident.[54]

Coterminous with these notable public scandals was the denunciation of police investigative techniques. Of particular concern was detective use of the 'third degree'.[55] In 1936 the Chief Justice of the Victorian Supreme Court, Sir Frederick Mann, denounced police criminal investigation methods as crude, untrained and overly reliant upon informers and physical coercion.[56] As one newspaper editorial noted, detectives were under pressure to solve crimes and apprehend offenders. Nevertheless, lacking adequate training and the assistance of modern scientific techniques, they were easily tempted to 'procure convictions by the rough-and-ready method of extorting confessions rather than ascertain the truth through painstaking investigation'.[57]

---

[52] *Victoria Parliamentary Debates*, vol. 191, 1933, pp. 1232–51.

[53] Report of the Board of Inquiry appointed to Inquire into Certain Allegations and Complaints made against Certain Members of the Police Force, including the Chief Commissioner of Police, *Victorian Parliamentary Papers*, vol. 1, 1933.

[54] Haldane, *People's Force*, pp. 211–14.

[55] For definition of the 'third degree', see Jerome H. Skolnick and James J. Fyfe, *Above the Law: Police and the Excessive Use of Force* (New York: Free Press, 1993) pp. 43–44.

[56] *Argus*, 19 June 1936, p. 11.

[57] *Argus*, 22 June 1936, p. 8; Haldane, *People's Force*, p. 216.

The denunciation of investigative techniques accompanied a broader discussion about the relationship between science and criminal investigation. In 1930 there were already concerns that Victorian detectives received no special training in criminal investigation. Senior officers suggested scientific experts should be taken directly into the Criminal Investigation Branch without prior policing experience. Such suggestions were rejected by detectives, who advanced earlier notions of detective work as the monitoring of a criminal class. Street knowledge, one detective claimed, was the backbone of the detective's craft. The detective remarked that when crimes were solved quickly:

> it may seem ... that some very clever detective work has been done, but I am afraid it is nothing so romantic. The arrests are made simply because the police force is always 'on the job' and because detectives, by their experience, know by what members of the underworld certain crimes are likely to have been committed.[58]

Little appeared to have changed since Christie's day. The scandals surrounding detectives in the mid-1930s compounded the impression that Victoria lagged behind international developments in criminal investigation. In 1936, following the judicial criticisms of the Criminal Investigation Branch, the Victorian Government engaged Chief Inspector Alexander Duncan, head of Scotland Yard's flying squad, to conduct an investigation of the Victorian Police Force. Duncan had considerable experience in criminal investigation and recommended extensive reforms of the Criminal Investigation Branch, including the introduction of a training course for detectives and the adaptation of scientific detection methods (see illustration 6.2).[59]

The subsequent opening in October 1938 of a training school for detectives was accompanied by significant publicity suggesting rapid modernisation and the advance of scientific technique. The school was directed by Fred Hobley who was noted for his university training and knowledge of ballistics and other 'methods of scientific detection of crime'. Lecturers at the school included Duncan himself, newly appointed as Victoria's Chief Commissioner of Police, in addition to the Government Pathologist and the Government Analyst. The emphasis of courses was also firmly upon scientific method, with instruction given in chemistry, physics, ballistics and photography.[60]

In the same year a Detective Training School was established, the highly publicised murder of shoe manufacturer and pillar of the community, William Sherry, appeared to provide incontrovertible evidence of the power of science to combat crime. In September 1938 Sherry was shot and killed by two payroll

---

[58]   *Argus*, 8 January 1930, p. 8.
[59]   Haldane, *People's Force*, p. 217.
[60]   *Argus*, 10 October 1938, p. 10.

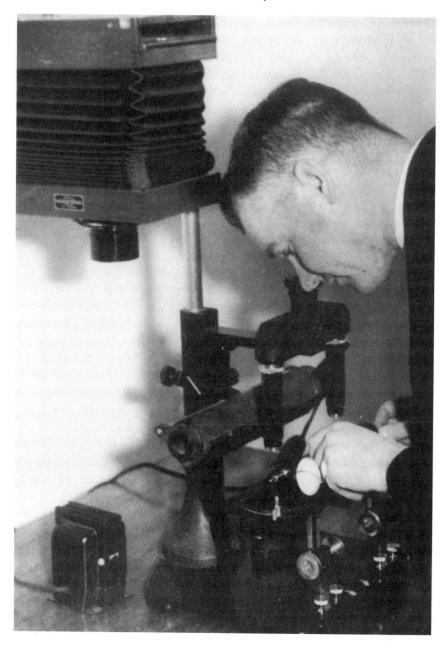

Illustration 6.2 **The science of detection: Fred Hobley, Director of the Victorian Detectives Training School (1938).**

bandits in Clifton Hill, a northern suburb of Melbourne. Sherry's murder shocked the Melbourne public, and seemed to suggest that the sleepy southern city was not immune from the sort of criminal violence usually associated with Chicago or Sydney.[61] Occurring just as the newly appointed Chief Commissioner Duncan was reorganising the Detective Branch, the Sherry case provided an opportunity to prove the efficiency of Victorian detectives. In the initial investigation the traditional methods of shoe leather and criminal contacts prevailed, as detectives staked out pubs, brothels and private residences thought to harbour potential suspects and sources of information. Old-fashioned detective work appeared to yield results, and a 22-year-old man, Selwyn Wallace, was subsequently arrested and charged with murdering William Sherry. Wallace finally revealed the identity of his accomplice, Edward Jenner, who was later apprehended after having fled to Sydney.[62]

Despite both suspects having signed confessions detectives remained uncertain that there was sufficient evidence to secure a conviction. The testimonies of Wallace and Jenner contradicted one another, with both denying that they had carried a gun. The newscientific instruments of the CIB were subsequently engaged. Sherry's sedan was examined and fragments of the bullet that shattered its windscreen were found. Microscopic examination showed the fragments to have come from a .22 calibre weapon and not the .32 calibre pistol that had killed Sherry.[63] During the five-day trial the scientific evidence proved crucial. Both Wallace and Jenner had signed confessions placing them at the scene of the crime. However, it was microscopy that had proven both had been carrying weapons, contrary to the information they had given detectives. The jury found Jenner guilty of murder and Wallace guilty of being an accessory to murder.[64]

The Sherry case demonstrated that the practice of criminal investigation remained an amalgam of old and new methods. It was still the old-fashioned skills of criminal contacts and 'street knowledge' that had ferreted out Sherry's killers. Nevertheless, the case also demonstrated the power of science and technical knowledge in crime-fighting, and especially in gathering evidence towards a conviction, a notion that continued to receive enthusiastic support from the Chief Commissioner of Police. By 1939, Chief Commissioner Duncan proclaimed that the Victorian detectives possessed scientific equipment 'better than any other in the

---

[61] Alex Castles, 'Detective Work', in Bill Gammage and Peter Spearritt, eds, *Australians 1938* (Sydney: Fairfax, Syme & Weldon, 1987) p. 319.

[62] Castles, 'Detective Work', pp. 323–24.

[63] Castles, 'Detective Work', p. 324.

[64] Castles, 'Detective Work', p. 325.

world'. Duncan told members of the Insurance Institute about the virtues of scientific policing, adding that 'the development of science as an aid to crime detection had led to remarkable results, and many crimes were solved because it was now possible to link up the most minute particles left behind and identify them with the criminal'.[65]

Conclusion

However, limited in its impact on detective practice, the imagery of science was intimately bound to the representation of detective work as procedural, bureaucratically constrained, consistent and efficient. Detectives applying scientific method contrasted sharply with the imagery of the nineteenth-century detective, who operated beyond organisational strictures and followed an individuated path. Indeed, Duncan's vision of the scientific detective incorporated the notion of the detective as an accountable functionary rather than a potentially rogue individual. Detective training was to include the correct means of interviewing witnesses and suspects and 'proper methods of contact between detectives and public'.[66] The symbolism of science then was one response to some very old dilemmas inherent in the covert nature of detective work. How were detectives to be made accountable and how could they be monitored and constrained? Scientific method suggested extricating the detective from the shadowy world of informers, 'fiz-gigs', bribery and forced confessions. The imagery of the scientific detective suggested an ethically neutral investigative practice, where disembodied clues and carefully maintained records marked out a rational path to the capture of the offender. The reality of criminal investigation remained different. The work of detectives continued to evade the bureaucratic gaze and skirt the margins of legality into the later twentieth century and beyond, as successive Royal Commissions in the post period were to discover and chief commissioners required repeatedly to confront.[67]

---

[65]   *Argus*, 24 August 1939, p. 2.

[66]   *Argus*, 22 December 1936, p. 9.

[67]   See Haldane, *People's Force*, pp. 271–74 and 290–91, on the succession of inquiries and political eruptions in the 1970s over police corruption associated with the criminalisation and prosecution of abortion. At the time of writing (mid-2004) the Victorian police, and especially the detective branch, is deeply embroiled in corruption allegations associated with policing of the drug trade and related gangland wars in which 24 alleged criminals as well as a police informer and his partner, supposedly under witness protection, have been killed in the last five years: *The Weekend Australian*, 29–30 May 2004, p. 21.

Chapter Seven

Local 'Demons' in New Zealand Policing c. 1900–55

Graeme Dunstall

Looking to an idealised model of the London Metropolitan Police, critics of New Zealand detectives in the early 1930s urged that there be an interchange of British and New Zealand officers, or that two detectives be sent to London each year to get a 'thorough grip of English methods of crime detection'.[1] In 1935 two experienced detectives, William McLennan and Henry Murch,[2] were sent to observe the methods and practices taught at the London Metropolitan Police College and employed at New Scotland Yard as well as at various stations and divisional headquarters. While methods of investigating crime in London did not vary greatly from those employed in New Zealand, there were clearly significant differences in the size, organisation and context of policing. The detectives noted particular practices which they recommended be adopted in New Zealand, but they were definite in their view that training New Zealand police in England was 'not of any particular advantage' – it could be provided 'equally as effectively in New Zealand, by experts and practical officers familiar' with its 'peculiar' conditions.[3]

What were the 'peculiar' conditions? From its origins in 1840, state policing was a visible part of the colony's cultural inheritance from Britain. Indeed, important changes in the organisation and ethos of policing in the two decades from 1898 could be seen as part of a broader process of New Zealand's 'recolonisation' – a tightening of links with Britain, especially between the 1880s and the First World War.[4]

---

[1]   *Dominion*, 12 April 1934.

[2]   William McLennan had joined the New Zealand Police Force in August 1920 and been appointed Detective in February 1924; Henry Murch had joined the Force in 1923 and was appointed detective in May 1926.

[3]   New Zealand National Archives, Wellington (hereafter NZNA) P 36/1, Report of [Detectives] William McLennan and Henry Murch Relative to Period of Training at Hendon Police College and New Scotland Yard, London, 26 April 1936, pp. 4 and 40.

[4]   James Belich, *Paradise Reforged. A History of the New Zealanders* (Auckland: Allen

Nonetheless, geography, demography, one centrally-controlled police force (since 1877), the development of a local criminal code and pattern of social regulation (especially between 1893 and 1920), and an Australasian ethos of egalitarianism together with growing administrative inertia and insularity of outlook during the 1920s and early 1930s shaped an antipodean variant of the English model of policing. Interpreted broadly the issue of 'peculiar' conditions shapes a discussion of the organisation, work and status of New Zealand detectives in the first half of the twentieth century.[5]

Influences from London

In the decade from 1898 the New Zealand Police Force was more consciously modelled than hitherto on the London Metropolitan Police. In the face of mounting pressures to reform its police force, the New Zealand government looked overseas in 1897 for a commissioner. In the 1860s the Victoria Police had provided the model and personnel for revamping some of the colony's provincial police forces; by the 1890s, the 'more benign style' of London's police was perceived to be more appropriate for the transition from frontier turbulence to settled communities.[6] John Tunbridge, a retired chief inspector from 'The Met's' Criminal Investigation Department became the first professional policeman to head the national police force.[7] He was succeeded in 1903 by Walter Dinnie, another retired detective and chief inspector from London.[8] Together the two imported commissioners laid the basis for a pattern of policing that was to endure until at least the mid-1950s.

In his first annual report, Tunbridge reasserted in the colony the basic precept of London's police that the 'primary duty' was to 'prevent crime'.[9] In fact, from the outset, the basic mode of the colony's policing had been surveillance by uniformed patrolmen. The new commissioner looked to increase the efficiency of the preventive

---

Lane, 2001) pp. 29–30 and 53–86.

[5]   This chapter draws on research presented in Graeme Dunstall, *A Policeman's Paradise? Policing a Stable Society, 1918–1945* (Palmerston North: Dunmore Press, 1999), especially from local newspapers and letters to the author from and/or interviews with 93 men who joined the New Zealand Police before 1945.

[6]   Richard S. Hill, *The Iron Hand in the Velvet Glove: The Modernisation of Policing in New Zealand, 1886–1917* (Palmerston North: Dunmore Press, 1995) p. 47.

[7]   Richard S. Hill, 'Tunbridge, John Bennett', *D[ictionary of] N[ew] Z[ealand] B[iography]*.

[8]   Richard S. Hill, 'Dinnie, Walter', *DNZB*.

[9]   *Appendix to the Journals of the [New Zealand] House of Representatives*, Annual Report [of the New Zealand Police Force], 1898, p. 2.

police by an increase of numbers and pay, establishing a training depot for recruits, improving supervision and discipline, and introducing a pension scheme (together with compulsory retirement). From 1886 the police force had been divided into preventive and detective branches. Symptomatic of the ethos of preventive policing however, detectives (fluctuating in number between 14 and 20) averaged about 4 per cent of the newly centralised force during the early 1880s.[10] Indeed, the uniformed branch's confidence in the effectiveness of detectives declined during the late 1880s to the point where Commissioner Walter Gudgeon considered abolishing their separate organisation.[11] On the eve of Tunbridge becoming commissioner in 1897, the number of detectives had fallen to 12, some 2.3 per cent of the police force.

The former London detective looked to reinvigorate the local detective branch by increasing their numbers (to 20 by 1900) and seeking to improve the quality of their work. He selected men who had shown their abilities in surveillance of 'doubtful characters' and making good 'catches' while on plain-clothes duty in the uniformed branch; he had detectives account more fully for their movements, and improved their supervision by chief detectives. While he believed his detectives' work to be improving, especially in surveillance, Tunbridge continued to be embarrassed (as his predecessors had been) by botched investigations which suggested that local standards of detection were lower than those of Scotland Yard. However, Tunbridge was initially sceptical of the value of fingerprinting (recently adopted by 'The Met') as a means of improving detection by identifying and registering criminals.[12]

The initiative for introducing Edward Henry's classification system into New Zealand came from Colonel Arthur Hume, head of the prison system (and Tunbridge's predecessor as commissioner), who was concerned about 'habitual criminals' and saw fingerprinting as means of identifying them, including those who crossed the Tasman. Accordingly, a Finger Print Bureau was established in 1903 modelled on that introduced a year earlier in New South Wales for gaol inmates. Lascelles Ward, appointed as a prison official to establish the system, was keen for comprehensive coverage and looked for those arrested by police to be included. Now appreciating the scheme's potential to improve detection, Tunbridge cooperated while having concerns at a lack of legal authority to force people in custody to have their fingerprints taken. Police at all stations were notified of methods of taking prints and instruction given to recruits at the Training Depot. Thus a scheme of gathering and classifying fingerprints was in place when Walter Dinnie arrived from London to take over from Tunbridge.[13]

---

[10]   Calculated from the Annual Reports.

[11]   Hill, *The Iron Hand in the Velvet Glove*, pp. 49–53.

[12]   Hill, *The Iron hand in the Velvet Glove*, pp.119–25, and 167.

[13]   Hill, *The Iron Hand in the Velvet Glove*, pp.166–69; John Pratt, *Punishment in a Perfect*

The new commissioner was an enthusiast for the new technology which he saw as a part of a wider system of criminal registration, including photographs, as had developed at New Scotland Yard. Dinnie soon had the Prisons' Finger Print Branch transferred to police control as the Fingerprint Bureau at the Wellington headquarters and put (from the 1906 until 1947) under the direction of his son who had been trained in fingerprinting in London. By 1911, the chief detective overseeing the Criminal Registration Branch could claim, rather extravagantly, that fingerprints had 'revolutionised' the work of detectives in the 'past few years'.[14] The mystique of a 'scientific' system of detection was established locally by a small but growing number of convictions from 1905 on the basis of fingerprint evidence and reinforced by a publicity campaign instigated by the commissioner.[15] It served to enhance the 'profile and status of detective work'.[16] So too did Dinnie's appointment of a growing number (and proportion) of detectives,[17] including the colourful chief detectives Charles Broberg and W.B. McIlveney.[18] Their heightened activity – in surveillance of 'undesirables' entering the country and at public events, prosecuting thieves and spielers, tracking down fugitives, and raiding gambling dens[19] – caught the eye of the press, and especially the Wellington-based populist weekly, *New Zealand Truth* which gave the ambiguous slang 'Ds', 'dees', 'D-man' and 'demon' (recorded earlier in the colony than elsewhere) wider currency during the decade before the First World War.[20]

Issues of status

While Tunbridge and Dinnie had heightened the role of detectives within the Force, they had not resolved long-standing issues of their status and relationship with the preventive branch. Jealousies and resentments remained – amongst uniformed men

---

Society: The New Zealand Penal System 1840–1939 (Wellington: Victoria University Press, 1992) pp. 159–62.

[14]   *Evening Post*, 2 November 1911.

[15]   Annual Reports, 1904–9.

[16]   Hill, *The Iron Fist in the Velvet Glove*, pp. 169–71, 201 and 370–72.

[17]   The 35 detectives in 1909 comprised 4.5 per cent of the Force, double the proportion of 1897. Not included are 'acting detectives', probationers appointed from 1906 who continued to be listed as constables in the Annual Reports. If acting detectives are included, the number of detectives in 1909 would be 52 or 6.7 per cent of the Force.

[18]   Sherwood Young, 'Broberg, Charles Robert', *DNZB*; Graeme Dunstall, 'McIlveney, William Bernard', *DNZB*.

[19]   Hill, *The Iron Fist in the Velvet Glove*, pp. 186 and 200.

[20]   H.W. Orsman, ed, *The Dictionary of New Zealand English* (Auckland: Oxford University Press, 1997) pp. 202 and 204.

concerning the elite status, higher pay and perquisites claimed by detectives; and amongst detectives at the lack of a career structure with equivalent ranks and opportunities for promotion within their (much smaller) branch by comparison with those of their uniformed colleagues. A consensus was not reached until 1919 when the findings of an internal committee of inquiry (composed of senior representatives of both branches chaired by a magistrate) were adopted by Commissioner John O'Donovan. The committee recognised that 'a detective on appointment acquired a status somewhat higher than a constable' and was senior to all constables associated with him on an inquiry. Nonetheless, it found a detective equal in rank to a constable and recommended a common rank structure and seniority list for promotion purposes, the interchange of men between the two branches and 'equal pay for equal ranks' – with the unusual work and expenses of detectives being recognised by special allowances. By comparison with constables at city stations, detectives' duties could be construed as 'special, their hours more irregular, and their responsibility varies according to the work they have in hand'. Yet the 'relative value' of work done by detectives or uniformed men could not be fixed. Both branches were 'equally necessary in order to secure an efficient police service'.[21] The committee's sagacity (reflecting an antipodean egalitarian ethos) prevented jealousies and elitism developing to the extent that has been observed of the 'Met's' CID.[22]

The policy of equality between uniformed men and detectives in terms of status, pay and career opportunities established in 1919 was broadly reflected in the patterns of promotion to the ranks of officers and commissioners during the next thirty years. Walter Dinnie was the last policeman from outside the Force to be recruited as commissioner.[23] From 1912 all commissioners (with one exception) rose through the ranks of the New Zealand police – in contrast to the 'Met' during the inter-war years, and to Victoria where three successive chief commissioners in the 40 years from 1925 were 'outsiders': two military men and a former head of Scotland Yard's 'Flying Squad'.[24] A quarter of those promoted from NCO to commissioned officer between 1918 and 1939 were detectives who, excluding acting-detectives, comprised 4.2 per cent of the Force in 1918, and 6.3 per cent by 1939. In fact, after the common

---

[21] Report of Committee of Inquiry, *New Zealand Police Gazette*, 1919, pp. 418 and 422–26.

[22] Dick Hobbs, *Doing the Business: Entrepreneurship, the Working Class and Detectives in the East End of London* (Oxford University Press, 1989) pp. 41–45.

[23] Dinnie resigned in December 1909 after a commission of inquiry depicted him as incompetent. The under-secretary for justice, Frank Waldegrave, assumed Dinnie's responsibilities until the appointment of the most senior inspector, John Cullen as commissioner in April 1912.

[24] Robert Haldane, *The People's Force. A History of the Victoria Police* (University of Melbourne Press, 1986) p. 183.

seniority list was established in 1919, being a detective brought no discernible advantage in rising to higher ranks, with the exception of the controversial acceleration in seniority received by one detective sergeant in 1921.[25] The disproportionate representation of former detectives amongst officers by the 1930s reflected their greater willingness or ability to sit the qualifying examinations for promotion (introduced in 1913) and their length of service. Of the eight commissioners appointed between 1912 and 1949 (essentially on the basis of seniority with sufficient length of service remaining of between four and seven years) three were former detectives. Length of service meant that in the experience and outlook of officers, whatever their background, traditions of nineteenth-century New Zealand policing persisted well into the twentieth. During the inter-war years the New Zealand Police Force came to be led by officers who knew at first hand only its local practices and traditions, and who saw little need to change them. The organisation and conditions of police work established by 1920 would remain largely unchanged for nearly 40 years.

Local influences on policing

During the inter-war years, patterns of New Zealand policing were shaped by other local factors. With over three-fifths of its population in towns by 1936, New Zealand was highly urbanised in world terms, but less so than Britain or Australia.[26] As an outcome of its geography and farm-based economic development, there was not yet one dominant metropolis, but rather four metropolitan areas (or 'main centres') scattered over two islands – by contrast with England and Wales, and each of the Australian states. Moreover, the country's small population (just over 1.5 million in 1936 – roughly equal to the West Yorkshire or Clydeside conurbations) meant that the combined 'main centre' population (of 577 000) was only a fraction (7 per cent) of London's in 1936, while the numbers in the largest main centre, Auckland (210 000), were a sixth of Sydney's and a fifth of Melbourne's. With a quarter of its population dispersed throughout the country in towns of between 1000 and 20 000, New Zealand had more of a rural/small town society than did most of the Australian states. Upon this distinctive demographic pattern, 1289 police were relatively thinly spread through 339 stations, 240 of which were sole charge (one-man) and 33 two-man stations in 1936. The ratios of police to population, in urban areas (1 to 866 in Auckland in 1936) as well as over the country as a whole (1 to 1283), were much higher by comparison

---

[25]   Graeme Dunstall, *A Policeman's Paradise?*, pp. 66, 127 and 225.
[26]   Campbell Gibson, 'Urbanisation in New Zealand: A Comparative Analysis', *Demography*, 10, 1 (1973) pp. 71–84.

with both England and Wales and the Australian states. Politicians and police commissioners were aware of such a disparity, but accepted it during the inter-war years as an adequate balance between the costs of a national police force and the particular conditions of New Zealand society, apparently more orderly than hitherto and with little 'serious crime' in comparative terms. As Commissioner Wohlmann put it when defending the adequacy of the existing police facilities in 1934:

> We have to bear in mind, in addition to the relatively small population of New Zealand, its geographical conformation, its absence of large cities, its relatively uniform diffusion of population, and its insular position.
>
>   The problems in New Zealand differ from those in largely populated countries. The inauguration of mobile squads [which New Zealand then lacked] in London, ... Melbourne and Sydney, were to meet the menace of organised gangs of criminals, which we have not in this country.[27]

A distinctive demographic pattern and local perceptions of crime were reflected in the organisation of the detective branch and its work. In 1936, three-quarters of New Zealand's 77 detectives (not counting acting detectives) were concentrated at the central stations of the police districts encompassing the four main centres, with the largest number (24) at Auckland. One or two detectives were also deployed at each of the headquarters stations in the main provincial towns of the remaining 11 police districts. Clearly, as in Britain and Australia, the contrasting milieux of city and rural/small-town policing influenced local relationships between detectives and uniformed men, and produced variations on a common pattern of detective work. In the largest detective offices of the main centres, especially Auckland, a sense of superiority and distinctiveness (along with a belief in a separate career structure with faster promotions) persisted amongst staff, reinforced periodically by *New Zealand Truth* which constructed images of detectives as 'sleuths with greater intelligence and skill' than the ordinary 'John Hops'.[28] In the provincial centres there was probably greater equality of esteem where the few detectives needed to work closely with their uniformed colleagues, especially those at sole charge stations who generally made the initial inquiries and possessed vital local knowledge.[29] Whether in the cities or the small towns, the small numbers of detectives made most of them generalists – usually working alone or in pairs and involved in a wide range of investigations rather than specialising in some types of crime. Furthermore, the effects of comparatively small

---

[27]   *Press* (Christchurch), 11 April 1934.

[28]   *Dominion*, 16 November 1923; Charles Belton, *Outside the Law in New Zealand* (Gisborne: Gisborne Publishing Company, 1939) pp. 252–53; Richard S.L. Joblin, 'The Breath of Scandal: *New Zealand Truth* and Interwar Society, 1918–1939', unpublished MA thesis, University of Canterbury, 1990, pp. 214–16.

[29]   Belton, *Outside the Law*, pp. 157–60, 186–87, 191–92 and 197.

numbers and of a common seniority list with the uniformed branch also meant that there was a different balance of ranks amongst New Zealand detectives from that in the London Metropolitan Police. In 1936 Detectives McLennan and Murch noted that the CID (with its own career structure and more rapid promotion) had 180 officers, 463 detective sergeants and 476 detective constables.[30] In New Zealand there were three 'senior detectives' (detective senior sergeants), 15 detective sergeants and 59 detectives. Before sub-inspectors were appointed in Wellington and Auckland from 1930[31] and Christchurch from 1940 to take charge of the local detective office, senior detectives had this role. McLennan and Murch observed that a detective sergeant or a 'detective of experience' in New Zealand did 'similar work' to that of a detective inspector in English police forces; indeed, they conducted murder investigations which in London could only be led by detective chief inspector. 'In the majority of cases Detective Sergeants in New Zealand have had more service than the average Detective Inspector in England'.[32]

To the two New Zealand detectives it seemed that their work and methods in investigating crime and securing convictions were fundamentally the same as those of their counterparts in England.[33] That said, the development of a New Zealand legal code (through statute and local case law) provided local definitions (of larceny and car conversion, vagrancy, gaming and opium offences, indecent and subversive publications, as well as the law of evidence, for example) which influenced local approaches and priorities in policing.[34] To McLennan and Murch, attending the CID Officers course at the London Metropolitan Police College, the instruction on English law and its practical application was 'useless for us ... due to the vast differences between the Common and Statute law of England and the Statute laws of New Zealand'.[35] Nevertheless, the only formal instruction in New Zealand law received by detectives was of the rudiments which had been given to them at the Training Depot as recruits on joining the Force.

There was no formal induction or training for New Zealand detectives – by contrast to the courses provided at the Hendon Police College for 'Aids to the CID' (constables on probation in the CID) and inspectors from both the London and provincial forces. Would-be detectives in New Zealand – constables selected for six

---

[30] 'Aids to the CID' and other probationers were not included; NZNA, P 36/1, Report of Detectives, pp. 30–31.

[31] There had been a sub-inspector in Wellington in charge of the detective office from 1924 to 1926.

[32] NZNA, P 36/1, Report of Detectives, pp. 3 and 21–22.

[33] NZNA, P 36/1, Report of Detectives, pp. 29 and 40.

[34] Francis B. Adams, ed, *Criminal Law and Practice in New Zealand* (Wellington: Sweet and Maxwell, 1964).

[35] NZNA, P 36/1, Report of Detectives, p. 3.

months' trial in a main centre detective office – were usually 'thrown in at the deep end', unlike (it seemed to McLennan and Murch) the experience of the 'Aids to the CID' in London who could not investigate cases, except when supervised by detectives, and whose duties, in practice, were 'very minor and consist mainly of patrol work'.[36] From the outset, the New Zealand probationers were usually given mundane files for inquiry with (retired men recalled) little more than a few words of advice from the chief detective or one of the more experienced men on the procedures of inquiry and the methods of reporting on an investigation, or 'writing off' a file when nothing was detected. Otherwise, when the opportunity arose, the new recruit might assist a detective sergeant and pick up, by observation and experience, the techniques of investigation, interviewing suspects, and preparing 'tidy' files with the evidence necessary for prosecution.[37] After six months' trial, constables were eligible for appointment as acting detectives who in turn could apply, after two years, for appointment to the prized status of detective. In his memoir, Charles Belton claimed that, during nearly three years in the Auckland detective office before his appointment as detective in 1930, he had 'handled several hundreds of investigations which had in all cases involved the writing of statements and reports as well as making the numerous inquiries and personal interviews involved in each case'.[38] Belton, like his colleagues, continued to learn on the job by observation and experience and in self-preparation for the qualifying examinations for promotion – often, in the process, keeping newspaper clippings of their cases in scrapbooks.[39] McLennan and Murch considered that these examinations required 'much more study and the necessity for a much wider knowledge, both theoretical and practical, than any of the examinations conducted at the College'.[40] Belton echoed a similar parochial view in comparing the work of a New Zealand detective (who 'must of necessity be able to handle even complicated cases from the start to the finish') with that of 'a Scotland Yard detective' seen to be 'often only one of number doing one set portion of the investigation'.[41]

---

[36] NZNA, P 36/1, Report of Detectives, p. 2.

[37] This account (as with other parts of the discussion of details of detective work) is based on information from letters from and/or interviews with retired detectives listed in Dunstall, *A Policeman's Paradise?* p. 497. See also Belton, *Outside the Law*, pp. 55–57.

[38] Belton, *Outside the Law*, p. 99. Charles Belton was born in Ireland and had previous experience in the British Gendarmerie in Palestine and as a clerk before he joined the New Zealand Police Force on 1 July 1927, aged 22 years. He was appointed detective at Auckland on 1 December 1930 and transferred to Hamilton in December 1934 and then to Gisborne in November 1936. He resigned from the Police on 2 February 1939. His book is the only memoir of a New Zealand policeman published before the 1980s.

[39] Graeme Dunstall, 'Cummings, Denis Joseph'; 'Cummings, James'; 'Young, John Bruce', *DNZB*.

[40] NZNA, P 36/1, Report of Detectives, p. 4.

[41] Belton, *Outside the Law*, p. 175.

Patterns of work

For New Zealand detectives as for their counterparts in England and Australia, the main focus of their work was on acquisitive crimes and those traditionally perceived most likely to commit them: 'vagrants' and 'bad characters'. It was a pervasive belief of mid-nineteenth-century settler society that New Zealand (unlike Australia) had no criminal class – no 'criminals whose trade is crime, [who are] educated in it from their earliest infancy and systematically trained to be thieves', according to a New Zealand judge in 1864.[42] Nevertheless, the notion of a criminal class was part of the operational code of 'preventive' policing recreated in the colony.[43] While there might not be many home-grown professional criminals, fears persisted that such could arrive from across the Tasman.[44] By the 1920s, detectives still found safe-blowers and sneak thieves, pickpockets and 'spielers' frequenting the main centres or crossing the Tasman in search of opportunities;[45] yet the notion of a 'criminal class' was losing its force (see illustration 7.1). Much of the growing volume of 'crimes against property' recorded by police during the inter-war years (increasing from 5429 cases in 1919 to a peak of 12 188 in 1932) could not be explained in these terms. Detective Charles Belton, for one, sought a psychological rather than a sociological explanation for the behaviour of recidivist burglars and thieves, seeing them as 'mentally sick' – 'suffering under, what is up to the present, an incurable disease'.[46] Furthermore, many acquisitive crimes were apparently opportunist – as implicitly recognised by the offence of car or bicycle 'conversion' created by the Police Offences Amendment Act, 1919. Such offenders, Belton observed, 'are nearly always youths or very young men' who 'appear to commit such offences mostly through a spirit of adventure' and who 'reform to a greater or lesser degree as they grow older'.[47] By the inter-war years (and probably earlier), it appears that most of those apprehended and prosecuted by the police were not known to have offended previously. And, in common with patterns of arrests for property crimes at other times and places, they were disproportionately

---

[42]   Peter Spiller, *The Chapman Legal Family* (Wellington: Victoria University Press, 1992) p. 107; Miles Fairburn, *The Ideal Society and its Enemies. The Foundations of Modern New Zealand Society 1850–1900* (Auckland University Press, 1989) pp. 61–67 and 245–50.

[43]   Maxims adopted from the London Metropolitan Police and issued to the New Zealand Police Force in 1886 instructed constables to 'Obtain a knowledge of all reputed thieves, and idle and disorderly persons' and to 'Watch narrowly all persons having no visible means of subsistence and repress vagrancy'.

[44]   Richard S. Hill, *The Colonial Frontier Tamed: New Zealand Policing in Transition, 1867–1886* (Wellington: Government Printer, 1989) p. 342; Hill, *The Iron Fist in the Velvet Glove*, pp. 125, 186 and 197.

[45]   *Dominion*, 12 January 1923.

[46]   Belton, *Outside the Law*, p. 110.

[47]   Belton, *Outside the Law*, p. 110.

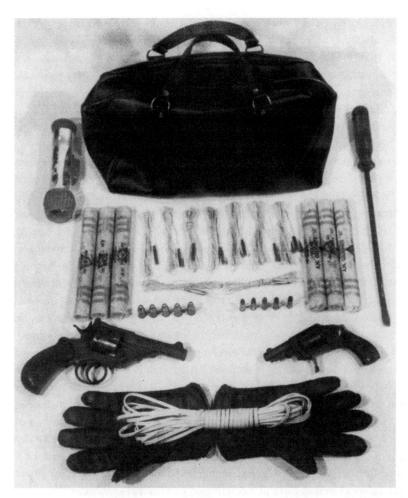

Illustration 7.1   This kit of a safe-blower arrested by Auckland detectives in 1956 was exceptional amongst the local 'professional' criminals, few of whom carried revolvers.

youthful, male, working class and (from the 1920s) Maori. However, the growth in prosecutions of often 'white collar' offenders for fraud and false pretences (rising from 288 in 1919 to 920 by 1932) indicated that the investigation of crime was not confined to a distinct social group. 'Sometimes', Belton noted, 'a highly respected man in the community is arrested for some crime – the cream of to-day may be sour tomorrow'.[48] Indeed, the fact that 'criminals' could be found in all walks of life, that there were 'various types' and 'fresh offenders keep cropping up' compounded the difficulties of detection.[49]

As Belton's memoir (and the unpublished reminiscences and scrapbooks of retired detectives) makes clear, New Zealand detective work entailed a wide range of routine jobs (as it did in England and Australia). A basic diet of petty theft and burglary (shop and housebreaking) cases was interspersed with a variety of other types: typically car conversion, false pretences, forgery, bigamy, indecent assaults or exposure, gaming and opium smoking/possession cases, the occasional sudden death, manslaughter and (not in Belton's memoir) murder. Stories of petty thefts predominate in Belton's account – suggesting the range of opportunities for criminals, as well as presenting a self-image of perseverance and skill in detecting them in a similar manner to overseas detective memoirs discussed by Paul Lawrence:[50] a missing alarm clock, bicycle thefts by children, thefts of money (especially from residents in boarding houses), thefts from a college cloakroom, cars, dwellings, shops, building sites, telephone boxes as well as business premises broken into. After Belton is transferred from the 'the large, happy and noisy family' of detectives in Auckland to join two other detectives at the rapidly growing provincial town of Hamilton, the scope of his stories broadens to include investigating rural thefts of poultry and animals, the extortion of money by a Maori woman from an Indian hawker, a 'hit and run' case by a drunken rabbiter driving a truck, the suicide of an isolated farmer, the sudden death of a farmer's wife from an overdose of quinine, gaming and fortune-telling at Agricultural and Pastoral shows as well as cases of incest, bigamy and carnal knowledge.[51]

In the absence of detective notebooks, a precise measure of an individual's workload is difficult to obtain. However, from the time he entered the Wellington detective office soon after joining the Force in 1922, Bill Murray kept a record of all the cases he dealt with that led to prosecution.[52] This provides only a partial view of

---

[48]   Belton, *Outside the Law*, p. 96.

[49]   Belton, *Outside the Law*, pp. 73, 96 and 110.

[50]   Paul Lawrence, ' " Scoundrels and Scallywags and some honest men": Memoirs and Self-Image of French and English Policemen c.1870–1939', in Barry Godfrey, Clive Emsley and Graeme Dunstall, eds, *Comparative Histories of Crime* (Cullompton, Devon: Willan, 2003).

[51]   Illicit sexual intercourse with a girl under the age of 16 years.

[52]   William Robert Murray was born in England in 1896, arrived in New Zealand in 1920 and was appointed constable at Wellington in March 1922 and detective in November 1924.

Murray's workload since his cases that did not come to court are not recorded. Nevertheless, some patterns may be observed. Between June 1922 (while still a constable) and September 1937 (when he became a detective sergeant, still at Wellington), he prepared 360 cases for prosecution. Just over half these cases occurred between 1925 and 1930. By the mid-1930s, Murray briefed only a third as many cases for court annually as he had a decade earlier. In part this was a consequence of being given increasingly complex cases, especially those involving false pretences and fraud, for which he showed an aptitude, but also, perhaps, there was a growing proportion of insoluble cases which were not recorded. In 1931 Murray also played the leading role in a successful murder investigation, being commended for 'exceptional work'. Of Murray's recorded cases between 1922 and 1937, nearly 46 per cent related to fraud, false pretences, forgery, and theft of money while in a position of trust; 30 per cent were undescribed thefts; only 3.5 per cent involved breaking and entering with theft; 8.6 per cent were gaming cases; just over 10 per cent concerned sexual offences (including bigamy) and barely 1 per cent related to vagrancy. By contrast, as a proportion of all acquisitive crimes recorded by police in 1932 (the highest number recorded during the inter-war years) fraud, false pretences, forgery and theft by servants comprised only 12 per cent, all other thefts 71 per cent, and burglaries 14 per cent. The contrast between the balance of Murray's prosecutions and that of the main categories of reported acquisitive crime recorded in Police Force annual reports reflects differences in the degree of difficulty in detecting offenders and police methods in achieving convictions.

Interrogation and confessions

For Bill Murray and Charles Belton, and their counterparts in Australia and England, a key element of success lay in securing an admission of guilt from a suspect by interrogation. Belton attributed his 'considerable amount of success' to the 'confessions [made] to me without which there would have been little evidence'.[53] Such admissions were more easily gained from some types of offenders than others.

Promoted to detective sergeant in September 1937, he was transferred to take charge of the Hamilton detective office in 1941 and promoted to senior detective in July 1945. He became sub-inspector in charge of the Christchurch CIB in 1950 and then took charge of the Gisborne police district as Inspector in 1953. Three years later he took charge of the Auckland CIB as superintendent and retired in 1958 as chief superintendent in charge of the Auckland police district. The following discussion is based upon his 'Record of Cases' [1922–50], a typescript, and his scrapbooks of newspaper cutting and personal papers. See Graeme Dunstall, 'Murray, William Robert', *DNZB*.

[53] Belton, *Outside the Law*, p. 58.

In 1932 the clear-up rate for recorded burglary cases was 61 per cent, and 93 per cent overall for fraud, false pretences, forgery and theft by servants. These relatively high clearance rates (by comparison with those of a London police division visited by McLennan and Murch and the New Zealand clearance rates from the 1960s, based on stricter procedures for record keeping) reflected considerable latitude taken in excluding 'petty offences' and in determining whether there had been an offence.[54] Nevertheless, those who broke into shops and dwellings, for example, were not only hard to catch, but seasoned burglars were less likely to confess than other thieves unless there was a trade-off. Partly for this reason, there were few breaking and entering cases amongst Belton's accounts of successful detection and in Murray's cases that came to court. By contrast with cases of theft and burglary, complainants of breach of trust by employees or of false pretences could name a suspect – and generally there was damning evidence. By the time Murray interviewed those accused in such cases, many were ready to admit their offences to the adroit interrogator. Indeed, without such assistance in 'clearing up the defalcations', Murray conceded during one case, 'the police would have been put to very great difficulty and trouble', which was evident in the few of Murray's cases where the evidence was contested.[55] Compliance could also be stimulated by a detective's willingness (threat or inducement) on occasions not to press the most serious charge possible, thereby allowing the chance of a 'lenient' sentence – in one of Murray's cases, for example, the judge told an accountant who had pleaded guilty to misappropriating a large sum of money that he 'was lucky in the way the charge was framed. But for that, said his Honour, he would have imposed a heavier sentence'.[56]

As elsewhere, police methods in identifying and interviewing suspects were subject to criticism during the inter-war years. Following criticism in the Supreme Court by both judge and jury of the 'unfair' manner in which suspects had been identified by complainants, Commissioner McIlveney felt it necessary to issue a circular in 1926 specifying the procedure to be observed in conducting identification parades. Occasional criticism continued; for his part, Belton portrayed an identification parade in one of his stories as being fair.[57] McLennan and Murch recommended that two aspects of the practice in London be adopted in New Zealand: that the officer in charge of the case be present to note what was said (if anything) by a person identified, and that the witness or complainant did not have to go up and touch the suspect, but merely point to him – thereby making identification parades 'more

---

[54]   Dunstall, *A Policeman's Paradise?*, pp. 132–34; NZNA, P 36/1, Report of Detectives, pp. 40–41.
[55]   *Truth*, 12 May 1937.
[56]   *Evening Post*, 18 July 1932.
[57]   Belton, *Outside the Law*, pp. 117–18.

successful'.[58] By contrast, however, there was no 'daily line up' of those in custody for scrutiny by police at the London divisional stations as there was at the central stations of the main centres in New Zealand; McLennan and Murch considered the New Zealand practice a 'distinct advantage'.[59]

More persistent were allegations of threats made, inducements offered, and unfair methods used by some police when interviewing suspects and securing statements. There were contemporary parallels with criticisms of police methods elsewhere – notably in Victoria where judicial condemnation of prolonged detention for questioning led in 1936 to a review of the use of the 'third degree' in local criminal investigation.[60] In New Zealand such allegations were most likely to be made in cases relating to indecent assault, abortion, burglary and theft where the accused denied the charge, other incriminating evidence was not strong, and inherently there was pressure on detectives to get a conviction. Publicly expressed concerns focused more on the manner in which some statements were induced, rather than on the possibility of fabrication. A recurring complaint was the length of detention for questioning, sometimes with claims of bullying tactics and, occasionally, violence. Though Murray and Belton were probably perceived as 'white men' (of exemplary character), there were some rough and tough detectives, popularly recognised in fictional accounts, for example: 'When they got to the station a big demon walked into Joe's cell with his coat off'.[61] Commissioner McIlveney reminded all ranks in 1926 (in not the strongest terms) that 'even the greatest delinquents should not be brought to justice by unjustifiable means'.[62] Yet varied practices in dealing with suspects were to be expected, given the decentralised organisation of detectives, the extent to which successive cohorts of them learnt their skills on the job, and the lack of effective regulation and monitoring of the process of interrogation and the taking of statements. Certainly the extent to which detectives in the inter-war years knew of, or even felt bound to follow, the English 'Judges Rules', first formulated in 1912, is not clear. At the Training Depot, recruits were told only of the local Evidence Act, 1908. To critics, section 20 of this Act, which varied the common-law rules on the admissibility of confessions, seemed to leave a loophole for what they dubbed 'the third degree'. Much depended on the discretion of judges in particular cases.[63] In 1929 (after local publicity on the varying extent of the application of the Judges Rules by English

---

[58] NZNA, P 36/1, Report of Detectives, p. 10.

[59] NZNA, P 36/1, Report of Detectives, pp. 32–33.

[60] Haldane, *The People's Force*, pp. 215–17; Mark Finnane, *Police and Government: Histories of Policing in Australia* (Melbourne: Oxford University Press, 1994) pp. 86–87.

[61] Cited in Orsman, *Dictionary*, p. 204.

[62] *New Zealand Police Gazette*, 1926, p. 275.

[63] *Press*, 30 August 1930; Adams, ed, *Criminal Law and Practice in New Zealand*, pp. 690–96.

police which was reported by Royal Commission on Police Powers and Procedures) leading defence lawyers managed to have a remit adopted by the annual Law Society conference recommending that the Minister of Justice investigate 'the whole system of taking statements by the police'.[64] Nothing came of this. Criticism of police methods was often seen as a ploy by defence counsel, and was thus discounted by some magistrates and notably by Justice Herdman, a former Minister in charge of the Police (1912-18) on the Supreme Court bench at Auckland for most of the period between 1918 and 1935: 'You must not make observations like that about a member of the police force. To say that subterfuge and falsehood were employed ... is contrary to my thinking, is not to be allowed, and I will not permit it.'[65]

Ninety-three per cent of Bill Murray's cases that came to court in Wellington between 1922 and 1939 (when he was transferred to Hamilton) culminated in a conviction. (By comparison, 83 per cent of breaking and entering cases, 80 per cent of theft cases, and 97 per cent of fraud and false pretences cases tried in New Zealand Magistrates' Courts during 1932 resulted in convictions). The high conviction rate achieved by Murray marked him out as an effective detective, though the rate did not include an unknown and probably sizeable number of burglary and theft files that were 'written off'. Success in court also reflected the nature of Murray's cases which had a high proportion of confessions. The degree of success also reflected his skill in preparing cases and as a witness. Like other experienced police, Murray managed to convey an aura of fairness when giving evidence in court. Belton was not alone in maintaining a self-image that 'I always mentioned everything I knew in favour of the accused'.[66] (However, this practice, to the extent that it occurred in the Magistrates' Court, was more likely for first offenders than for those with long list of previous convictions or charged with a serious offence). Most cases brought to court by detectives were dealt with summarily by a small group of stipendiary magistrates who came to know and respect many of the police who appeared before them as witnesses. Typically, E.M. Page, the stipendiary magistrate in Wellington, commented: 'The work of the detectives and police is responsible, arduous, difficult and sometimes dangerous. My experience of their methods which extends over a decade, is that they carry out their duties with conspicuous fairness, and I have no reason to believe than they have departed from that in this case ... '.[67] Where there was a conflict of evidence, that of the police was usually preferred. Not always, however. Auckland stipendiary magistrates looked critically, for example, at the testimony of detectives who sought during 1933 to have various showmen, labourers and seamen convicted as

---

[64]   *New Zealand Herald*, 6 April 1929.
[65]   *New Zealand Herald*, 9 February 1923.
[66]   Belton, *Outside the Law*, p. 58.
[67]   *New Zealand Herald*, 3 December 1924.

vagrants for being 'idle and disorderly persons who habitually consorted with reputed thieves'.[68] Similarly, Murray was not alone in finding it difficult to secure convictions on charges of *attempted* false pretences and *conspiracy* to defraud, and that Supreme Court juries could be reluctant to convict those charged with offences relating to abortions, or motorists on serious charges such as manslaughter.

Surveillance, entrapment and raids

The currency given to the slang 'dees' and 'demons', especially amongst those who experienced at first hand the attention of detectives during the inter-war years, arose from images and fears not just of interrogation but also of police undercover work and raids to secure incriminating evidence of gambling, opium smoking by Chinese, or sedition. Particularly amongst male wage-earners for whom gambling was well-entrenched as a pastime, the 'dees' were adversaries.[69] Some 15 200 gaming cases were prosecuted between 1918 and 1949, representing a significant proportion of detectives' work yet only a fraction of the potential offences. By the inter-war years, most gaming and betting practices were illicit, except for some 'art unions' and betting on totalisators at racecourses; in particular, the business of bookmaking and betting with 'bookies' was illegal. Inevitably, given the national passion for betting on horse races, illicit betting with bookies was widespread and in varying degrees covert – in workplaces, offices, shops (especially tobacconists), hairdressing and billiard saloons, hotel bars, suburban dwellings, and (by novices and the audacious) at racecourses. A hierarchy of bookmakers had developed by the late 1920s, ranging from the 'big men', protecting themselves from prosecution by using telephones and agents amongst a variety of small shopkeepers, to the 'small fry' (or 'hotel rats' in detectives' argot) who frequented public bars and billiard saloons. Detectives focused on the agents of the big men as well as the 'small fry'. Not infrequently complaints (often anonymous) helped to identify bookies, but that was the limit of assistance; detectives had to seek the necessary evidence. Once under suspicion or convicted, a bookmaker became subject to periodical surveillance, especially by selected new constables from the Training Depot (such as Belton) who spent some weeks on undercover work to secure incriminating betting confirmation slips. Once these were obtained, detectives procured a search warrant from a JP and made the arrest, hopefully catching the bookie (or his agent) red-handed with his notebook and double charts on race days. Especially during the popular race meetings of the Christmas and New Year summer holiday season, simultaneous raids by detectives and constables on a number of shops

---

[68] Graeme Dunstall, *A Policeman's Paradise?*, p. 162

[69] This paragraph is based on Dunstall, *A Policeman's Paradise?*, chapter 7.

and offices were usual. Ostensibly there was no let-up, with growing numbers of gaming offences (not just related to bookmaking) being recorded by detectives in a wave-like pattern of prosecutions with ever higher peaks until the mid-1940s.

In Frank Sargeson's novella *That Summer*, written between 1938 and 1941, and set in Auckland during the Depression of the early 1930s, 'a tall bloke', who had been 'sitting on his own listening' at a hotel bar to a ship's cook sounding 'bolshy' while talking politics, 'came over and asked the barman what the cook's name was'. The barman repeatedly said he did not know, despite the 'tall bloke' enlisting the aid of 'the boss'. When the stranger left, 'the barman winked at me and said he was a demon', but then lost his job for 'not letting that bloody dee bulldoze' him.[70] From 1920, the development of peacetime political surveillance by detectives added another dimension to the popular perception of 'demons'.[71] By contrast with the London Metropolitan Police, however, there was no 'Special Branch', designated as such, until December 1949. During the inter-war years, a detective in each of the four main centres was selected for full-time political surveillance work, monitoring individuals and organisations broadly perceived to be potentially 'revolutionary' and the extent to which 'revolutionary propaganda' was being disseminated. The approach was both legalistic in looking for offences and pragmatic in seeking to detect threats to public order. In the provincial centres and country districts, local detectives and constables reported as necessary on strikes, and on the movements and activities of those thought to have 'revolutionary tendencies'. In Auckland and Wellington in particular, the sole detectives on surveillance work soon found they needed assistance in attending the variety of meetings where there was potential for 'seditious utterance', and in gathering information, especially at times of industrial conflict and as demonstrations of the unemployed increased during the early 1930s. In the early 1920s, the main focus of political surveillance was on public meetings to detect prosecutable seditious utterance and literature. From April 1921, with the development of a local Communist Party which became more circumspect following police prosecutions, covert surveillance became increasingly important. Detectives' methods paralleled those used to suppress gambling – with undercover constables (rather than recognised 'demons') infiltrating meetings and becoming members of Communist organisations. As growing Communist activity amongst the unemployed heightened a sense of crisis in the mind of Commissioner Wohlmann during the early 1930s, there were successive raids on Party premises and the homes of prominent members, followed by prosecutions for 'seditious offences'. By 1933 many of the leading activists were incapacitated by imprisonment.

---

[70]   Frank Sargeson, *Collected Stories* (introduction by Bill Pearson) (Auckland: Blackwood and Janet Paul, 1964) pp. 167–68 and 178.

[71]   This paragraph is based on Dunstall, *A Policeman's Paradise?*, chapter 10.

Informants and 'suspicious' persons

Altogether then, the basic methods of interrogation, surveillance, entrapment and raids remained fundamental to securing convictions – the *raison d'être* of detective work. While the identification of suspects by complainants or witnesses was crucial in many cases (and in most of Belton's stories), the extent to which informers or 'fizgigs' were cultivated and used by detectives is not known. Such relationships existed (at least one Auckland detective in the 1930s did not go on gaming raids so as not to compromise his links with informants), but they were covert and apparently informal. After hearing a 'special lecture' by Chief Inspector A.M. Duncan[72] on 'informants and street thieves', McLennan and Murch recommended that the New Zealand Police follow Scotland Yard's practice and have a fund to pay rewards for information, at the discretion of the Commissioner. They had 'no doubt that a class of person exists who can and will supply valuable information from a police point of view, on the promise of reward'. At the 'Met', the identity of the informant was supposed to be known only to the detective who received the information and who in turn paid a reward from the fund (after conviction of an offender), obtaining 'a receipt from the informant under a fictitious name'.[73] There was no official response to this recommendation, nor any evidence that such a fund was established before 1956 when a central rewards file was begun at Police Headquarters – and this dealt only with rewards and possible indemnity from prosecution offered publicly ('as a tactic of last resort') for information regarding specific crimes. By the 1980s Scotland Yard's more liberal policy of 50 years earlier had been adopted: during 1989 police paid $140 000 to 'people, mainly from the underworld, or on its fringes, for dobbing in their mates'.[74]

In the view of McLennan and Murch, the sanctions of the vagrancy laws against 'suspicious' persons were also not so liberally applied in New Zealand as in London. It seemed that section 11 of the (English) Vagrancy Act 1824 was 'used extensively by the Metropolitan Police in dealing with suspected persons who are found loitering about motor cars, shops etc.'. Indeed, the New Zealand detectives were told by 'senior CID officers' that section 11 was 'open to abuse' by 'Aids to the CID' who were 'anxious to justify their appointment by the number of arrests made', and so 'persons have been arrested without the necessary evidence to justify a conviction'. After listening to such cases presented in court, McLennan and Murch believed '[m]uch more evidence would be required in any New Zealand Court to secure a conviction'.[75]

---

[72] Soon afterwards Duncan was to investigate the 'third degree' in Victoria and become Chief Commissioner of its Police.

[73] NZNA, P 36/1, Report of Detectives, p. 18.

[74] *Evening Post*, 4 April 1990.

[75] NZNA, P 36/1, Report of Detectives, pp. 36 and 41.

Certainly by 1936 the number of arrests for vagrancy (207) in New Zealand was only a quarter of its inter-war peak in 1927, and had declined steeply since 1932, reflecting a change in social and political climate. However, police statistics on 'vagrancy' (with categories of 'idle and disorderly persons', 'rogues and vagabonds' and 'incorrigible rogues' as defined by the Police Offences Act 1927) encompassed a wide variety of offences, making it impossible to assess the extent to which New Zealand detectives employed section 52 of the Police Offences Act (relating to suspected persons and reputed thieves frequenting public places) which broadly paralleled section 11 of the English legislation. When Belton went on patrol in Auckland he 'kept a close eye on vagrants loitering about the town' or 'consorting' with reputed thieves (section 49 of the Police Offences Act). When detectives' 'vag reports' were sufficient, arrests might be made. 'Naturally', Belton assured his readers, 'great discretion is exercised before arresting even a vagrant'.[76] Thirty years later, according to one commentator, detectives still regarded section 52 as 'the most useful of the vagrancy provisions'.[77]

Technology and science

In New Zealand the application of technology and science – of cars and wireless, 'technical aids' and forensic science – to the craft of detective work was in its infancy in the early 1920s, as it was in British and Australian forces. A decade later, scientific aids and expertise were being increasingly used by police, locally and abroad, in solving major crimes; but in other important respects New Zealand police continued long-standing practices, by contrast to developments in the organisation and technology of surveillance and investigation adopted in overseas metropolitan centres, notably in Melbourne and London.

That fingerprints were 'a most valuable part of detection', was the conventional wisdom of New Zealand detectives during inter-war years.[78] In reality, however, they remained only a minor aid in the solution of crime. Certainly there were some dramatic identifications as the result of fingerprints, notably in securing a conviction for murder in 1920.[79] Yet very few New Zealand murder trials hinged on fingerprint identification. In accord with the initial conception of the Fingerprint Bureau (later renamed the Criminal Registration Branch) as focusing on 'habitual criminals', burglars were the most common category of offender identified by fingerprints. When

---

[76]   Belton, *Outside the Law*, p. 116.

[77]   G.P. Curry, 'Vagrancy – The Exercise of Discretions by the Police', in R.S. Clark, ed, *Essays on the Criminal Law in New Zealand* (Wellington: Sweet and Maxwell, 1971) p. 200.

[78]   *Press*, 28 July 1945.

[79]   Dunstall, *A Policeman's Paradise?*, p. 165.

so identified, burglars generally confessed and would also often admit to earlier offences. Overall the results were meagre, given the considerable labour involved in gathering, classifying, recording, and searching prints. In the best inter-war year (1936), when 1063 burglaries were recorded, 51 offenders were identified and prosecuted on the basis of their prints; the annual inter-war average was 25. The main value of fingerprints lay in helping detectives keep tabs on some recidivists (an average of 234 prisoners annually). To this end the Criminal Registration Branch regularly exchanged prints and photographs with their counterparts in Australian and British forces. However, the 'Henry' classification system involved searching prints of all fingers. McLennan and Murch noted that Scotland Yard had a single fingerprint classification ('Battley') system which was said to be 'most valuable' in clearing up crimes where portions of single prints were found, and save time in searching.[80] Soon after they reported to the Commissioner in April 1936, E.W. Dinnie began the 'long and tedious task' of applying the Battley system to the New Zealand collection of more than 51 000 prints.[81]

McLennan and Murch were also impressed with the card index systems of the Criminal Registration Office at Scotland Yard, and particularly with the modus operandi system which indexed reported crime according to its peculiarities and the idiosyncrasies of known criminals. There were associated indexes of photographs and of cars possessed by 'all known criminals'. The detectives were 'firmly of the opinion' that a similar system should be 'introduced in New Zealand at an early date'. Twelve years earlier, after visiting Scotland Yard, Bill Murray had recommended an 'MO' system in a report to Commissioner Wright who did not see New Zealand conditions as warranting such elaborate record keeping.[82] Such scepticism remained. Nevertheless, the first steps were taken at Auckland in 1937 to establish a local modus operandi system which began to be more fully developed and implemented in the other main centres from 1950.

A modus operandi system would have been of little assistance to detectives in clearing up homicides, since most of those accused of murder had no criminal history in the eyes of the police. In the police statistics for the period from 1921 to 1939, 177 murders were recorded, with numbers ranging from two in 1928 to 22 in 1933. At least 14 homicides (including five unidentified new-born children) remained 'unsolved'. However, it was the unsolved murders of an Auckland taxi driver and of a Christchurch hotelier in 1933 which caused considerable public disquiet, mounting

---

[80] NZNA, P 36/1, Report of Detectives, p. 17.

[81] Annual Report, 1937, p. 5.

[82] Murray interview. In 1951 Murray himself was sceptical of the need for such an elaborate system in New Zealand, Report of Sub-Inspector W.R. Murray, 2 October 1951. NZNA, Police file P 22/3.

criticism of the organisation and methods of detective work, and calls for detectives to be sent to London for specialised training and to be given more up-to-date scientific aids. In fact, New Zealand detectives did not lack access to scientific expertise. After attending lectures on forensic science at the Police College and visiting the Metropolitan Police Laboratory attached to it, McLennan and Murch made few comments on new knowledge and no recommendation other than that already noted: such lectures could be given equally as effectively in New Zealand by local experts. While English police had established a number of forensic science laboratories by the late 1930s, New Zealand detectives continued their long-standing practice of turning to specialists outside the Force, especially public hospital pathologists and the Government Analysts in the four main centres.[83] Local gunsmiths and professors of chemistry and physics were also used until the police appointed its own ballistics expert in 1935.[84] The availability and effectiveness of a range of technical and scientific expertise was demonstrated in the conviction of W.A. Bayly for murder in 1934.[85] What also made this investigation exceptional (and successful) was the scale of the police effort: beginning as a routine investigation with a couple of detectives and three constables using a borrowed car, and eventually involving more than 50 police as well as inspectors (now in the uniformed branch) with prestige as former successful detectives. In this investigation the Commissioner had something to prove to his critics.

In fact, the exceptional police effort in the Bayly case underscored later detailed observations by McLennan and Murch about the conduct of murder investigations by Scotland Yard detectives. Their success was

> attributed to the fact that at the outset the staff is organised in a proper manner [under a chief inspector]; the murder investigation takes precedence over all other inquiries; every facility available [including 'motor cars kept in readiness'] is placed at the disposal of the officer in charge of the investigation; no expense is spared from the very commencement of the inquiry; the co-operation of the press is invited whenever considered necessary for the purpose of locating persons the authorities desire to interview ....[86]

Conferences of all police involved in a murder investigation were 'frequently held' to obtain 'any suggestions'. 'Murder bags' (which 'should be kept at all principal head-quarters stations in New Zealand') were considered essential at Scotland Yard. These

---

[83] P.P. Lynch, *No Remedy for Death: The Memoirs of a Pathologist* (London: John Long, 1970).

[84] G.G. Kelly, *The Gun in the Case* (Christchurch: Whitcomb and Tombs, 1963).

[85] H.J. Wilson, ed, *The Bayly Case* (Wellington: National Magazines, 1934); L.P. Leary, *Not Entirely Legal* (Christchurch: Whitcoulls, 1977).

[86] NZNA, P 1/36, Report of Detectives, p. 35.

and other comments stood in implicit contrast with the usual practice of New Zealand detectives which was shaped by their small and dispersed numbers, a decentralised organisation of detective work, on-going pressures for economy during the inter-war years, and a degree of institutional inertia stemming from an inbred leadership. The 'administrative system of this department could not be described as progressive', a political scientist observed of the Police Force in 1948.[87]

Nonetheless, small changes were made, besides those already indicated, to enhance the efficiency of detective work and policing more generally. From 1937 a modest system of in-service training began, first in Auckland and later in the other main centres: a compulsory course of fortnightly lectures at district headquarters by local officers in 'practical duties' for three separate classes of detectives, uniformed sergeants and constables.[88] Smaller districts were to have lectures at least monthly. This coincided with a renewed emphasis on training by most Australian police commissioners. Where they focused (in post recruit training) on the formal instruction of detectives through special courses in the capital cities (notably in Victoria and Queensland), the New Zealand commissioner attempted to reach all his staff 'at convenient places'. He felt he could not afford to transfer men to the Wellington Depot for further training. Nor (following the observations by McLennan and Murch) did he see any advantage in more detectives going to London. An exchange of detectives with Australian forces (favoured by Belton) was not yet considered. Also from 1937, new equipment was acquired for forensic ballistics and microphotography, and the police headquarters library was 'brought up to date' (coinciding with similar developments at the New South Wales Police headquarters). Like their counterparts in Sydney, New Zealand detectives continued to look to scientists outside the Force. However, the New Zealand Police continued to lag behind the larger Australian forces, and London Metropolitan Police, in using modern communications. Few cars were available for detectives who continued to resort to bicycles, public transport, or (when permitted) hiring taxis or using their own cars on mileage allowances. Though experiments began in 1938 with wireless communication, it was not until 1946 that the first radio-controlled patrol cars were introduced in Auckland and Wellington.[89] Despite piecemeal changes, Charles Belton was frustrated at the working conditions, slowness of promotion, and inadequate training and equipment.[90] Ambitious and

---

[87] Leslie Lipson, *The Politics of Equality: New Zealand's Adventures in Democracy* (University of Chicago Press, 1948) p. 471.

[88] J.B. Young, 'Notes on Criminal Investigation', typescript, 1937; Graeme Dunstall, 'Young, Jock Bruce', *DNZB*.

[89] Details in this paragraph have been drawn mainly from Annual Reports of the New Zealand Police and from 'Notes of Commissioner's address to the 1937 Police Association conference', NZNA, Police file P 13/1.

[90] Belton, *Outside the Law*, pp. 209–55.

active, he resigned from the police in 1939 and became a successful real estate agent in Auckland.

Conclusion: Crisis and innovation

A fundamental shift in the organisation and training of detectives came only after a crisis brought in an outsider to head the Force with a mandate for change. The crisis was precipitated by the promotion in 1952 of a former detective, Sub-Inspector E.H. Compton over the heads of 35 senior officers to the newly-created post of assistant commissioner, and then to commissioner, thereby breaking the long-standing convention of promotion by seniority. Seeking to meet the government's expectations of a shake-up, but with little expertise in administration, Compton's ill-judged actions compounded a sense of resentment amongst police. His authority was further eroded by allegations of improper conduct, especially as a detective investigating bookmaking. A commission of inquiry found that Compton had twice tapped telephones before his methods were made illegal in 1948, but found no evidence that he or any other detectives had received 'hush money' from bookmakers. When a conference of senior officers passed a motion of no confidence in him, Compton was forced to retire. The unprecedented crisis was resolved by the appointment in May 1955 of a leading civil servant, S.T. Barnett, as Controller-General of the Police Force.[91]

Barnett had already overhauled the administration of the Education and Justice departments, he was to do the same – comprehensively – for the Police. To Barnett (who had visited British police forces) 'the major problems of the Police are not going to be resolved with aid of overseas experts'.[92] Instead he drew on staff from other government departments and on ideas from younger officers within the Force. He saw the 'detective force' (now renamed the Criminal Investigation Branch) as 'the attacking force on crime', but he found it to be 'under-staffed, inadequately equipped, and insufficiently trained'.[93] That training 'on the job' had been inadequate was a point reinforced by a commission of inquiry in 1955 into the interrogation of two

---

[91] Graeme Dunstall, 'Compton, Eric Henry', *DNZB*; First Interim Report of the Commission of Inquiry ... Into Certain Matters Relating to the Conduct of members of the Police Force, *Appendix to the Journals of the [New Zealand] House of Representatives*, 1954, H–16A; Second Interim Report..., 1954; Third and Final Report..., 1955.

[92] Comment in the transcript of a press interview which is undated but was made soon after Barnett became Controller-General; NZNA, Police file, P 1/1/1.

[93] Where not otherwise acknowledged, quotations in this paragraph are from the Annual Reports of the Police Force, 1956–59.

Maori youths by Auckland acting detectives.[94] Thus courses for detectives were a priority at a new Police Training School opened in 1956.[95] Short 'refresher courses' were quickly held for experienced detectives in which 'techniques were revised' and the 'systems now in use reviewed' – establishing a pattern for periodic reassessment of detective work. Henceforth, after more systematic inservice training, acting detectives had to take a ten-week 'qualifying' course. A range of specialist courses (such as for investigating homicides) were also developed, as well as courses for NCOs and officers. To promote a 'co-ordinated national endeavour' from dispersed sections of the CIB, Barnett appointed a detective superintendent (a new rank) as a 'controlling officer' at national headquarters, and the organisation of each 'provincial group' was surveyed and 'realigned to being about quicker and better results'. In effect picking up McLennan and Murch's recommendation of a 'murder bag' 20 years earlier, a 'special kit' was sent to all district headquarters as 'standard equipment in the investigation of major crimes'. To enhance the 'application of scientific method to police work', Barnett saw no need for a police laboratory but, instead, for better liaison with the Department of Scientific and Industrial Research. However, a recasting of the police statistics so as to obtain 'a more comprehensive account of crime' meant much less favourable clear up rates.

In essence (and only partially sketched here) Barnett's regime, lasting three years, laid the basis for an on-going pattern of innovation in New Zealand policing – in contrast to the long period of virtual stasis during the inter-war years. By the 1980s at least, many aspects of New Zealand policing, including the organisation and more technologically sophisticated methods of criminal investigation, had come to resemble more closely those of London, Melbourne and Sydney – though clearance rates for property crime had not necessarily improved.[96] Though perceptions of detectives remained ambiguous, 'demon' was no longer a commonplace in the argot of the policed.

---

[94] Report of Commission to Inquire into the Prosecution by the Police of Donald James Ruka and Murdoch Campbell Harris, *Appendix to the Journals of the [New Zealand] House of Representatives*, 1955, H–16A.

[95] Margaret Gordon, 'Police Training 1869–1992', in Sherwood Young, ed, *With Confidence and Pride: Policing the Wellington Region, 1840–1992* (Wellington: Wellington Police Trust, 1994) p. 106.

[96] Graeme Dunstall, 'Police in New Zealand', in Dilip K. Das, ed, *Police Practices: An International Review* (Metuchen, N.J.: Scarecrow Press, 1994).

Chapter Eight

The Image of the Gestapo: As Revealed in Retrospective Surveys and Interviews with Ordinary Germans[1]

Eric A. Johnson

Strange as it might seem, the Secret State Police (*Geheime Staatspolizei* or Gestapo for short) of Nazi Germany appears to have enjoyed a rather positive image among large numbers of ordinary Germans during the years of the Third Reich.[2] For an American this is particularly difficult to fathom as the word *Geheim* in the acronym Gestapo alone (or 'secret' as it is translated into English), let alone *Staatspolizei* (or 'state police'), conjures up sinister images of surreptitious spying that send shivers up the spine. But to a German living in Nazi Germany this may not have been the case. The word *Geheim* had longed been coupled in German parlance with words like *Rat* (as in *Geheimrat*), and, when it was, it did not necessarily convey something particularly nefarious or scary. Thus the *Geheim* in the word *Geheimrat* means more 'privy' than it does 'secret', for the normal English translation of the legions of German governmental advisers of the past who held the post of *Geheimrat* is indeed 'privy councillor' not 'secret councillor'.

Indeed, even after the Second World War had ended and the Third Reich had vanished and both German and the rest of the world's citizens had been well informed about the stupendous crimes against humanity that the Gestapo and other Nazi henchmen had perpetrated, former Gestapo officers standing trial or simply

---

[1]   An earlier draft of this essay was originally presented to the European Social Science History Association Convention in The Hague, The Netherlands, on 2 March 2002.

[2]   While the Gestapo was principally concerned with political and race matters there was also the *Kripo* (the *Kriminalpolizei*), the detective branch of the regular police. From the summer of 1936 these two institutions were brought under the supervision of the same centralised police office under the direction of Reinhard Heydrich. Technically their roles were different, yet increasingly their missions were driven by Nazi ideology and their methods overlapped.

undergoing denazification proceedings commonly received such positive character references from their fellow German citizens that both allied as well as German prosecutors more often than not decided to let them off the hook. For just a few examples of these *Persilscheine* (the ironic German word used for these character references at the time; Persil was a kind of German detergent that in these 'Scheine' or testaments was used figuratively to wash the brown off the people they were written for) we might consider the postwar denazification proceedings of Richard Schulenburg, who had been the former head of the Jewish desk of the Krefeld Gestapo (see illustration 8.1).

On 27 February 1947 the leader of the Catholic Church in the city of Krefeld penned a letter to the Krefeld denazification authorities on Schulenburg's behalf that stated:

> Mr. Richard Schulenburg was head criminal secretary in the political section of the police force. When the police force was nationalised it was compulsory for him to remain with the state police. Here he was exceedingly humane and just in carrying out his duties. As an almost 'permanent guest' of the Gestapo, I heard this repeatedly from various sides. I was told the same especially by many persecuted Jews who came to me in great numbers as I was entrusted with the care of Jewish relics. Schulenburg was in charge of the 'Jewish Department' and as the Jews told me, he always treated them decently and, as far as he was able, offered them many possibilities. Any injustice, hardness and ill-treatment was incompatible with the decency of his character. I am glad to be able to issue this evidence for a gentleman who belongs to the Protestant community.[3]

On 24 March 1950 Schulenburg received a similar letter written on his behalf from the head of Krefeld's Protestant Church stating that 'Yes, we can attest that if Herr Schulenburg had not held the position he had held that we would have had to face many difficulties from which we remained spared. In those days, we often feared that they would transfer him to another [Gestapo] post because of his conduct'.[4] Both prior to and after this letter Schulenburg received character references from a considerable number of other Krefelders who were held in high regard, like that of the city's mayor in May 1949 that called him a 'humane and blameless man' who was also 'upstanding and modest'.[5]

With character references like these, Richard Schulenburg was able to return to civilian life after the war and in the 1950s to receive his full police pension with his 12 plus years of Gestapo service included without ever having to suffer any punishment for his crucial role in the persecution, deportation, and murder of

---

[3]　Cited in Eric A. Johnson, *Nazi Terror: The Gestapo, Jews, and Ordinary Germans* (New York: Basic Books, 1999) p. 31.

[4]　Ibid, p. 473.

[5]　Ibid.

Illustration 8.1   **Krefeld Gestapo Jewish Desk Head (circa 1936).**

hundreds of Krefeld Jews and his leadership position in the functioning of the Krefeld Gestapo organisation generally. Incredible as it seems, his was a rather typical case for a Gestapo officer in post-war Germany. In the course of my research for a book I published in 1999 on the subject of terror in the Third Reich, I investigated the backgrounds and fates of scores of Gestapo officers of all ranks from Krefeld and other German cities and never came across a single former Gestapo officer who did not receive similar glowing references from respected German citizens saying that they were 'humane' and 'fair' and 'upstanding' and 'just' and the like.

Did these *Persilscheine* tell the truth about these Gestapo officers? As I argued at length in my book, the answer most definitely is no. But that does not mean that some or even many of the character references were not meant in earnest by those who formulated them. There are many reasons for this. Among them are that Gestapo officers were in a position of power and authority that made it possible for them to do many favours for people and those who had received such favours were understandably thankful for them. But another important reason that I want to address in this essay is that, by their own admission, most ordinary German citizens had not lived in fear and dread during the years of the Third Reich and many believed that the Gestapo served primarily to protect them from harm and to rid their country of people they considered undesirable. Indeed, a major part of the powerful appeal of Nazism for ordinary German citizens is that it provided a strong sense of order and security while at the same time allowing considerable latitude for ordinary citizens to vent their frustrations without undue worry that they might be forced to suffer persecution or prosecution like the declared enemies of the Nazi regime.

In my book *Nazi Terror* I made this argument by relying primarily on the archival record as revealed in Gestapo case files, court records, and other written documents pertaining to the workings of the Gestapo and the everyday lives of German citizens in three Rhineland communities: the cities of Cologne and Krefeld, and the small town of Bergheim. Here I will treat quite different types of evidence: oral-history interviews and written surveys I and my German colleague Karl-Heinz Reuband have conducted over the last decade with German citizens from nearly all corners of the country who had spent important parts of their lives in Hitler's Germany. I will begin with a brief discussion of two interviews that I consider to be representative of the nearly 200 in-depth interviews that we conducted and then I will turn to an analysis of some of the most pertinent findings of our written surveys with several thousand respondents.

Interviews with Reinhart Koselleck and Hubert Lintz

On 8 December 1998 I interviewed the renowned German historian Reinhart Koselleck in a public forum at the Netherlands Institute for Advanced Study.[6] Two and a half years later, I interviewed an expatriate German physicist named Hubert Lintz in the privacy of his American home outside Ann Arbor, Michigan. Both interviews lasted for about one and a half hours and were recorded on audio tape.

Born in 1923 and spending his childhood in the largely Protestant city of Kassel in central Germany, Koselleck hailed from a highly educated, upper-middle-class family with moderate to liberal political views that had not originally supported Hitler and the Nazi Party. Reaching his early twenties before the end of the Third Reich, Koselleck had spent several years in the Hitler Youth and later had served as soldier in the German army before being taken prisoner near the end of the war by the Soviets. Five years younger than Koselleck, raised in the predominantly Catholic Rhineland city of Cologne, and a child of economically-strapped workers and salespeople that strongly supported the Nazi movement (his father joined the Nazi Party in 1933 and eventually rose through the ranks to become a mid-level Party functionary, *Ortsgruppenleiter*), Lintz had joined the Hitler Youth at the age of seven and risen to be a Hitler Youth Leader by the age of 17 at the war's end.

Although these two men are of somewhat different ages, come from different parts of Germany, have family backgrounds that differ in social status and political leaning, and have lived the balance of their adult lives in two different countries, the answers they gave to questions I asked them about everyday life, popular support for Hitler and the Nazi regime, and the nature of terror in the Third Reich bore marked similarity, just as they did to the answers given by numerous other former citizens of Nazi Germany from a wide variety of backgrounds that I and my associates have interviewed over the past several years. Thus, for example, both men divulged candidly that they had been deeply impressed by Hitler in their youth and had led what they had considered to be quite normal and even happy lives during most of the years of Nazi Germany. This notwithstanding, they both admitted that they had possessed some knowledge about the persecution and eventual murder of the Jews and other Nazi crimes against humanity and that members of their own family had occasionally committed various small infractions against the laws of the Reich, such as listening to illegal BBC broadcasts during the war. Nevertheless, neither of them had believed that they personally had any reason to fear the Nazi terror apparatus, had not felt that they had been spied upon,

---

[6]   The transcript of the Koselleck interview has subsequently been published in English under the title of 'Recollections of the Third Reich: Interview with Reinhart Koselleck', *NIAS Newsletter*, 22 (1999) pp. 5–16, and in a somewhat abbreviated Dutch translation: 'Duitsers onder de nazi-terreur', *Historisch Nieuwsblad*, 1 (February 2000) pp. 40–45.

were not encouraged to spy upon others, and had held little fear of denunciations from the civilian population around them.

As Hubert Lintz explained in detail: 'In my ten years as a member of the Hitler Youth, I never heard anybody suggest that you spy on your parents or that you spy on anybody else ... I don't know anybody in my environment who ever finked on [denounced] somebody ... [Denunciations] weren't even talked about. It was so taboo, you didn't do that'. When I asked him if he had perceived that ordinary Germans had lived in a climate of fear in Nazi Germany, he replied abruptly, 'No, absolutely not'. He then went on to explain that he and his family had lived for many years in a small apartment building with a Gestapo officer as a neighbour, whom he described as 'very friendly. He was very friendly to me — to everybody'.

Although Koselleck, on the other hand, said that his own father had once been arrested and held prisoner for a while by the SA in 1933 and that his own mentally ill aunt had been killed in the Nazi's euthanasia programme, he too stated firmly that he himself had also not lived in fear of the Gestapo or the police even though he had known from quite early on about the existence of concentration camps. Discussing some jokes he had heard about Dachau concentration camp while he had lived for a time in nearby Munich before the war, he explained: 'We thought that Dachau was a place for criminals'. In an article entitled 'Germans under Nazi Terror', based on the Dutch translation of my interview with him that was published in the February 2000 issue of a Dutch popular history magazine, this comment was placed prominently in half-inch-high red letters as the lead-in to the article.

Taken, rather unfortunately, out of context for reasons of drawing interest to the interview as it was, this quote does indeed express what great numbers of ordinary Germans thought about the Gestapo and Nazi terror while they lived in Nazi Germany. They knew that they had been loyal to the regime even if they had occasionally transgressed against it and that the regime and its policing organs had drawn sharp distinctions between the specified minorities that constituted targeted enemies and the overwhelming majority of German citizens. The written surveys that Karl-Heinz Reuband and I have conducted with thousands of German citizens who had experienced the Third Reich at first hand like Reinhart Koselleck and Hubert Lintz provide more systematic evidence to support this argument.

Survey evidence

Karl-Heinz Reuband, who is a professor of sociology at the University of Düsseldorf and an expert in opinion research, and I began our project of surveying elderly German citizens about their everyday lives in the Third Reich and their experiences with and observations about the functioning of Nazi terror in a pilot survey we administered in the fall of 1993 to a random sample of 300 Cologne citizens born in or before 1928. After we had completed and analysed the results of this pilot survey in which 188 people responded, we made some limited revisions in our survey questionnaire for purposes of accuracy and clarity and mailed it out a year later in the fall of 1994 to a random sample of 3,000 Cologne citizens and an additional 1,500 Krefeld citizens. Three years later in 1997 we conducted a similar survey with a random sample of 1,500 elderly citizens of Dresden and in 2000 we mailed out an additional 2,000 questionnaires to elderly residents of Berlin. Tables 8.1 through 8.4 summarise a preliminary analysis of these four surveys.

We chose these four cities because we thought they represented a broad cross section of the German population. Thus they involve German citizens coming from both western and eastern parts of Germany and from communities with different religious majority populations and communities with different types of economic bases. It should also be mentioned that although about one half of the population of each of these cities had lived their lives during the period of Nazi Germany in the cities that we included in our surveys, the other half had lived in communities spread geographically across the entire landscape of what before 1945 had constituted Nazi Germany.

When we take allowance for the people who could not have answered the questionnaires because they were either already dead when we mailed them out or were too ill to respond, we calculate that there was a response rate of about 50 per cent for each city. Also one should mention that of the 938 people from Cologne, 404 from Krefeld, 678 from Dresden, and 923 from Berlin who responded to our surveys, the majority in all but Berlin were women (at a rate of about 60 per cent females to 40 per cent males). The reason that our Berlin respondents varied from this with 56 per cent male and 44 per cent female respondents is that in this survey we decided to send out our questionnaires to a population that was equally divided along gender lines, whereas in the other three cities we sent out our questionnaires to a truly random sample of the population, which, for well understood reasons, contained larger numbers of women than men. As the Berlin survey shows (see Table 8.1), the response rate among men was somewhat higher than that of women, thus accounting for the higher proportion of men that responded in that city. Finally, in terms of the background variables provided in Table 8.1, it is to be noted that the median age of the respondents was similar in all four cities with the average person who answered the questionnaires born around 1920. This means that roughly half of the respondents were in their mid-twenties or older when the Third Reich came to the end, but that the other half varied in age between 17 and 25 in 1945. Although the ages of these people did account for some differences and we will certainly control for these when we publish our findings in a forthcoming

Table 8.1 Background variables of respondents

	Cologne	Krefeld	Dresden	Berlin
1. Number of Cases	938	404	678	923
2. Year of Survey	1994	1994	1997	2000
3. Median Birth Year	1920	1920	1921	1922
4. Gender				
% Male	38	41	38	56
% Female	62	59	62	44
5. Religion				
% Protestant	39	40	79	80
% Catholic	61	60	9	12
% None or Other	0	0	12	8

Table 8.2 Involvement in illegal activity by respondents (in %)

	Cologne	Krefeld	Dresden	Berlin
1. Illegal youth group	5	6	2	4
2. Foreign Radio Broadcasts during the War	41	43	36	50
3. Criticised Hitler	13	14	13	11
4. Criticised Nazis	19	19	15	16
5. Distributed Anti-Nazi Flyers	3	3	2	2
6. Helped Nazi Victims	11	13	10	11
7. Told Illegal Jokes	30	32	22	32
8. Active Resistance	1 (11 people)	1 (2 people)	1 (5 people)	1 (8 people)
9. Other	0	1	2	4
10. None of the Above	33	32	39	43

Table 8.3 Fear of arrest in Third Reich among respondents (in %)

	Cologne	Krefeld	Dresden	Berlin
1. Constant	5	6	5	3
2. Occasional	19	17	19	13
3. Don't remember/ Other	0	0	3	6
4. None	76	76	73	78

Table 8.4 Arrested or interrogated by Gestapo or police in Third Reich (in %)

	Cologne	Krefeld	Dresden	Berlin
A. Respondents Themselves				
1. Yes	3 (25 people)	1 (5 people)	1 (5 people)	1 (12 people)
2. No	97	99	99	99
B. Family Members of Respondents				
1. Yes	8	7	8	8
2. No	92	93	92	92

book on the subject,[7] we do believe that all of these people were old enough when they had lived in Nazi Germany to be able to provide meaningful answers to the questions we asked of them.

Of main interest to the argument of this essay, however, are the results of our surveys displayed in Tables 8.2, 8.3, and 8.4. In the first of these tables we report on the answers that the respondents in the four cities gave to a battery of questions we asked about their own personal involvement in illegal activities during the Third Reich. Here and in the other two tables the answers the respondents gave in the different cities are strikingly consistent. As one notes in the bottom of Table 8.2 under number 10, only a minority of the respondents listed that they had never taken part in illegal activity in Nazi Germany. Thus, even though it could theoretically have landed them in jail or concentration camp or possibly cost them

---

[7]   Eric A. Johnson and Karl-Heinz Reuband, *What We Knew: Everyday Life, Terror, and Mass Murder in the Third Reich — an Oral History* (New York: Basic Books, 2004).

their lives, most people had trespassed against Nazi laws at one time or another. Nearly one half of the respondents in each city answered, for example, that they had listened to outlawed foreign radio broadcasts like those of the BBC during the war years and nearly one-third had told illegal jokes critical of the Nazi regime, Nazi leaders, or Nazi policies. Smaller but still significant numbers of people had been members of illegal youth groups like the primarily working-class Edelweiss Pirates or the usually middle-class swing youth, or had provided aid and support to targeted enemies of the regime like, above all, Jews. But it is important to stress that very few of the survey participants considered that these or any other activities they had been involved in at any time had constituted active resistance against the Nazi regime. Therefore, only one per cent of the participants in each of the cities responded that they had taken part in what they themselves defined as 'active resistance' against the regime.

Supporting the argument that the Gestapo and the other policing organs of Nazi Germany distinguished between true enemies of the regime and generally loyal citizens who sometimes violated Nazi laws is the evidence presented in Tables 8.3 and 8.4. In Table 8.3 one finds answers to a question we asked about people's fear of arrest by the Gestapo or the Nazi police. Even though the majority of the participants had answered that they had sometimes acted illegally, only a small minority responded that they had ever feared being discovered and arrested. Roughly three-quarters of the participants responded that they had held absolutely no fear whatsoever of being arrested in Nazi Germany and the great majority of those who had ever had any fear at all answered that they had only had occasional fear of arrest, for only about five per cent of the people in each city answered that they had held constant fear of arrest, and here it must be remembered that many of these people had come from communist or socialist backgrounds or were members of other types of persecuted minority populations.

In Table 8.4 one notes that it indeed makes sense that so few people had harboured fear of arrest in Nazi Germany because only a very small minority of the populations of these cities (a minority even smaller than of those who had answered that they had lived in constant fear of arrest) answered that they had ever been actually arrested or even interrogated for wrongdoing at any time during the years of Nazi Germany. In three of the four cities, only one per cent of the participants had ever been arrested or even interrogated at any time, and in Cologne only three per cent (representing a total of a mere 25 out of the 938 survey respondents of that city) answered that this had happened to them.

In sum, therefore, our surveys and oral-history interviews point to a German population that had entirely different perceptions of and experiences with the Gestapo and other Nazi policing organs than those of Jews and other targeted minorities in the Third Reich. In the view of most Germans, the Gestapo was certainly not all knowing, all powerful, and out to get them. That large numbers of Germans believed that the Gestapo could even be counted on to be quite understanding in their own personal cases is supported by a great deal of evidence. Some, like Hubert Lintz, even thought they knew 'friendly' Gestapo officers. Many, probably most, actually did believe that 'Dachau was for criminals' and certainly not for them.

Chapter Nine

'Hard-Headed, Hard-Bitten, Hard-Hitting and Courageous Men of Innate Detective Ability …' From Criminal Investigation to Political and Security Policing at End of Empire, 1945–50

Georgina Sinclair

'I was a Police Officer, a CID officer and a Special Branch Officer either or all of which were a normal function in the enforcement of law and order at this time'.[1]

'It is hardly the job of a Police Force to talk in terms of "going on to the offensive." At the same time, I was not alone in thinking that we had been purely defensive for far too long'.[2]

Following the Accra riots in Gold Coast in February 1948 the Governor, Sir Gerald Creasy, wrote to the Colonial Secretary, Arthur Creech Jones, deploring a situation in which he was 'labouring under [the] difficulty of extremely poor intelligence work'.[3] Indeed, the Watson inquiry that emerged from these events was quite clear that the Gold Coast Police needed 'to organise and strengthen' their Intelligence Branch.[4] This should have come as no surprise to the War Office who had in the

---

[1]   This is taken from J.J. O'Sullivan's responses to an aide memoir within the 1982 Oxford Development Records Project 'Law Enforcement in former British-African territories' held at Rhodes House Library, Oxford. O'Sullivan, RHL MSS. Afr. s. 1784, Box VII, f. 12. This manuscript collection contains written contributions and supporting evidence of former police officers who served principally in the police forces of British Colonial Africa. In future, references to these sources will be given as RHL MSS Afr. s. 1784.

[2]   Bernard Fergusson, *The Trumpet in the Hall, 1930–1958* (London: Collins, 1970) p. 221.

[3]   Public Record Office/National Archives, London (hereafter NA) CO 96/795/6 Creasy to Creech Jones, telegram, 5 March 1948.

[4]   *Report of the Commission of Enquiry into Disturbances in the Gold Coast* (Watson

previous year sent the Chief of the Imperial General Staff, Field Marshal Montgomery, on a tour of Africa to report on the state of British defence and security. Montgomery had concluded that 'at present the civil intelligence system is in very poor shape ... a well organised Communist movement amongst the Africans could make our position very unpleasant.[5] Regarding intelligence as predominantly a civil, rather than a military matter, the War Office wrote to the Colonial Office urging 'an improvement in the local intelligence services so as to ensure an early warning ... of widespread trouble'.[6] These suggestions would appear to have been largely ignored until after the Gold Coast riots. By the end of 1948, the British had hastily withdrawn from Palestine. In Malaya the declaration of an emergency signalled the start of a bitter twelve-year-long struggle against the Malayan Communists, which overlapped with the Korean War. The early 1950s brought rioting and public disturbances to much of British Colonial Africa shattering any illusion there might have been of post-war stability. Britain had entered its post-war era of decolonisation.

In their introduction to *Policing and Decolonisation*, David Anderson and David Killingray noted that the policing of end of empire took place within the wider concerns of post-war British security and strategy.[7] British foreign policy concerns underpinned a colony's security profile. Ironically it was as colonial rule was crumbling that Britain turned its attention to colonial development, addressing the need for reform programmes, which extended to the Colonial Police Service[8] and its intelligence systems. Crucially, these reforms would entail the export of the *British* policing model as a final gesture of paternalistic goodwill. This, it was hoped, would prepare the police forces for their future role as independent member states of the expanding British Commonwealth. Up until this period little consideration had been given to a concerted central policy from Whitehall regarding police organisation and its role within the colonial state.

Following a posting to the Uganda Police in the late 1930s, Christopher Harwich wrote of how 'police work at Entebbe could not be described as either exciting or arduous. Apart from the almost routine murders, usually reported by the aggressor, the only other crime of consequence was petty larceny ...'.[9] Indeed,

---

Commission) (London, 1948), para. 7.

[5]   NA, WO 216/675, Montgomery, 'Tour in Africa Nov./Dec. 1947', Memo, 19 December 1947, paras. 12 and 51.

[6]   NA, CO 537/2760/2, Major-General Gerald Templer, WO to Andrew Cohen, CO, 27 November 1947.

[7]   David Anderson and David Killingray, eds, *Policing and Decolonisation: Politics, Nationalism and the Police, 1917–65* (Manchester University Press, 1992) p. 14.

[8]   The Colonial Police Service was set up in 1936 following the 1930 creation of the Colonial Service.

[9]   Christopher Harwich, *Red Dust* (London: Vincent Stuart, 1961) p. 7.

when considering the role of colonial policing up until the Second World War, there would appear to have been no great need for a separate Special Branch unit. Whilst the setting up of a Criminal Investigation Department (CID) often coincided with the creation of a colonial constabulary, these units did not evolve into separate Special Branches until a much later stage. Overall the regular police and CID provided sufficient resources to deal with crime and internal security. In some territories, notably within the rural areas of British Colonial Africa, the police were ably assisted in their intelligence gathering duties by the native authority or tribal police. The need for greater political policing came principally in the aftermath of the Second World War as the colonies jostled for independence with vigorous displays of public unrest. It was a time when all colonies were faced with peculiar law-enforcement problems arising from societies caught in transitional periods.

The sweep of colonial territories prevents a detailed analysis of individual territories. This essay will, therefore, focus essentially upon the police forces of late British Colonial Africa, whilst making more general comments from a Colonial Office perspective. Details surrounding the development of police intelligence systems during this period are still partially shrouded owing to the dearth of official documents available. Many of the relevant papers were destroyed at independence, and those that survive are not always open for public scrutiny. To complement official documents, further information has been drawn from the papers and oral testimonies of former colonial policemen.

Early colonial police intelligence systems

Police intelligence systems have typically been installed to prevent threats to national security through major outbreaks of public disorder, and to identify political 'dissenters' and political 'deviance'. The latter can loosely be defined as *political policing*, an important function of policing the modern state.[10] The traditions and history of the Colonial Police Service stemmed from its military character, the gazetted ranks comprising 'Europeans' and the rank and file being made up of local people. It was formed in the first instance to protect the colonial administration and provide an efficient means of enforcing government policy. Colonial policing was in essence the strong right arm of government and generally considered its eyes and ears, whilst remaining subordinate rather than complementary to the entire political process. Despite this fact, political policing colonial-style was developed at a slower pace than in Britain through the establishment and then the strengthening of Special Branch units.

---

[10]   Jean-Paul Brodeur, 'High Policing and Low Policing: Remarks about the Policing of Political Activities', *Social Problems*, 30 (1983) p. 513.

The most obvious precedent for these intelligence units was the Metropolitan Police Special Branch, which came about in embryonic form in 1881[11] and was formally established in January 1887. Its creation was sparked principally by the Fenian bombing campaigns of 1881–85. With the cessation of bombings, Special Branch was retained for use in monitoring Irish political groups, anarchists, Indian students and other 'aliens'.[12] Within the British Empire it was the Indian Police that followed suit, with their early central and provincial 'Special Branches' created in 1887–88 following increasing communal tension towards colonial rule.[13] Lord Dufferin's police reforms in India at this time made use of the London experiences of combating the Irish Dynamiters. Edward Jenkinson, the Royal Irish Constabulary spymaster, had been despatched to the Met in 1885 to assist the fledgling Special Branch. Correspondence between Jenkinson and the Home Secretary, Sir Richard Cross, provided the guidelines under which the Indian police would operate their intelligence systems in the future.[14] The Irish Constabulary developed within Ireland's 'quasi colonial' niche, mirrored the environment found throughout the Empire, with intelligence gathering remaining a fundamental part of its work.[15]

CID units, operating prior to 1939, were primarily concerned with serious crime and internal security matters that ranged from the investigation of smuggling to the confiscation of seditious literature. Even then, they were smallish outfits, often headed by one officer of gazetted rank. In Uganda, for example, CID was set up in 1906 but was not officially recognised as a separate unit until 1923. Thereafter, its activities focused primarily upon the work of the Criminal Record Office and the Finger Print Bureau at police headquarters under the command of one gazetted officer.[16] The CID branch of the Nigeria Police Force was set up as late as 1936.[17] (It had been loosely based upon a unit known as the Eastern and

---

[11]   Initially this was the 'embryo political arm' of Metropolitan Police CID. Bernard Porter, *The Origins of the Vigilant State: The London Metropolitan Police Special Branch before the First World War* (London: Weidenfeld & Nicolson, 1987) p. 42.

[12]   Tony Bunyan, *The History and Practice of the Political Police in Britain* (London: Quartet Books, 1977) pp. 104–5.

[13]   David Arnold, *Police Power and Colonial Rule, Madras 1859–1947* (Oxford University Press, 1986) pp. 186–87.

[14]   R.J. Popplewell, *Intelligence and Imperial Defence; British Intelligence and the Defence of the Indian Empire 1904–24* (London: Frank Cass, 1995) pp. 46–47.

[15]   W.J. Lowe and E.L. Malcolm, 'The Domestication of the Royal Irish Constabulary, 1836–1922', *Journal of Irish Economic and Social History*, XIX (1992) p. 29.

[16]   RHL MSS. Afr. s. 1784, Box XVIII, f.49, Anderson. G.A. Anderson served in the Met and then in the Uganda Police CID from 1950–64.

[17]   The Nigeria Police (NPF) was formed on 27 February 1930 following the unification of the Northern and Southern Forces of the 1917 Ordinance. Quite differently to other colonial territories, the NPF was headed by an Inspector-General, with two Assistant

Western Preventative Service established in 1931 with the sole task of preventing smuggling.)[18] When Alan Saunders was transferred from Palestine as Commissioner of the Nigeria Police, he increased the size of CID through a network of district branches. Saunders also modernised the criminal record system by adapting the Palestine model, which remained the basic system in use up until independence.[19] John Coles, who had also served in the Palestine Police, recalled that in the Gold Coast it was deemed that 'no internal security problems existed prior to 1948 ... the disparate nature of the territorial and tribal composition of the country and particularly the constitutional differences made any countrywide rising improbable ... [Besides] the chiefs of the Gold Coast Colony proper ... had, after all invited British rule in 1844 ...'.[20]

Throughout the Empire Provincial and District Commissioners shouldered much of the responsibility for supplying central government with the intelligence they needed. In British Colonial Africa, this would be supplemented by members of the native or tribal police. This term covered the policing practice of constables empowered to enforce local by-laws and traditional practices. The size of these forces varied as much as their general efficiency and depended upon the degree of supervision exercised by the district commissioner and the extent to which the regular police were prepared to assist in training. Common offences that took place in rural areas, such as burglary, housebreaking, theft and assaults, were typically tried in African courts as contraventions of native law and custom. The native authority or tribal police also derived authority from the local chiefs, and carried out such law and order duties as serving summonses and making arrests. In terms of gathering intelligence for the colonial administration, these local policemen possessed greater knowledge of the local people, tribal customs, traditions and dialects than the regular police. Courtney Gidley, former Commissioner of the Nigeria Police, commented: 'it seemed to me that there was no need for a Special

---

Inspector-Generals for the North and South regions respectively. In addition, a Commissioner was appointed for each of the 17 Provinces. In 1938 these titles were changed and the Inspector-General became Commissioner, Commissioners became Superintendents and so on. By the Second World War the NPF numbered some 5000 officers. In the north and west of the country, the NPF was assisted by the local Native Administration/Authority Forces (NAP). Typically, the NPF policed the urban areas, including the commercial and government areas, and the NAP the rural areas. W.R. Shirley, *History of the Nigeria Police* (Lagos: Government Printer, 1950) p. 36.

[18] The *Nigeria Police Magazine* in 1938 recorded that the Eastern Preventative Service was concerned with the prevention of tobacco smuggling. Anthony Clayton, *Thin Blue Line; Studies in Law Enforcement in Late Colonial Africa* (Oxford: Oxford Development Records Project, 1985) pp. 34 and 36.

[19] RHL MSS. Afr. s. 1784, Box VII, f. 9. Hodge. J.E.

[20] RHL MSS Afr. s. 1784, Box I, f. 31. Coles, J.F.G. Coles became Acting Deputy Commissioner of the Gold Coast Police from 1956–60.

Branch. We [the regular police] knew everything that was going on from the rank and file. The Native Authority Police passed intelligence on to the District Officers. It seemed to be down to a question of trust between them and us'.[21]

The possibility for change within the existing intelligence systems came with the advent of the Second World War. The influence of the war on many colonies was governed by military considerations. Wartime police intelligence focused not only on internment and increased security threats but also, in some colonies, rising crime. In the Gold Coast, for example, a chronic shortage of consumer goods led to widening corruption and the proliferation of crime, often unchecked by the police.[22] In some instances, new units were established to cope specifically with the registration and internment of aliens. From the available documentary evidence it would appear that some of these 'new' police intelligence units were drawn from existing CID, whilst others were created as new entities. In many colonies, civil intelligence and security units were established to carry out wartime duties alongside the regular police in dealing, for example, with the internment of aliens and the supervision of the prisons. Some colonial police officers even took to describing these units as Special Branch rather than CID, such as Michael Macoun, former Inspector General of the Colonial Police service, who described his posting to Special Branch in Tanganyika in 1939. This had been redesignated under war conditions as the Department of Intelligence and Security.[23] Similarly in Nyasaland a Political Intelligence Bureau was set up and enemy aliens were arrested and interned. At the same time a 'small special force' was raised to guard key installations.[24] In Kenya, the police were expanded to help guard the Northern Frontier territories against the Italian armed forces. Their role was essentially to gather intelligence, act as guides and interpreters, and, on occasion, serve as fighting units.[25]

The Second World War certainly influenced the creation of new police or civil intelligence systems in some colonies. However, by the same token CID units were faced with manpower shortages as officers were either posted to other units or seconded elsewhere for the duration of the war. In Uganda at the outbreak of war, local CID units were shut down due to lack of staff. Indeed, by 1941, an 'insufficiency of the present staff' made any prospect of decentralising CID into

---

[21]   Taken from an interview with Courtney Gidley (Acting Dep. Insp. – Gen. Nigeria Police, rtd., 1942–63), 28 August 2003.

[22]   RHL MSS Afr. s. 1784, Box I, f. 20. Coles, J.F.G.

[23]   M. Macoun, *Wrong Place, Right Time; Policing the End of Empire* (London: The Radcliffe Press, 1996) p. 17.

[24]   Clayton, *Thin Blue Line*, p. 90.

[25]   W. Robert Foran, *The Kenya Police 1887–1960* (London: Robert Hale Limited, 1962) pp. 107–15.

the provinces unfeasible.[26] With some officers being posted away from police headquarters at Kampala, CID officers were being used to undertake 'miscellaneous duties' ... they were having to 'take their hand in traffic duties ... and as patrol officers', despite a reported rise in 'serious and intricate crime'.[27] In Nigeria, CID officers felt that their 'true task of detecting, preventing and suppressing subversive conspiracies and activity' floundered owing to a lack of time to collate and assess intelligence as a result of carrying out other police duties which took precedence.[28] Ian Proud, who served in the Nigeria Police, noted how police duties were 'out of place'. He described some policemen as 'revenue collectors' for 'motor vehicle licensing, testing learner drivers, inspecting vehicles for road-worthiness, weights and measures inspections etc. ... in fact revenue collection seemed to be of greater importance than measures for the prevention and detection of crime'.[29]

A noticeable increase in crime trends continued in the aftermath of the Second World War. This was particularly noted in colonies that had suffered social upheaval throughout enemy occupation or overall food shortages. In some African colonies, the continuing food shortages provoked general unrest and as a result increased crime, whilst in others this was blamed on a rising population within urban areas within both local and European quarters. Within Nigeria the bloody 'Leopard Society' murders that occurred from 1945–48 within Eastern Nigeria resulted in the killings of 196 people. Whilst these murders were perceived as neither political nor as a threat to the legitimacy of British rule, they nonetheless forced the commissioner to create a specific crime unit consisting of four Assistant Superintendents, two Inspectors and 95 rank and file. At the same time, John Hodge, who became Assistant Commissioner of the Nigeria Police, noted that by early 1946 CID headquarters in Lagos had acquired larger premises to accommodate growing fingerprinting and photograph sections. By the end of that year, CID records contained 127 000 fingerprint sets, with an average yearly addition of 16 000. A training team drawn from CID was established to run courses in conjunction with the trainers specialised in 'major' and 'complicated' crime. To boost training, CID officers were sent to Britain to the Detective Training School at Wakefield from the late 1940s.[30] Austin MacDonald, who also served in the Nigeria Police, stated that regional CID units were provided with up-to-date

---

[26]   In fact the Uganda CID was not fully decentralised until 1960 when officers stationed in the districts were given the same powers as those at headquarters. RHL MSS Afr. s. 1784, Box XVIII, f. 116, Anderson.

[27]   RHL MSS Afr. s. 1784, Box XVIII/Appendix E, ff. 29–30. Minutes Meeting Police HQ Kampala, 31 January 1941, Anderson, G.A.

[28]   RHL MSS. Afr. s. 1784, Box VII, f. 9. O'Sullivan.

[29]   RHL MSS. Afr. s. 1784, Box VII, f. 4. Proud.

[30]   RHL MSS. Afr. s. 1784, Box VII, ff. 9–12. Hodge.

equipment in 1945, with investigation squads formed to tackle serious crime outside the capital.[31]

No lessons learned from Palestine?

Despite tentative moves to develop CID in some colonies, the situation faced by many in the aftermath of the Second World War showed how ill-prepared they really were. The serious disturbances that took place in Kampala in Uganda in January 1945 had caught the police unawares and pointed to the lack of a police intelligence system capable of predicting public disorder.[32] This would be mirrored a few years later in Accra. But curiously the British had not drawn on the experiences of the Palestine Police by this stage. In the event, the lessons of Palestine would be transferred by former policemen to other colonies rather than through official channels.

Throughout its relatively brief history the Palestine Police[33] remained an 'armed Force responsible for the internal security of [the] country ... '.[34] During this period, the Palestine Police had placed great reliance on its CID branch for the collection of intelligence. Palestine CID was formed alongside the Palestine Gendarmerie in 1920 under Eugene Quigley. Alongside the setting up of a records system and a fingerprint branch for the collection of criminal intelligence, Quigley acquired a reputation for his development of a political intelligence gathering system that resembled the Metropolitan Police Special Branch. The early use of 'pseudo gangs' possibly stemmed from this period involving CID members penetrating the villages and desert areas of Trans Jordan dressed as Arabs. Their brief was not only to collect intelligence on drug smuggling but also on local politics and security issues.[35] In 1930, Harold Rice took over as head of CID, increasing the number of CID offices in each district to enable a channel of command from headquarters down to district level. Divisional headquarters became responsible for new departments, which included a specific 'political section'. District CID branches mirrored this, adding in newer sections that included immigration and emigration work. By the end of that year, the number of CID officers had risen from 30 to 52. In increasing its duties Rice was carving out a new role for CID. Alongside the investigation of crime, CID was responsible for

[31] RHL MSS. Afr. S. 1784, Box VII, f. 4. Macdonald, A.E.

[32] RHL MSS. Afr. S. 1784, Box VIII, f. 7. Akker, M.K. Akker served in the Kenya Police from 1954–65 and became Assistant Commissioner.

[33] Palestine Gendarmerie 1920–26, Palestine Police 1926–48.

[34] NA, CO 733/174/1. A.S. Mavrogordato (then Inspector General of the Palestine Police) to Chief Secretary, Enclosure II, 1 June 1929.

[35] Edward Horne, *A Job Well Done; A History of the Palestine Police Force 1920–1948* (Leigh-on-Sea: The Anchor Press, 1982) pp. 262 and 465.

intelligence on all subversive organisations, including communists. In terms of the Palestine's external security, CID was to liaise with the police forces of the Middle East, Egypt, Cyprus and India, and Scotland Yard.[36] Following the 1936 Arab Revolt, CID expanded its District Investigation Branches still further to encompass a Jewish Affairs section to gather intelligence on Hagana (a 'self defence' organistion, Hagana meaning defence) and its breakaway groups such as Irgun Zvai Leumi (meaning National Military Organisation) as the so-called 'Jewish Troubles' took hold.

A decade later, William Moffat, a Royal Ulster Constabulary Inspector, accompanied Sir Charles Tegart on his 1946 mission to Palestine to recommend CID reforms (Moffat had, in fact, been in charge of the Special Crime Squad in Northern Ireland for some years).[37] In his report, Moffat argued 'to combat terrorism, reliance must be placed chiefly on the CID'. To this end it was vital that the 'Political Branch' of CID outweighed the 'Non Political Branch' in terms of its size, calibre of officers recruited and allowances on 'the generous side'.[38] Moffat's most important recommendation was that CID should be an elite branch of the police. This would be reflected in the high quality of officers recruited and their length of stay within the force. In effect, Moffat was recommending that Palestine CID, for the short remainder of their existence, encompass both CID and Special Branch duties. CID would, for example, remain responsible for 'Illegal Organisations' and anti-terrorist duties.[39]

It was then that the development of police political and security intelligence in Palestine took a strange turn as terrorist attacks intensified and the situation worsened. Colonel Nicol Gray, who became Inspector-General in March 1946, developed police undercover units. Gray, an ex-marine, found the wartime successes of new organisations such as the Special Air Service (SAS) and the Special Operations Executive (SOE) highly appealing.

Gray appointed Brigadier Bernard Fergusson, who had served in Burma, as Assistant Inspector General to form these units, under the banner of the Palestine Police, and to be responsible for their training and organisation. Early in 1947, Fergusson was dispatched to London to recruit leaders for these so-called squads. He chose two of his former pupils from his instructor days at Sandhurst, Roy Farran and Alastair McGregor. Both men had served in the embryonic SAS.[40] The

---

[36]   Horne, *Job Well Done*, p. 470.

[37]   NA, CO 537/3847/8, Wickham to Cunningham, 20 August 1946.

[38]   NA, CO 537/2269/54, W. Moffat, 'Criminal Investigation Department Report', 1946.

[39]   RHL MSS. Afr. s. 1784, Box XVII, f. 3. O'Sullivan, J.J.

[40]   Gerald J. Green (ex Palestine Police) to Edward Horne, 10 Aug. 1998, Horne, Private Papers. See also Roy Farran, *Winged Dagger: Adventures on Special Service* (London: Collins, 1948) a memoir of Farran's wartime service in SAS.

squads themselves comprised members of the Palestine Police, the British army and air force.[41] From Spring 1947, Farran's squad operated in the Jaffa-Tel Aviv area and McGregor's in the Jerusalem area with great success.[42] Fergusson had intended that these former 'specially trained' servicemen would train the police in modern weaponry and survival techniques as practised by commando troops, alongside their other duties. Yet aside from this there is evidence that, despite repeated warnings from Gray, these squads operated outside the law. Edward Horne noted that they were 'to disappear into the Jewish areas ... the main object being to flush out terrorist nests and then either arrest or shoot to kill'. He points out that they were, *theoretically*, accountable to the law like any other police officer.[43] In reality, however, the squads had operational free rein. Farran noted that he had 'to all intents and purposes [been given] a *carte blanche* (sic) ... a free hand for us against terror when all others were so closely hobbled!' Using the unorthodox 'Grant-Taylor methods' of close quarter combat, the squads were encouraged to tackle the Jewish underground movements Irgun Zvai Leumi and the Stern Gang. Counter-terrorism and intelligence were seen as entirely the domain of the police, the army being used essentially for guard duty and assistance with cordons and curfews.[44]

In the event darker aspects of their work emerged with the so-called 'Farran Affair' and his implication in the murder of Alexander Rubowitz, a member of *Lehi* (acronym for 'Fighters for the Freedom of Israel') who vanished in 1947. As a result of the ensuing scandal, the squads were ordered to stand down and all operations in progress were suspended. Fergusson was forced to resign his police commission,[45] In the event, Farran was found not guilty of murder and the death of Rubowitz remained unproven.[46]

On disbandment of the Palestine Police in June 1948, a number of ex-CID officers were posted to other colonial territories taking their experience with them. Rice, for example, brought his experiences of dealing with the Arab Revolt to the Kenya Police. This was also true of Kenneth Haddingham who later was

---

[41]   Known by the Palestine Police as 'Special' or 'Snatch' Squads, the following members of the Palestine Police were known members: Carson, Carter, Cade, B. O'Dell, W. Pilkington, Birch, O'Regan, Tompkins, R. Long, Clarke, Murphy, Burke, E.C. Nickels, Reilly, W. Abraham, J. Faulkner and E. Barlow. These squads also comprised five former members of the SAS, two former Commandos, one former 'Cavalry Sergeant' and one former RAF pilot. Edward Horne, 'Ferguson's Special Squads 1947', Palestine Police Data Sheets, p. 93, Horne, *Private Papers*.

[42]   Fergusson, *Trumpet in the Hall*, p. 227.

[43]   Horne, *Job Well Done*, p. 565.

[44]   Farran, *Winged Dagger*, pp. 348–51.

[45]   Fergusson, *Trumpet in the Hall*, p. 228.

[46]   *Palestine Post*, 3 October 1947.

responsible for police CID operations in Nairobi. A number of former Palestine policemen were highly influential within both CID and Special Branch of the Kenya Police with others becoming scenes of crime officers, photographic and fingerprint officers and forensic specialists.[47] John Fforde, who joined the Palestine Police in 1933 rose to become deputy Inspector General by 1946 and head of CID. He then went on to the post of Commissioner of the Sierra Leone and then Northern Rhodesia Police forces. As commissioner he used his Palestine experiences to bring change and modernisation not only to the CID branches but also to the entire force. He believed that Palestine was a valuable training ground for the colonial police, in general, as well as providing many senior and experienced officers in dealing with colonial unrest.[48] Significantly, events in Palestine during the 1930s and the build-up to the British withdrawal in 1948 did not trigger any significant changes to the police intelligence systems in other colonies. It took a combination of events that occurred that year threatening British colonial security to bring this issue to the fore.

The 1948 watershed

1948 was the watershed in terms of Colonial Office attitudes towards colonial policing. This brought revived attempts to reform and standardise the Colonial Police Service. Yet it appears to have been a question of too little and too late. The majority of police forces had suffered from a lack of reform and modernisation by this period, brought about by the pressures and financial consequences of the Second World War. This included intelligence systems.

War Office recommendations to the Colonial Office in 1948 proposed that intelligence systems should be in place to provide adequate warning of public disturbances. Andrew Cohen, Assistant Under-Secretary of State with responsibility for Africa, requested regular political intelligence reports to view 'the progress of political development ... the growth of nationalist movements ... because of the very much greater interest in the Colonies now existing both in this country and internationally'. At that time, Cohen noted that the *African Affairs Fortnightly Review* from Uganda summarising intelligence matters, was the 'only one we receive'.[49] Cohen asked Colonial Governors to make distinctions between

---

[47]   Taken from an interview with Derek Franklin (Kenya Police, Bahrain State Police, Lesotho Police, Botswana Police, Deputy Head SB, Sen. Sup., rtd., 1953–81), 12 October 2001.

[48]   RHL, MSS Afr. S. 1784, Box XV, f. 22. Fforde, J.P.I.

[49]   The events that took place in Uganda in January 1945 had taken both the government and the police 'completely by surprise'. They were 'not in possession of any

political as compared to *security* reports. The police would provide political intelligence summaries that would include the 'general political situation … that is nationalist movements, tribal relations, activities of local societies, race relations, the attitude of the press and public to government policy and influential personalities'. The section dealing with external matters would consider communist activities and relations with neighbouring territories.[50] The Colonial Office would then prepare a synthesis of the material giving 'a really good birdseye view of political trends in the colonies'. The real change stemming from this proposal was that the Colonial Office was now in direct receipt of intelligence summaries rather than relying on other intelligence channels.[51] Relevant information concerning communist activities within the colonies would be passed on to the Foreign Office who viewed the earlier Gold Coast disturbances as a clear signal that an 'overhaul of the security and intelligence arrangements' was needed within the colonies.[52] This change in circumstances underlined the importance of the police in terms of their intelligence gathering duties.

Indeed, the following year, Henry Gurney, High Commissioner in Malaya, pointed to this whilst noting that 'good police work, as is well known, demands an intimate knowledge of individuals and of everything that goes on'.[53] Gurney, along with many Colonial Governors, believed in the police taking more active frontline role, which included intelligence gathering, considering that the 'opposition' would have more to fear from the police than from the army. 'The Police are the only force possessing the information and intelligence necessary for the conduct of an underground war', he wrote. 'An effectively trained Police Force takes a longer time than the formation, say, of a battalion of infantry and is not something that can be left to a late state … [Besides] without information the large sums spent on the police and troops will be useless'.[54] With the ongoing emergency in Malaya some 200 Chinese detectives were brought in on the advice of an 'expert' from Scotland Yard advising on all aspects of police intelligence work.[55]

But clearly reinforcement was needed in *all* territories to ensure that adequate police intelligence was provided. An immediate solution was the despatch of

---

information which would suggest the possibility of the disturbances…' *Report of the Commission of Inquiry into the Disturbances which occurred in Uganda during January 1945* (Entebbe, 1945) para. 28. This contributed to the need for a 'Fortnightly Review'.

[50]   NA, CO 537/2686/1, Cohen to all Governors in Africa, Secret despatch 15 March 1948.

[51]   NA, CO 537/2677, Colonial Political Intelligence Summaries 1948, Minutes.

[52]   NA, CO 537/2760, Colonial Political Intelligence Summaries 1948, Minutes.

[53]   NA, DEFE 11/33/297, Gurney to Malcolm MacDonald, Colonial Secretary, 11 April 1949.

[54]   NA, DEFE 11/33/2, Gurney to Arthur Creech Jones, 30 May 1949.

[55]   NA, DEFE 11/33/169, Report on the Malayan Police Force, July 1949.

Alexander Kellar, head of MI5's E Branch, to West Africa to offer assistance.[56] On his return, Kellar recommended the permanent posting of an MI5 officer 'to provide ginger' to the local police intelligence services. The Colonial Office felt that this measure would offer some solution.[57] MI5 officers were subsequently posted to the West, Central and East African regions and assisted in the development of Special Branches and their liaison with MI5 in London. Many have been described as colourful and peripatetic characters collecting intelligence within their vast territories in whatever manner they saw fit.

From this time, monthly intelligence reports were sent from each and every colony. Until the expansion of Special Branches, they were often prepared by CID or Defence Security Officers. Typically, intelligence was collated from reports sent in from a district or a high level committee meeting comprising the senior members of the police, army and administration. They were sent from even the smallest such as the Falklands, although it was soon recorded that there was 'no political situation at all' in that area.[58] Cohen's request for monthly reports to be produced across the board highlighted the Colonial Office's increasing interest in political developments throughout the Empire. It also pointed to the Foreign and Colonial Offices' concerns about mounting Cold War tensions.[59] The growing interest in the gathering and delivery of this type of intelligence contributed to the development of Special Branches.

On 5 August 1948, Arthur Creech Jones, then Colonial Secretary, had sent out a circular despatch to all Colonial Governors highlighting his particular concern about the security situation in Malaya and, to a lesser extent, in Gold Coast. He requested that a 'review of the present state of efficiency, in numbers, organisation, equipment, [and the] Security forces' be undertaken. The Governors were asked specifically to outline 'the existence or otherwise of intelligence and special branches'.[60] This was followed by a further despatch on 20 August, stressing once more the need for intelligence organisations but suggesting that they could be based upon the needs of an individual territory.[61]

---

[56]   NA, CO 537/2760, CO Minutes May 1948; NA, CO 537/3653, Sir M. Logan, 'Political Intelligence Report West Africa': Reports on Communism, 14 July 1948.

[57]   NA, CO 537/2760, J.C. Mangan, Minute, 20 May 1948.

[58]   NA, CO 537/2677, Colonial Political Intelligence Summaries, 1948, Minutes.

[59]   'The Secretary of State for Foreign Affairs has called for periodical surveys of communist activities in countries outside the Soviet Union. The Foreign Office has asked that any material in relation to Colonial territories which may be relevant to these reports should be provided every fortnight'. NA, CO 537/3653, Lloyd, CO, to Gormusch, FO, 26 May 1948.

[60]   NA, CO 537/2770, Creech Jones, 'Colonial Police Forces', Circular despatch, 5 August 1948.

[61]   NA, CO 968/727, Creech Jones, Circular despatch to all Governors, 20 August 1948.

Overall, though, the Colonial Office placed greater importance on the need for further standardisation within the Colonial Police than on the development of intelligence systems within individual territories on an *ad hoc* basis. An important measure came on 1 November 1948 with the appointment of William Johnson, a former Inspector of Constabulary as police adviser. Johnson was seconded from the Home Office, with Sir George Abbiss appointed as an assistant adviser, the following month.[62] Johnson's primary task as police adviser was to provide an ongoing review of the 'organisation, methods, administration, discipline and technical efficiency of all Colonial Police Forces'.[63] Secondly, he was expected to advise colonial governments and their Commissioners of Police on methods of improving and modernising their police forces. Thirdly, he was to advise the Colonial Secretary and the colonial governments on all aspects of intelligence gathering and dissemination and, finally, to liaise with British police authorities.

Johnson's appointment was followed by a series of visits throughout the colonies that culminated in a report submitted to the Colonial Secretary on 28 December 1949.[64] In general Johnson concluded that the level of administrative and operational efficiency varied considerably from one territory to another, but 'regarded as a whole it leaves much to be desired'. His report was highly critical of the colonial police. He claimed that the organisation, methods and equipment used were 'completely out of date' when compared to the home forces. Most importantly, Johnson perceived that intelligence and security within these territories was inadequate despite the formal introduction of Special Branch units within some territories. O'Sullivan, serving with the Nigeria Police CID, noted that their 'sparse intelligence coverage had not gone unnoticed' by Johnson. As a result, funds were gradually made available to increase personnel and equipment and provide more training.[65] As a result, Security and Special Branch courses at MI5 and Scotland Yard were set up. By 1950, 31 colonial police officers had attended these courses.[66] Thereafter, as more funds were made available, middle-ranking Special Branch officers, both European and locally recruited, were invited to attend courses in Britain.

Johnson's report was made available to all the colonial constabularies he had visited. Many senior officers were highly critical of its contents and considered that the Inspector-General had little grasp of the realities of colonial policing

---

[62]   NA, CO 537/5440W, C. Johnson, Police Adviser to the Secretary of State for the Colonies, *Report on the Colonial Police Service*, 28 December 1949.

[63]   NA, CO 537/2770, Terms reference for Police Adviser to Colonial Secretary, 1948.

[64]   In 1949, Johnson visited Cyprus, the Gambia, Sierra Leone, Gold Coast, Nigeria, Hong Kong, Singapore, Malaya, North Borneo, Brunei and Sarawak.

[65]   RHL MSS. Afr. s. 1784, Box XVII, f. 28. O'Sullivan, J.J.

[66]   G.J. Morton, *Just the Job: Some Experiences of a Colonial Policeman* (London: Hodder & Stoughton, 1957) p. 273.

particularly in view of the turmoil that some colonies were facing.[67] Overall, 42 territories came under the Colonial Office's wing and, therefore, intelligence networks could hardly be improved overnight. The need for a separate and efficient Special Branch was recognised but would take time to implement in every colony. And those facing colonial unrest would take priority. In Malaya, for example, in 1949, the ongoing emergency situation increased the need to maintain internal security. In a top secret report the colonial government expressed the need for 'an efficient Special Branch which will in fact be the eyes and ears both of the Government and the Police themselves. It must work in the closest co-operation with other intelligence organisations and the intelligence branches of the armed forces in the territory'. However, it was noted that very few colonial Special Branches were proficient in political intelligence gathering 'or can be relied upon to draw the right deductions from it ... the task now demanded of the Special Branch demands a very high standard and a great deal of research and study, but it must be attempted'. Without this, the huge sums spent on building up the police and the army would be squandered.[68]

Essentially the building up of intelligence systems within the colonies depended upon an increase in spending on police bodies to bolster their effectiveness in ensuring order. However, the Colonial Office was asking Colonial Governments to make 'a maximum contribution towards the costs of defence' at a time when they were struggling to resolve post-war financial issues, and to deal with ongoing security issues.[69] Indeed, the 1949 Defence White Paper stressed the need for Britain to assist in internal security arrangements 'as Colonial governments are feeling the draught when it comes to providing finance'. This would prevent political embarrassment and would 'leave no room for doubt [that] we were very willing to help ...'[70]

The creation of Johnson's post coincided with the setting up of separate desks within the Colonial Office to co-ordinate matters of defence, security and intelligence. Colonial officials with police intelligence portfolios collaborated with those working on legal and defence matters. The Home Office and MI5 were

---

[67] Taken from an interview with Neil Hadow (Ceylon, the Gambia, Sierra Leone, Uganda Police, Com., rtd., 1935–58), 10 January 2002 and Ted Eates (Nigeria, the Gambia, Sierra Leone, Hong Kong, Com., rtd., 1946–69), 25 June 2001. 'Johnson had the grace to admit later, when he had been around more, that his early criticisms were due to his ignorance at the very different conditions under which we operated'. RHL, MSS Afr. s. 1784, Box XV, f. 177. Fforde.

[68] NA, DEFE 11/33/148, Malaya Federation, Despatch No. 5.

[69] NA, CO CAB 130/44, 'Financing of Colonial Defence', Cabinet Committee meeting, 10 December 1948.

[70] NA, DEFE 11/413, G.T. Gavalan, Defence to Mr Donaldson, Colonial Office, Minute, 18 January 1949.

consulted whenever needed and provided considerable input into the development of Special Branches in many colonies during the 1940s and 1950s.

The development of colonial special branch units

The difficulty in maintaining law and order and state security in the post-war years was mirrored throughout the British Empire. As to the development of police security and intelligence systems, the influence came predominantly from the changing face of global security with the onset of the Cold War and the crisis of decolonisation. The rapid turn of events sparked widespread nationalism and colonial unrest, prompting a sharp increase in the strength of colonial constabularies and their auxiliary units. In the Gold Coast, for example, the events of 1948 clearly demonstrated that the police force was inadequate both in size and in its intelligence gathering capacity. As such it was increased to a force of some 8,000 men with 560 officers serving within the so-called Emergency Security Organisation. This period also saw the creation of the Fraud Squad, Special Branch, Signals and Traffic Branches and an Immigration Branch within the regular police.[71]

The development of police intelligence systems within the colonies centred upon the partial translation of colonial office policy into working practice. In most cases this necessitated the disentangling of an existing department within CID in order to create a separate unit. These sections of CID had been known as the 'Political Intelligence Bureau', for example in the case of the Nyasaland Police,[72] or, in Nigeria, as the 'Intelligence Section', known within the force as 'I' Branch, an unofficial title that was not used outside the police owing to concerns of political criticism.[73] In Uganda, the guiding principle during the earlier period was that the so-called Special Branch section of CID 'enquired but did not prosecute',

---

[71]   RHL MSS. Afr. s. 1784, Box XVIII, ff. 20–23. T. Jenkins served in the Northern Frontier, 1935–46, the Gold Coast Police, 1947–50 and the Kenya Police, 1951–56 with the rank of Chief Inspector.

[72]   The Nyasaland Police was established in 1920. CID was set up the same year. Nyasaland Special Branch was set up in 1949/50.

[73]   Gidley, 28 August 2003. Sullivan, who worked within 'I' noted that its duties did not meet with the approval of the Police Commissioner 'as it seemed the Government feared that there might be hostile reaction in the Legislative Council and the local press'. Indeed, in some circles, this unit was referred to as CID (S), although 'nobody seemed to know whether the "s" meant "secret", "security" or "special"'. Duties after the Second World War were mainly taken up with producing a 'Daily Intelligence Report' to be dispatched chiefly to the Chief Secretary, the Commissioner and the GOC. RHL MSS. Afr. s. 1784, Box XVII, f. 8, f. 15. Sullivan.

this being left to CID in order to keep Special Branch work firmly under wraps. The Special Branch of the Uganda Police had its origins in the Second World War as a section of the CID, which was expanded after the events in Uganda of 1945 and then the watershed of 1948. By the mid-1950s, Special Branch staff operated at all provincial and some district headquarters.[74]

Following the creation of separate units the new roles of CID and Special Branch had to be defined. Typically, the function of Special Branch was to procure, collate, assess and disseminate intelligence that potentially affected the security of a colony or the maintenance of public order. This involved the investigation of subversion, espionage, sabotage and other deemed unlawful, unconstitutional or violent activities which might endanger the safety of the state.

The creation of separate Special Branch units ran parallel to the expansion, and often decentralisation, of CID branches. In Tanganyika it was felt that urban unrest and the emergency situations in other colonies necessitated an expansion of CID into eight provinces with the later creation of Special Branch.[75] Denis Brockwell, a former CID officer who served with the Northern Rhodesia Police (NRP), noted an increase from two CID gazetted officers and 16 inspectors to 16 gazetted officers and 67 inspectors by 1949. Numbers of African constables were augmented in line with these figures. Brockwell commented on how this increase in CID staff corresponded to its gradual relinquishing of Special Branch duties. Yet it was not until 1949 that a Special Branch officer was formally appointed. He described operations in 1948 and 1949 where CID duties were 'combined with a covert operation which required prolonged surveillance, including travel and sensitive screening of documents ...' The NRP had uncovered a communist 'cell' set up by Simon Zukas and other Europeans who organised secret meetings. In the event, this proved to be the first communist cell in Central and East Africa, Zukas having joined forces with the banned South African Communist Party and helped trigger the creation of a Special Branch.[76] Douglas Cracknell, who served in Eritrea at this time, wrote of how 'terrorist activity in the urban areas began to occur. Young elements of the pro-Ethiopian Unionist Party directed attention to the Italian community with hand grenade attacks, shooting and one or two cases of kidnapping ...' This prompted the creation of Special Branch in 1950 as a separate unit from CID.[77]

---

[74] RHL MSS. Afr. s. 1784, Box XVIII, ff. 60–68. Anderson.

[75] The Tanganyika Police was established in 1916 with CID set up the same year. An independent Special Branch was set up in 1953. Blake, J.D. in RHL MSS. s. Afr. 1784, Box XX, f. 130. Macoun, M.J.

[76] RHL MSS. Afr. s. 1784, Box XV, ff.6–11, Brockwell, 'Secret letter from CID HQ to Com. NRP', 11 March 1949,

[77] RHL MSS. Afr. s. 1784, Box X, f. 9. Cracknell.

In the Gold Coast, Jenkins noted that:

> The Convention Peoples Party pursued a vigorous and militant self-government campaign. Special Branch and the police were heavily committed to controlling large political meetings and demonstrations held with increasing frequency throughout the colony after 1948. Militant trade union leaders supported the campaign by encouraging unrest amongst organised labour and sporadic outbreaks of violence inevitably occurred. The authority of the chiefs was systematically undermined and their control of the youth was eroded ... under these circumstances the need for a constant flow of reliable intelligence was paramount. Unlike Special Branch in Kenya (until the outbreak of the Mau Mau emergency), the organisation in the Gold Coast had been established in every province. This was necessary if the heavy intelligence commitments were to be met.[78]

The crisis of 1948 and the changing nature of intelligence gathering implied immediate reinforcement of CID and Special Branch and the setting up of an 'Intelligence Co-ordination Committee' to meet weekly at police headquarters. Within many colonies, intelligence and security organisations comprised a 'central' intelligence committee responsible to the administration, the police and the army, a security division of the Chief Secretary's office, Special Branch and its district subsidiaries. It was generally the role of Special Branch to collect security intelligence (i.e. about any groups or individuals taking part in subversive activities that threatened internal security) and political intelligence regarding specific political parties. The distinction between security and political intelligence certainly became less than clear during this period and the two frequently overlapped.

Public order disturbances as a result of rising nationalism within this period forced a reconsideration of the role of CID across the board. By the time events were getting out of hand in the Gold Coast, the Nigeria Police's Special Branch element of CID was still struggling to produce a daily report of intelligence gleaned from newspapers articles, the odd contact with political and trade union activists and, for the most part, gossip acquired from government officials, police and military officers. On instruction from Whitehall, a 'Central Intelligence Committee' of police, military and administrative members had been set up, overseeing the developing Special Branch arm of CID, the Security Division of the Chief Secretary's office and their contacts throughout the colony. O'Sullivan, who would go on to head up Special Branch, recalled how matters were dealt with reactively, rather than proactively, hence their lack of success. The onset of the Cold War meant that the perceived threat was Marxist infiltration. Prior to the formal creation of Special Branch, the unit was progressively increased in size to

---

[78]   RHL MSS. Afr. s. 1784, Box XVIII, ff. 20–23. Jenkins, T.

meet the intelligence requirements arising from self-government throughout the provinces, Africanisation of the government structures, political and tribal unrest and penetration of perceived foreign subversives. However, it was not until as late as March 1959, that CID and Special Branch were officially separated within the Nigeria Police. CID became 'D' Department and the Special Branch and 'Aliens Branch' amalgamated as 'E' Department.[79] This was prompted, in part, by the advent of a new Inspector-General, Kerr Bovell. The occurrence of an emergency situation in Nigeria may well have prompted the earlier development of a separate Special Branch unit.

The same was true in Kenya where by 1954, with the onset of the Mau Mau emergency, Special Branch consisted only of three Europeans, one Asian officer and a handful of rank and file, working solely within Nairobi. The Kenya Police Special Branch had been set up in the early 1940s as a unit of CID, but the two were separated in 1945 after it was found that 'this arrangement suffered from one fundamental defect. The detection of crime [is] urgent; the collection of political intelligence appeared less urgent, and consequently suffered'.[80] The Special Branch also had the drawback in that it did not operate outside Nairobi and Mombasa and, therefore, had to rely on information supplied by local administrative and police officers. Much of the intelligence information was supplied by District Intelligence Teams, bodies which consisted of 'officers of all departments whose work brought them in contact with the people'. These teams were established in 1950 and were chaired by District Commissioners as a result of the Kolloa affray in Western Kenya causing the deaths of members of the general public and the police.[81]

When questioned as to effectiveness of these emerging police intelligence units during this period, former Special Branch officers have commented on their ability to pinpoint successfully foreign or local subversives. The evidence, however, remains largely anecdotal as O'Sullivan reflected:

> The Czech, Egyptian, Ghanaian, Russian Embassies were actively engaged in recruiting agents for subversion, espionage and propaganda projects and in each case had established contacts intended for immediate or future exploitation as 'agents of influence' and appropriate action was taken when security was endangered or the bounds of diplomatic behaviour transgressed. There were other undesirables detected by the Special Branch including within the government Service and members of the British Communist Party and others with communist connections in most but not all cases quiescent, a British fascist who was identified when he commenced to circulate fascist propaganda and inflammatory literature and an ex IRA man who had parachuted into Ireland as a German agent and spent the rest of the war in internment there ... There was an Ethiopian diplomat who took an undue

---

[79]   RHL MSS. Afr. s. 1784, Box XVII, ff. 22–33. O'Sullivan.
[80]   NA, CO 822/1222, Corfield Report, chapter 3, 1940–52 (1960).
[81]   NA, CO 822/1222, Corfield Report, chapter 3, 1940–52 (1960).

interest in the military and the police and was found to be a some time resident of Cuba and with an unsavoury record. Incidents of this or a similar nature were frequent enough to entail a godly amount of time in detection, investigation, surveillance, arrest, search interrogation and disposal ... Special Branch engaged in the production and processing of intelligence and counterintelligence operations ... It was not a secret service but nevertheless operated in secrecy.[82]

Conclusion

In 1954, Winston Churchill wrote that an 'efficient police force and Intelligence service are the best way of smelling out and suppressing subversive movements at an early stage, and may save heavy expenditure on military reinforcements'.[83] Ironically as it would seem the development of police Special Branch capable of assisting a colony in its 'vital "cold war" battleground'[84] was a question of too little and too late. Practical steps were not taken on an immediate basis. Despite the Inspector-General of Colonial Police's protestations in 1949 that intelligence systems should be improved, it took colonial unrest and emergencies to force a gradual reassessment and reorganisation of the policing bodies concerned. Even at the 1951 Conference of Colonial Commissioners of Police, the question of improving police intelligence was totally ignored.[85] And then, once again, the following year the inadequacies of intelligence were forced out into the open with the declaration of a state of emergency in Kenya. It was perhaps fortunate for the Colonial Office that they were able to draw on a pool of former Palestine policemen with experience not only in security and intelligence work, but also in counter-insurgency warfare. They took their experience to Malaya and Kenya and then to other colonial constabularies as unrest and emergency situations became the normality of end of empire. But still this did not suffice. When General Sir Gerald Templer was asked to review all aspects of colonial security in 1955, he reissued a familiar message after the Accra riots, that there was 'the greatest need' for the improvement of intelligence in the colonies.[86]

The development of police intelligence systems within the colonies came at a time when the Colonial Office was attempting to inject notions of Britishness within colonial policing. This was somewhat countered by rising nationalism

[82] RHL MSS. Afr. s. 1784, Box XVII, ff. 49–50. Sullivan.
[83] NA, CO CAB 128/27, Churchill, 'Defence Policy', Cabinet memo, 3 November 1954.
[84] NA, CAB 129/72, Harold Macmillan, 'Internal Security in the Colonies', Cabinet memo, 29 December 1954.
[85] NA, CO 537/6941, First Colonial Police Commissioners Conf. (1951).
[86] NA, CAB 129/76, Templer, Report on Colonial Security, Ch. II, 1955.

throughout the colonies that disrupted existing mechanisms of consent and collaboration between the police and the local communities. The concept of political policing took on a more important role, which in some instances confused the very nature of the security service of a democracy with the political police of an apparently autocratic state. Policing procedures acquired a different momentum after 1948, indicating that the very nature of the colonial state had changed. Special Branch emerged, in essence, as an alternative and additional source of information gathering and processing, dedicated to the pursuit of political and security intelligence, once the domain of CID.

The development of political and security policing contributed towards an extension of police powers and independence within individual territories undergoing emergency situations. This had its darker sides with which the policing of end of empire has been more commonly associated. Palestine saw the emergence of auxiliary intelligence units attached to the police and the development of the concept of the infamous 'pseudo-gangs'. Their members were despatched to gather information about the operational aspects of terrorist movements and to capture and turn terrorists. The general idea of these units stemmed partially from the need to relieve Special Branch of operational duties to allow them the freedom to concentrate on the political problems of subversion. So emanating from Special Branch units came the growth of irregular or special forces throughout this period operating a type of warfare that paved the way for what became known as the 'dirty war' in Northern Ireland in the 1970s. In Malaya, for example, by 1950 the so-called 'Ferret Force', comprising 136 police and military officers became an important intelligence provider. From Ferret Force came the creation of jungle squads whose lengthy sojourns within the jungle permitted contact with native aborigines and intelligence as to the whereabouts of the Malayan communists. This was followed up by search and destroy missions.[87] From Malaya these ideas were taken to Kenya where members of Special Branch became involved in pseudo gang and tracker team operations against the Mau Mau (see illustrations 9.1 and 9.2).[88] Their operations culminated in the formation of the 'Blue Doctor' Pseudo teams in the late 1950s made up principally of highly experienced Special Branch Officers under the leadership of Ian Henderson. Their final missions included the search for Dedan Kimathi and Stanley Mathenge,

---

[87]   Taken from an interview with Jim Godsave (Palestine Police, Malaya Police, Dep. Sup. 1946–60), 30 July 2001. Godsave served in 20 Jungle Company in Malaya.

[88]   Pseudo gangs were made up of members of the Kenya Police, the Kenya Police Reserve, the Kenya Regiment and members of Special Branch. Tracker teams also comprised members of the regular police, police reserve and 'White Hunters'.

Illustration 9.1   Kenya Police pseudo-gang in the Aberdane Range (1956).

Illustration 9.2   Kenya Police tracker team (1956).

senior Mau Mau leaders.[89]

The development of independent police intelligence systems within individual territories was a reflection of the gradual spreading of intelligence systems. Thus within situations of colonial conflict, Joint Intelligence Committee structures were put in place to oversee both police and army intelligence. This had the effect of developing police intelligence still further. Outside emergencies, some colonies experienced a move towards a newer type of intelligence system. Within the Federation of Northern and Southern Rhodesia and Nyasaland, the Federal Intelligence and Security Bureau (FISB), a federal intelligence *coordinating* body, as distinct from the intelligence *gathering* Special Branch bodies of each territory, was set up in 1954. This left the powers of the territorial governments in the field of internal security intact but created an overseeing body. Following the Unilateral Declaration of Independence in 1964, Rhodesia continued to develop its Central Intelligence Organisation (CIO) that increased police intelligence systems still further. The CIO brought the British South Africa Police (BSAP) Special Branch under its wing, increasing its membership and widening its role. The BSAP Special Branch was to play a crucial frontline role during the Rhodesian War of the 1970s.

Whilst colonial policing represented a very different model of policing to its English model, English liberalism no doubt contributed to the reactive rather than pro-active stance that was most often the initial position taken to the development of policing intelligence and security. Even then, as police intelligence systems were forced to develop in the light of decolonisation, some colonial officers still considered that British was still best. In 1959 O'Sullivan commented that ' ... after consideration of the corresponding orders of the Kenya, Tanganyika and Zanzibar Police Forces, [and] with due adaptation for local conditions we would be best served by an organisation similar to that of the CID of the Metropolitan Police, and of similar scope'.[90]

---

[89]   In the event, Kimathi was captured by the Kikuyu Tribal Police and Mathenge was never found. D. Franklin, *A Pied Cloak: Memoirs of a Colonial Police (Special Branch) Officer* (London: Janus Publishing Company, 1996) pp. 71–74 and correspondence with the author.

[90]   RHL MSS. Afr. S. 1784, Box XVII, f. 68. O'Sullivan.

Chapter Ten

'A Negative and Unwise Approach': Private Detectives, Vigilantes and the FBI Counterintelligence, 1910–72

John Drabble

The first part of this study traces an evolution in relationships between vigilantes and federal domestic security agents in the United States of America between 1910 and 1964. In the 1910s and 1920s moral panics regarding white slavery and radical unionism animated countersubversive efforts to preserve the moral fabric of the Republic. A nascent domestic security bureaucracy worked in tandem with private detective agencies and vigilante groups. This resulted in extensive violations of civil liberties during the First World War and the Red Scare and injury to democratic political processes. Under pressure to reform, J. Edgar Hoover professionalised the Bureau of Investigation (BI) in 1924, ending the practice of deputising vigilantes and breaking off overt ties with private detective agencies.[1] Henceforth, the BI would use covert surveillance and intelligence collection, as well as controlled informant penetration in its domestic security operations. During the Second World War and the early Cold War, the evolution of the Federal Bureau of Investigation (FBI) into a domestic security state forced existing incongruities in American countersubversive mechanisms to the surface, and this, in turn, led to further insulation of Bureau processes from racists and 'extremist' anticommunists. In 1964 the FBI launched COINTELPRO-WHITE HATE, a covert action programme that aimed to 'expose, disrupt and neutralise' the United Klans of America (UKA) and other 'extremist' organisations, which were attempting to thwart implementation of federal civil rights legislation through agitation and terrorist violence. This study examines the FBI's selection of targets for COINTELPRO-WHITE HATE, as well as the efforts to disengage vigilantes

---

[1]   The Bureau of Investigation was reorganised and renamed the Federal Bureau of Investigation in 1935. Richard Gid Powers, *Secrecy and Power: The Life of J. Edgar Hoover* (London: Free Press, 1987) pp. 184–85.

and other 'extremists' from an emerging network of cooperative law-enforcement agencies, patriotic organisations and system-supportive vigilante groups. In so doing, it provides an analysis of one critical permutation in the development of American domestic security strategies during the Cold War.

Ideological convergence and tactical divergence: The FBI and vigilante groups, 1915–64

During the first two decades of the twentieth century, Progressive reformers endeavoured to mitigate social conflict by enlisting government to combat urban social problems, promote greater political economic equality and subordinate vested and individual interests to the general welfare. While fear of class-conscious radicalism eventually allowed for limited tolerance of craft unions, local and national authorities suppressed social movements that remained dissatisfied by moderate reform. The discourses of the Progressive coalition also included desires by many native-born Americans to use social institutions and the law to restrain and direct the unruly masses, the foreign-born and African-Americans. Many Progressives focused on maintaining the values and moral assumptions that lay at the centre of conventional thought. While the social gospel that animated so many reforms was generous in spirit, it was often also intolerant of the social practices of those to be reformed. In keeping with this outlook, Progressives proscribed and restricted specifically disapproved modes of social behaviour and the 1910s especially saw a proliferation of restrictions on vice.

Beginning in 1910, legislation against trafficking in women, as well as the interstate transportation of prizefight films, obscene materials, narcotics and alcohol spurred the initial growth of the Bureau of Investigation. The BI first gained nationwide criminal jurisdiction in 1910, when the White Slave Traffic (Mann) Act made the interstate transportation of women over state lines for immoral purposes a federal offense. The Bureau soon gained jurisdiction in ever widening legislative attempts to regulate other vices.[2] The repressive anti-radical

---

[2]   Lawrence M. Friedman, *Crime and Punishment in American History* (New York: Basic Books, 1993) Chapter 6; Annual Report of the Attorney General, 1910 (Washington D.C., GPO, 1911) pp. 6 and 26; Max Lowenthal, *The Federal Bureau of Investigation* (New York: Sloane, 1950) pp. 10–13; Powers, *Secrecy and Power*, pp. 44 and 134; David J. Williams, '"Without Understanding": The FBI and Political Surveillance, 1908–1941', PhD, University of New Hampshire, 1981, pp. 50–51. On the White-slavery scare, see Frederick K. Grittner, *White Slavery: Myth, Ideology and American Law* (New York: Garland, 1990); David J. Langum, *Crossing Over the Line: Legislating Morality and the Mann Act*; (Chicago: University of Chicago Press, 1994); Ruth Rosen, *The Lost Sisterhood: Prostitution in America, 1900–1918* (Baltimore: Johns Hopkins University Press, 1982);

and anti-vice operations of the 1910s and 1920s, then, were undertaken by a newly created federal bureaucracy, which attempted to apply the modern techniques of scientific management to combat social problems.[3]

Enforcement of the White Slave Traffic Act was so zealous between 1917 and the late 1920s that historian David J. Langum described the Bureau of Investigation's operations as a moral crusade. Since the federal courts never restricted law enforcement to pursuing commercial vice investigations, many people who crossed state lines to pursue private sexual liaisons were also prosecuted under the law. Owing to popular support, the large majority of BI investigations in the 1920s pursued non-commercial sexual activity between consenting but unmarried adults. BI agents, moreover, used the traditional tactics of private detectives, employing spies among madams and prostitutes. These tactics had an important effect on the Bureau's dossier collection, as agents compiled unsubstantiated sexual allegations and registered the names, alleged failings and private affairs of hundreds of thousands of citizens.[4] In March 1925 J. Edgar Hoover created a secret file for 'obscene and indecent' materials, a file that could be exploited for other policy objectives.[5] White Slave Traffic intelligence files became a convenient tool for maintaining racial segregation, as federal officials prosecuted non-commercial vice cases against interracial couples in order to create examples of them.[6]

The metaphor of 'white slavery', according to Frederick Grittner, constituted 'a symbolic boundary reversal', in which Blacks and immigrants 'controlled plantations of vice populated by white women'. Long standing notions connecting whiteness with moral purity and blackness with moral depravity flourished in appeals to the prurient moralistic discourses of native born, middle-class Protestants'.[7] The myth of white slavery thus provided a forum in which concerns about immigration, urbanisation and changing gender relationships were linked to

---

Edward Bristow, *Prostitution and Prejudice* (New York: Schocken Books, 1983); Mark Thomas Connelly, *The Response to Prostitution in the Progressive Era* (Chapel Hill: University of North Carolina Press, 1980).

[3]   Martha Derthick and John J. Dinan, 'Progressivism and Federalism', in Sidney M. Milkis and Jerome M. Mileur, eds, *Progressivism and the New Democracy* (Boston: University of Massachusetts Press, 1999).

[4]   From 30 June 1922 through 30 June 1937, the FBI investigated 50 500 alleged violations of the Mann Act. Langum, *Crossing over the Line*, pp. 56, 87 and 180–86; Lowenthal, *Federal Bureau of Investigation*, pp. 16–17. On private detective tactics, see John Drabble, 'From Pinkerton to G-Man: The Transition from Private to State Political Repression, 1873-1956', *Journal of American Studies of Turkey*, 20, 3 (Fall 2004) pp. 57-82.

[5]   Athan Theoharis and John Stuart Cox, *The Boss: J. Edgar Hoover and the Great American Inquisition* (Philadelphia: Temple University Press, 1988) p. 96.

[6]   Grittner, *White Slavery*, p. 102.

[7]   Ibid, pp. 130–31.

contemporary concerns about race and the policing of interracial sexual relations became central to the Bureau's mission. The 1913 prosecution of black boxer Jack Johnson, an icon of black masculinity, who brazenly violated Progressive era racial codes, constitutes one dramatic example.[8]

Efforts, both private and public, to maintain white supremacy also characterised the Progressive period as a great black migration from southern plantations to northern cities unfolded, disrupting traditional relationships between the races and precipitating racial conflict. Between 1910 and 1940, virtually every northern and midwestern state, including states whose black populations were statistically insignificant, conducted hearings on anti-miscegenation statutes. The two decades before 1910 had been a period when white supremacist violence spread throughout the nation. In the American south, meanwhile, a diverse group of political leaders showed a willingness to use the power of the state governments in more active ways than before, implementing racial segregation, which they viewed as a modern, managerial approach to race relations.[9] Thus, Progressives in the New South linked the disenfranchising of blacks and racial segregation to anti-liquor and anti-vice crusades, all of which aimed to reduce political 'corruption'.[10]

Beginning in 1915 and accelerating through the 1920s, the Knights of the Ku Klux Klan also embarked on coercive moral-purity crusades against bootlegging, gambling and illicit sex. The Klan attracted grass-roots support from protestant Americans worried about a perceived decline in moral standards and alienated by social changes. The organisation drew from the broad middle of the American class structure and it most commonly mobilised support through campaigns waged on the theme of upholding community standards. Like BI vice investigators, Klansmen shared a fear of black independence that focused on the fear of miscegenation. They, too, worked to offer gender and race, rather than class, as appropriate categories for the organisation of collective identity.[11]

---

[8] Jeffrey T. Sammons, *Beyond the Ring: The Role of Boxing in American Society* (Chicago: University of Illinois Press, 1988) pp. 16 and 32–48; Randy Roberts, *Papa Jack: Jack Johnson and the Era of White Hope* (New York: Free Press, 1983) pp. 27, 31 and 150; Lawrence W. Levine, *Black Culture, Black Consciousness: Afro-American Folk Thought From Slavery To Freedom* (New York: Oxford University Press, 1977) pp. 420 and 430–32; Langum, *Crossing over the Line*, pp. 179–86.

[9] Edward L. Ayers, *The Promise of the New South: Life After Reconstruction* (New York: Oxford University Press, 1992) pp. 145–46, 413, 432–37 and 488 n.11. See also C. Van Woodward, *The Strange Career of Jim Crow* (New York: Oxford University Press, 1955).

[10] Alcohol and vice, it was argued, demoralised and debauched black men, reducing work efficiency and fueling a secret lust for white women. Dewey W. Grant, *Southern Progressivism: The Reconciliation of Progress and Tradition* (Knoxville: University of Tennessee Press, 1983) pp. 176–77.

[11] Grant, *Southern Progressivism*, pp. xv, xix, 14–17 and 411–15; Leonard J. Moore,

During the First World War and the Red Scare the Bureau of Investigation coordinated organised vigilante activity, as members of the Knights of the Ku Klux Klan, the American Protective League and other one hundred per cent American groups policed vice, rounded up draft dodgers and harassed radicals. The BI's antiradical work was made difficult, however, given that many private detective agencies that were contracted by corporations to infiltrate unions during this same period often employed agents-provocateurs.[12] Private labour spies, according to BI Director Bruce Bielaski, justified their employment through 'exaggeration and misrepresentation'.[13] In Philadelphia, for example, dozens of agents-provocateurs fomented trouble where it had not existed, selling questionable information to federal agents.[14]

After 1920, when famous private detective William J. Burns was appointed to the BI directorship, such tactics thoroughly corrupted BI security operations. Under his administration BI agents and operatives from his private detective agency worked together to suppress the International Workers of the World (IWW). The espionage director for seven Arizona copper mining companies convinced Burns to provide two federal agents to work within the Old Dominion Copper Company of Globe, Arizona. A provocateur named Haines became an IWW organiser in June 1923, and a second BI agent proceeded to intimidate and arrest a genuine organiser so that Haines could convince the latter to leave the union.[15] After local authorities arrested Haines, his successor, J.J. Spear, continued to sign up new members and collect union dues. Spears then set up arrests of militant workers by providing them

---

'Historical Interpretations of the 1920s Klan', in Shawn Lay, ed, *The Invisible Empire in the West: Towards a New Historical Appraisal of the Ku Klux Klan of the 1920s* (Urbana: University of Illinois Press, 1992); Leonard J. Moore, 'Historical Interpretations of the 1920s Klan: The Traditional View and the Populist Revision', *Journal of Social History*, 24 (Winter 1990); Kenneth O'Reilly, *Hoover and the Un-Americans: The FBI, HUAC and the Red Menace* (Philadelphia: Temple University Press, 1983) pp. 86–90 and 169; M.J. Heale, *McCarthy's Americans: Red Scare Politics in State and Nation, 1935–1965* (Athens: University of Georgia Press, 1998) pp. 296–301; Philip Jenkins, *The Cold War at Home: The Red Scare in Pennsylvania, 1945–1960* (Chapel Hill: University of North Carolina Press, 1999) pp. 210–14.

[12]   Drabble, 'From Pinkerton to G-Man'.

[13]   Theodore Kornweible Jr., *Seeing Red: Federal Campaigns against Black Militancy, 1919–1925* (Bloomington IN: Indiana University Press, 1998) p. 156.

[14]   Kornweible, *Seeing Red*, pp. 166–67.

[15]   Sidney Howard with Robert Dunn, *The Labor Spy* (New York: AMS Press, 1924) p. 144. On Burns's career, see William Hunt, *Front Page Detective: William J. Burns and the Detective Profession, 1880–1930* (Bowling Green OH: Popular Press, 1990); Gene Caeser, *Incredible Detective: The Biography of William J. Burns* (Englewood Cliffs NJ: Prentice-Hall, 1968).

with illegal IWW membership cards.[16] Burns also embarked upon a scheme to use the California legislature in order to put competitors out of business and allow Burns' private detective agency to take over control of industrial espionage in that state.[17]

BI agents also targeted outspoken critics of the Harding administration, placing legislators under surveillance and burglarising the offices of Congressman Oscar Keller and Senator William Borah.[18] William J. Burns was forced out in 1924, after Congressional investigators proved that Bureau agents had placed Senators Burton K. Wheeler, Thomas J. Walsh and their families and friends under surveillance. BI agents had tapped telephones, intercepted mail, broken into offices and homes and copied correspondence and private papers in an effort to blackmail them during the investigations of the Teapot Dome affair.[19]

After the 1924 election Attorney General Harlan Fiske Stone appointed J. Edgar Hoover to take over administration of the Bureau of Investigation. They agreed to dismantle the antiradical division and relegate the Bureau to strict pursuit of criminal investigations. They also terminated the practice of deputising vigilantes for federal raids on radical meeting places. Yet no full-scale Justice Department investigation of BI surveillance activities took place. Stone failed to order the BI to turn over or destroy documents relating to its investigations during 1919–20, because he, along with fellow cabinet officials and Congressional investigators, had mistakenly assumed that the pre-Burns BI had confined its investigations to socialists, communists, radical labour organisers and other subversive organisations.[20]

The BI had been forced to abandon overt intimidation and harassment, but surveillance of lawful political activities continued. Moreover, J. Edgar Hoover managed to circumvent legal restrictions for the next 15 years, as Bureau agents continued to monitor radical groups by collecting publications, attending meetings

---

[16] Ibid, pp. 150–52.

[17] Ibid, Chapter 8.

[18] Williams, 'Without Understanding', pp. 221–24; Theoharis and Cox, *The Boss*, p. 76; Curt Gentry, *J. Edgar Hoover: The Man and the Secrets* (New York: Norton, 1991) pp. 115–23; Powers, *Secrecy and Power*, pp. 139–43.

[19] The scandal involved oil-drilling contracts in the American West. Ibid; Lowenthal, *Federal Bureau of Investigation*, pp. 289–93; M.R. Werner, *Privileged Characters* (New York: Arno Press, 1935) pp. 162–65 and 311–14; Carl Solberg, *Oil Power: The Rise and Imminent Fall of an American Empire* (New York: New American Library, 1976) pp. 85–107.

[20] Williams, 'Without Understanding', pp. 253–59. On the 1924 changes, see Theoharis and Cox, *The Boss*, pp. 82–98; Powers, *Secrecy and Power*, pp. 144–69; Gentry, *J. Edgar Hoover*, pp. 124–44. On the 1919 raids, see Joan M. Jensen, *The Price of Vigilance* (New York: Rand McNally, 1978); Robert K. Murray, *Red Scare: A Study in National Hysteria 1919–1920* (Minneapolis: University of Minnesota Press, 1955).

and clipping press accounts of their activities. The Bureau supplied selective intelligence information to State prosecutors, local police, Military Intelligence, private detective agencies and organisations like the American Federation of Labor.[21]

Anticommunist countersubversive activity also characterised Klan operations during this period. Like the professional countersubversives, Klansmen had viewed the Bolshevik revolution in cultural terms and packaged it in nativist, racist and patriarchal discourses regarding control of sexuality and vice. Their primary charge against socialists was that they advocated free love. In contrast to Progressive anticommunists, Klansmen combated not only radicalism, but also unionism in general. Klan ideology pitted white supremacist Republicanism against political and social corruption, which they often equated with Catholic and Jewish office holding. Perhaps the most significant ideological difference for our purposes here was that the threats that Klansmen discerned came from above as well as from below. Klansmen perceived Progressive proposals for appointed city managers and commission governments, for example, as attempts to constrict popular control over the state so that it could better serve business interests. Klansmen's opposition to the religious liberalism that animated many Progressive campaigns was in keeping with their belief that the social gospel acted as the entering wedge of communism.[22]

The Knights of the Ku Klux Klan, moreover, was also the first national, sustained and self consciously ideological vigilante movement in American history. Bellicosity distinguished the Klan's brand of white supremacy from that of the professionals in the BI and Klansmen enforced white supremacy through vigilante violence.[23] The immediate goal of Klan vigilantism was to terrorise people out of particular behaviour and to subdue the lower classes. Vigilantism also served as notice that self-constituted groups of middling white men remained powerful social forces in their communities. Through vigilantism, Klansmen and other vigilante groups acted out their rejection of remote government, dramatising instead a version of paternalism enforced by a voluntary, local compact of white male households.[24]

---

[21]   Ibid; Powers, *Secrecy and Power*, pp. 161–69; Gentry, *J. Edgar Hoover*, p. 104.

[22]   Nancy MacLean, *Behind the Mask of Chivalry: The Making of the Second Ku Klux Klan* (New York: Oxford University Press, 1994) pp. 83–90, 93, 95–96, 118–19, 138 and 141–43.

[23]   MacLean, *Behind the Mask of Chivalry*, pp. 50–51 and 134, and Chapters 6–7; Glenn Allen Feldman, 'The Ku Klux Klan in Alabama, 1915–1954', PhD, Auburn University, 1996, pp. 10–12; David Chalmers, 'The Hooded Knights Revive Rule by Terror in the Twenties', *American History Illustrated*, 14 (February 1980) pp. 28–37.

[24]   MacLean, *Behind the Mask of Chivalry*, pp. xii–xiv, 102–3, 107, 114–15, 146–147 and 150. Kenneth T. Jackson, *The Ku Klux Klan in the City, 1915–1930* (Chicago: I.R. Dee,

The ritual expression of Klan ideology through vigilante violence was thus implicitly opposed to the BI's professional approach to subversion. J. Edgar Hoover emphasised this in 1922, when he declared that

> The Ku Klux Klan contaminates the courts – the very basis of our civic protection. It is bad enough when the pulpits and the legislative halls of the land are scourged with the course of Kluxism, but when the courts and processes of justice are directly attacked it is time for positive and drastic action.[25]

BI Director William J. Burns had also characterised the KKK as an illegitimate and potentially dangerous vigilante group and the BI investigated a fratricidal murder within the Klan leadership during the early 1920s.[26]

A second Klan investigation was prompted in 1922 because the Louisiana State Klan became so powerful that it was monitoring the governor's mail and tapping his phone. President Harding agreed with the governor that the BI should investigate the situation. BI agents found evidence that implicated Klansmen in a series of murders, but Klan-dominated local juries refused to convict. J. Edgar Hoover collected intelligence about the sexual practices of Edward Y. Clarke, the Imperial Kleagle of the Louisiana State Klan, who was indicted on a non-commercial white slavery charge in March 1923. He pled guilty and was fined $5000.[27]

Aside from these cases the BI seems not to have targeted Klan organisations in any systematic way before the Cold War. As late as the mid-1940s, when freelance private investigator Stetson Kennedy went to the Bureau with information on Klan activities, amused agents told him that they had never seen a Klan membership card.[28] Until economic and demographic shifts empowered African-Americans after the Second World War, national elites did not view Klan vigilantism as a problem significant enough to warrant suppression. Vigilantism had not yet been discredited in many American communities and high-ranking politicians, moreover, supported the organisation and its objectives. Klansmen were elected governor in Alabama, Georgia, Colorado and Indiana.[29] Thus, although the

1967) pp. 240–46.

[25]   Hoover to Burns, 28 October 1922, in FBI file 44–0–122 Ku Klux Klan.

[26]   FBI file 44–0–122, *passim.* For background on Klan infighting and the murder, see Wyn Craig Wade, *The Fiery Cross: The Ku Klux Klan in America* (New York: Simon and Schuster, 1987) pp. 186–93.

[27]   Langum, *Crossing Over the Line*, pp. 194–95; Powers, *Secrecy and Power*, p. 140.

[28]   Stetson Kennedy, *The Klan Unmasked* (Boca Raton FL: Florida Atlantic University Press, 1954) pp. 84–88.

[29]   Wade, *Fiery Cross*, p. 165; Michael and Judy Ann Newton, *The Ku Klux Klan: An Encyclopedia* (New York: Garland, 1991) p. x.

LaFolette Committee Hearings and the Wagner Act brought about a gradual end to union busting by private detectives in the late 1930s, anti-union violence by Klansmen and other vigilantes continued.

White supremacist regimes continued to sponsor Klan vigilantism in cities such as Birmingham Alabama, Atlanta Georgia and Tampa Florida. The political alliance forged between the New Deal and the labour movement provided communists with an opportunity to establish a legitimate social presence and this provided ammunition for the administration's enemies. As economic destitution, unionisation and New Deal relief and employment programmes combined to undermine white supremacy, Klansmen fused their racism and anticommunism with anti-federal government rhetoric. As Franklin Roosevelt redefined American liberalism in terms of active government and a welfare state, Klansmen charged that he was subverting American principles and destroying the foundations of States rights doctrine. Anticipating the anticommunism of the early Cold War, Klan Wizard Evans was one of the first public figures to charge that communists had infested the Congress of Industrial Organisations.[30]

The process by which liberals came to view Klansmen as un-American extremists was a long and complicated one, occurring at different times in different places. Pluralistic anti-Klan coalitions, which denounced the Order's racism, anti-Catholicism and anti-Semitism as 'un-American' discourses, first developed in the urban north of the United States during the 1920s.[31] Robert Ingalls traces a process by which, beginning during the First World War, members of the urban elite in Tampa, Florida took an organised stand against vigilante violence. Their emphasis on moderation and cooperation, by the mid-1930s, included conscious attempts to

---

[30] Jerome Auerbach, *Labor and Liberty: The LaFolette Committee and the New Deal* (Indianapolis: Bobs-Merrill, 1966); Diane McWhorter, *Carry Me Home: The Climactic Battle of the Civil Rights Revolution* (New York: Simon and Schuster, 2001) pp. 44–45, 52–55, 72–73 and 119; Feldman, 'Ku Klux Klan in Alabama', pp. 28–30 and 440–46; Glenn Feldman, 'Soft Opposition: Elite Acquiescence and Klan-Sponsored Terrorism in Alabama, 1946–1950', *Historical Journal*, 40 (September 1997) pp. 753–77; Charles H. Martin, 'White Supremacy and Black Workers: Georgia's Blackshirts Combat the Great Depression', *Labor History*, XVIII (Summer 1977); John Hammond Moore, 'Communists and Fascists in a Southern City, Atlanta, 1930', *South Atlantic Quarterly*, 57 (1968); Robert P. Ingalls, *Urban Vigilantes in the New South: Tampa 1882–1936* (Knoxville: University of Tennessee Press, 1988) p. xvii.

[31] Shawn Lay, *Hooded Knights on the Niagara: The Ku Klux Klan in Buffalo, New York* (New York: New York University Press, 1995) pp. 13–14 and 49–50; David J. Goldberg, 'Unmasking the Klan: the Northern Movement Against the KKK, 1920–1925', *Journal of American Ethnic History*, 15 (Summer 1996); Ezra A. Cook Publishers, *Ku Klux Klan Secrets Exposed* (Chicago, 1922).

avoid violence that might tarnish the city's progressive image and discourage capital investment.[32]

In the late 1930s, liberals and radicals worked to discredit far-right activists, isolationists and Klansmen, by attempting to link them to Nazi Fifth Column activity, highlighting flirtations with the German American Bund. According to Fifth Columnist hunter and New York Congressman Sam Dickstein, such 'collusion' threatened 'to destroy the Nation'. A 'Brown Scare' ensued, as the Roosevelt administration exploited fears of Nazi Fifth Column activity to revive FBI intelligence operation authority, and encourage the Bureau to monitor and discredit critics of the New Deal and internationalist foreign policy. In 1944 Internal Revenue service hit the Knights of the Ku Klux Klan with a $685,000 tax bill, effectively splintering the organisation into a number of competing groups.[33]

During the Second World War, J. Edgar Hoover mirrored public fears about Trojan horse activity and successfully gained control of domestic intelligence operations by raising the issue of vigilantes and the need to prevent mob violence.[34] He eliminated volunteer groups from active involvement in the fight against Fifth Columnists, as the President told citizens to turn over any evidence of suspicious activity to Bureau agents. The FBI established an 'American Legion Contact Program' to establish reliable informants, control intelligence gathering from within émigré communities and prevent vigilante operations like those of the APL during the First World War.[35] Importantly, Hoover was also careful to

---

[32]   Ingalls, *Urban Vigilantes*, pp. xvii, 203–4 and 214. On the subsequent period, see Steven F. Lawson, 'From Sit-In to Race Riot: Businessmen, Blacks and the Pursuit of Moderation in Tampa, 1960–1967', in Elizabeth Jacoway and David R. Colburn, eds, *Southern Businessmen and Desegregation* (Baton Rouge: Louisiana State University Press, 1982) pp. 257–81. On a similar process in St. Augustine, see David R. Colburn, 'The Saint Augustine Business Community: Desegregation, 1963–1964', in David J. Garrow, ed, *St. Augustine, Florida, 1963–1964: Mass Protest and Racial Violence* (Brooklyn: Carlson, 1989) pp. 211–35.

[33]   Brett Gary, *The Nervous Liberals: Propaganda Anxieties from World War I to the Cold War* (New York: Columbia University Press, 1999); Francis MacDonnell, *Insidious Foes: The Axis Fifth Column and the American Home Front* (New York: Oxford University Press, 1995); Geoffrey S. Smith, *To Save A Nation: American 'Extremism', the New Deal and the Coming of World War Two* (Chicago: Ivan Dee, 1990); Leo P. Ribuffo, *The Old Christian Right: The Protestant Far Right from the Great Depression to the Cold War* (Philadelphia: Temple University Press, 1983); Susan Canedy, *America's Nazis: A Democratic Dilemma* (Menlo Park CA: Margate Publishing Group, 1990); Wade, *Fiery Cross*, pp. 269–75.

[34]   Roy Talbot Jr., *Negative Intelligence: The Army and the American Left, 1917–1941* (Jackson: University Press of Mississippi, 1991) pp. 254–55.

[35]   Ibid; MacDonnell, *Insidious Foes*, pp. 158–59 and 180–81; Theoharis, *The Boss*, pp. 193–98 and 216; Athan Theoharis, 'The FBI and the American Legion Contact Program, 1940–1966', *Political Science Quarterly*, 100 (Summer 1985).

distance himself from freelance private investigators. In mid-1947 he tried to discredit the author of a sensational best selling exposé of the Fifth Column threat. He advised Hearst columnist Walter Pegler that Friends of Democracy's chief investigator, Avedis Derounian, had acted as Bureau informer only because the Attorney General had requested it and that the activist had contributed little of value. Pegler obliged, writing in his column that Derounian was 'not regular FBI man', but a 'snoop', and demanding a federal probe of the group's tax exempt status.[36]

Most liberals trusted J. Edgar Hoover, who had managed to avoid associating his Bureau with Martin Dies' more reckless House Committee on American Activities (HUAC) investigations during the 1930s. Committee investigators had resurrected the discredited tactics of the early BI, conducting vigilante raids with local police to seize documents for later use in Committee hearings. Investigator Edward F. Sullivan, moreover, had been dismissed from the HUAC in September 1938 after the LaFollette Committee revealed his record as a labour spy for the anti-Semitic Railway Audit and Inspection Company.[37] As conservatives exploited the communist issue for partisan purposes after 1945, liberal policymakers assigned internal security jurisdiction to the professional, non-partisan bureaucrats at the FBI.[38]

Fully accountable neither to Congress nor to the Justice Department, the Federal Bureau of Investigation became increasingly autonomous during the Cold War. Through alliances with congressional and state investigators, the FBI nurtured the growth of domestic anticommunism.[39] By 1951, however, even Hoover had become worried about anticommunist countersubversive activities conducted by ineffectual and incompetent state legislative committees. Concerned about state proposals to expand their police forces to combat communist subversion and fearing that state investigative squads might act irresponsibly and impinge on the FBI's jurisdiction, Hoover began supplying information on possible communist subversives working in government to governors and high level municipal authorities. By 1954, such charitable and private organisations as the March of Dimes, the Boy Scouts, the Damon Runyon Cancer Fund and NY Telephone were receiving material. FBI executives viewed this so-called

---

[36] O'Reilly, *Hoover and the Un-Americans*, p. 213.

[37] Ibid, pp. 38–41 and 44.

[38] William Keller, *The Liberals and J. Edgar Hoover, Rise and Fall of a Domestic Intelligence State* (Princeton: Princeton University Press, 1989) pp. 28–36.

[39] Ibid; Athan Theoharis, *Spying on Americans: Political Surveillance from Hoover to the Huston Plan* (Philadelphia: Temple University Press, 1978).

'Responsibilities Program' as an 'effective weapon of harassment of the Communist Party'.[40]

In 1956–57, however, the Supreme Court emasculated federal prosecutions of Communist Party leaders, by distinguishing between 'advocacy of abstract doctrine' and 'advocacy or teaching of action'.[41] In response, the Federal Bureau of Investigation launched COINTELPRO-CPUSA, a covert action campaign that aimed to destroy the Communist Party-USA.[42] Between 1956 and 1971, the Bureau would carry out a series of domestic covert action programmes (COINTELPROs) that endeavoured to vitiate organisations and activists deemed threatening to internal security.[43]

During this period, FBI institutionalised anticommunist countersubversion, utilising covert action to nurture political consensus. The period from 1910–71, then, can be characterised as one in which Progressive reformers and liberal politicians transformed the American countersubversive impulse into a professional, bureaucratic and covert apparatus of the federal government.[44] By focusing upon the question of which vigilante and far-right anticommunist groups

[40]   Cathleen Thom and Patrick Jung, 'The Responsibilities Program of the FBI, 1951–1955', *Historian*, 59 (Winter 1997) pp. 347-70.

[41]   Milton R. Konvitz, 'Yates v. United States', in Kermit L. Hall, ed, *The Oxford Companion to the Supreme Court of the United States* (New York: Oxford Press, 1992) p. 947.

[42]   U.S. Congress, Senate, *Final Report of the Select Committee to Study Governmental Operations with Respect to Intelligence Activities*, United States Senate, Ninety Fourth Congress, Second Session, Book II, pp. 10–14 and 66–67, Book III, pp. 15–17 (hereafter cited as Church Committee, Final Report); U.S. Congress, Senate. *Hearings before the Select Committee to Study Governmental Operations with Respect to Intelligence*, Activities of the United States Senate, Ninety Fourth Congress, First Session Vol. 6, pp. 6, 71 and 372 (hereafter cited as Church Committee, Hearings); Griffin Fariello, *Red Scare: Memories of the American Inquisition, An Oral History* (New York: Norton, 1995) pp. 202–3 and 236–38; Michael R. Belknap, *Cold War Political Justice: The Smith Act, the Communist Party, and American Civil Liberties* (Westport CT: Greenwood, 1977) p. 156; Powers, *Secrecy and Power*, pp. 295 and 336–41; Gentry, *J. Edgar Hoover*, pp. 443–44. In 1961, the techniques of foreign counterintelligence were also brought to bear on the Socialist Workers Party, a 'subversive' threat unrelated to a foreign government. Margaret Jayko, ed, *FBI on Trial, The Victory in the Socialist Workers Party Suit Against Government Spying* (New York: Pathfinder Press, 1988).

[43]   These files are available on microfilm: Athan Theoharis, ed, *COINTELPRO: The Counterintelligence Program of the FBI* (Wilmington DE: Scholarly Resources, 1978).

[44]   Michael Rogin provides the strongest argument for placing the countersubversive impulse at the centre of American politics. See his essays, 'Political Repression' and 'American Political Demonology: A Retrospective', in Michael Rogin, ed, *Ronald Reagan, The Movie and Other Episodes in Political Demonology* (Berkeley: University of California Press, 1987).

the FBI chose to target with covert action, the remainder of this piece will attempt to elucidate the completion of J. Edgar Hoover's Progressive mission to wrest control of the American countersubversion tradition.[45]

COINTELPRO-WHITE HATE and the counterextremist impulse to repress Klan vigilantism, 1964–71

In communities such as New Orleans and Baton Rouge, Louisiana; Atlanta and Augusta Georgia; Nashville, Tennessee; Dallas Texas; Jacksonville, Florida; Raleigh and Charlotte, North Carolina; and Columbia South Carolina, businessmen and moderate politicians began to accommodate black demands for desegregation and voting rights in the early 1960s.[46] By 1965–66, similar aspirations to attract industrial plants and capital investment motivated white moderates to break with massive resistance and seek compromise in Montgomery, Selma and Birmingham Alabama. As the implementation of the 1964 Civil Rights Act and the 1965 Voting Rights Act significantly reduced the amount of political capital to be gained from resistance, tacit support for Klan vigilantism declined, even in Mississippi (see illustration 10.1).[47] Yet juries continued to provide implicit sanction for vigilante violence against African Americans in the early 1960s by refusing to indict and convict Klansmen in a number of southern communities. Moreover, in central and southwest Mississippi, Birmingham Alabama, Bogalusa Louisiana and St. Augustine Florida, Ku Klux Klan groups often coordinated their night-riding activities with overt repression of civil rights demonstrations by local law-enforcement authorities.

---

[45] All FBI documents cited in the remainder of this study are located in COINTELPRO-WHITE HATE file (FBI file 157–59), unless otherwise indicated.

[46] Most cities in the upper south reached at least partial accommodation by spring 1963, but cities in the Deep South remained unbroken. David R. Goldfield, *Black, White, and Southern: Race Relations and Southern Culture 1940 at the Present* (Baton Rouge: Louisiana State University Press, 1991) pp. 132–34; Kim Lacy Rogers, *Righteous Lives: Narratives of the New Orleans Civil Rights Movement* (New York: New York University Press, 1993) pp. 84–87; Jacoway and Colburn, eds, *Southern Businessmen and Desegregation*; 'Dixie Businessmen Executives Seek Racial Amity as Clashes Peril South's Economic Rise', *Wall Street Journal*, 16 May 1963, p. 1.

[47] Ibid; J. Mills Thorton III, *Dividing Lines: Municipal Politics and the Struggle for Civil Rights in Montgomery, Birmingham and Selma* (Tuscaloosa: University of Alabama Press, 2002) pp. 10, 14–15, 33–37, 122–23, 139–40, 178, 203, 311 and 338–39; Joseph Luders, 'Countermovements, The State, and The Intensity of Racial Contention in the American South', in Jack A. Goldstone, ed, *States, Parties and Social Movements* (Cambridge University Press, 2003) p. 43.

Will The Real Kluxers Please Stand?

Illustration 10.1   FBI agents found this cartoon in the *Birmingham News*, 8 December 1969, and realised that the FBI could produce similar cartoons and use them as an effective weapon of ridicule.

In June 1964, after three civil rights workers disappeared in Neshoba County Mississippi, President Johnson pressured the FBI to suppress Ku Klux Klan violence. Liberals in his administration deemed covert infiltration of white supremacist groups and harassment of the members to be the most effective way to suppress Klan vigilantism.[48] As biographer Richard Gid Powers has pointed out, J. Edgar Hoover's view of KKK terrorism was also quite different from that of his liberal sponsors:

> For Hoover it was not the issue of racial equality that presented a moral issue ... it was the challenge Klan violence posed to legitimate authority, his own and that of the federal government ... in fighting (the Klan) he was not so much protecting black rights as putting down a white revolt against the law and against the authority of the national government. As an old Washingtonian with a Southern orientation Hoover would despise the Klan as a blot on the honor of the white race: The Klansmen, Hoover said were 'a group of sadistic, vicious white trash ... (one) can almost smell them where they live.[49]

Since local courts in many southern communities held little promise of convicting white supremacist vigilantes, FBI executives created COINTELPRO-WHITE HATE, a covert action campaign that discredited Klan leaders and thereby culled rank and file Klan membership and neutralised Klan activity.[50] The WHITE HATE programme was very successful, vitiating the nation's largest Klan organisations. The American Nazi Party (ANP) and the National States Rights Party (NSRP) were also extensively disrupted. COINTELPRO also targeted some members of the paramilitary, anticommunist Minutemen organisation, especially those who held membership in Klan groups.[51]

Much of the scholarship on COINTELPRO has downplayed the White Hate operation. Kenneth O'Reilly and David J. Garrow have documented the fact that the FBI primarily focused on disrupting leftist and civil rights groups and

---

[48]   John Drabble, 'To Ensure Domestic Tranquility: The FBI, COINTELPRO-WHITE HATE and Political Discourse, 1964–1971', *Journal of American Studies*, 38, 2 (August 2004) pp. 297-328; idem, 'The FBI, COINTELPRO-WHITE HATE and the Decline of Ku Klux Klan Organizations in Mississippi, 1964–1971', *Journal of Mississipi History*, 66, 4 (Winter 2004) pp. 353-401.

[49]   Powers, *Secrecy and Power*, p. 372; See also James Phelan, 'Hoover of the FBI', *Saturday Evening Post*, 25 September 1965, p. 32. Here Hoover labelled Klansmen 'white trash and yellow cowards'.

[50]   Drabble, 'The FBI . . . in Mississippi'; idem, 'The FBI, COINTELPRO-WHITE HATE and the Decline Ku Klux Klan Organizations in Alabama, 1964–1971' (working paper in possession of the author) posted at http://geocities.com/drabbs/workingpapers.

[51]   Drabble, 'The FBI . . . in Mississippi'; John Drabble, 'COINTELPRO-WHITE HATE, the FBI and the Cold War Consensus', PhD, UC Berkeley, 1996.

destroying Black Power organisations.[52] Frank Donner has explained the supposedly inadequate attention paid to the Klan with the following argument:

> The FBI's southern offices were staffed by nativist types who, if not in accord with the Klan's methods, endorsed its values from anticommunism to race hatred, from super-patriotism to Puritanism ... the roots of the modern Klan and the Hoover Bureau's anti-radicalism are entwined in the nativist soil of the twenties.[53]

It is certainly true that both the KKK and the FBI endeavoured to suppress African-American aspirations for full citizenship in the 1960s. Yet the tactics adopted by each group were very different. The FBI attempted to discredit civil rights organisations, and COINTELPRO aggravated dissention in the black power movement to such an extent that murderous internecine conflict resulted.[54] By contrast, Klansmen helped to maintain white supremacist regimes by perpetrating assaults, bombings and murders.

Biographers have attested to J. Edgar Hoover's Negrophobia, as well as his obsessions about interracial sex, but they have also pointed out that he was not viciously contemptuous of blacks in a socio-biological sense.[55] Hoover's paternalistic, Progressive ideology distinguished between so-called responsible Negro leaders, versus agitators who created confusion and consternation among the black masses.[56] By contrast, Klansmen demonstrated contempt for all African Americans, assaulting and murdering non-activists as well as civil rights workers.

---

[52] Kenneth O'Reilly, *Racial Matters: The FBI's Secret File on Black America, 1960–1972* (New York: Free Press, 1989); David J. Garrow, *FBI and Martin Luther King Jr.* (New York: Norton, 1981).

[53] Frank Donner, *The Age of Surveillance: The Aims and Methods of America's Political Intelligence System* (New York: Vintage, 1980) pp. 204–5; Powers, *Secrecy and Power,* pp. 17–20.

[54] O'Reilly, *Racial Matters*; Ward Churchill and Jim Vander Wall, *Agents of Repression: The FBI's Secret Wars Against the Black Panther Party and the American Indian Movement* (Boston: South End Press, 1988); idem, *The COINTELPRO Papers: Documents from the FBI's Secret Wars Against Domestic Dissent* (Boston: South End Press, 1990).

[55] Powers, *Secrecy and Power,* pp. 127–28, 324 and 461; William Sullivan with Bill Brown, *The Bureau: My Thirty Years in Hoover's FBI* (New York: W.W. Norton, 1979) pp. 121–26, 268–69 and 273; O'Reilly, *Racial Matters,* p. 13; Gentry, *J Edgar Hoover,* p. 500 n; Donner, *Age of Surveillance,* pp. 121 and 214 n.

[56] For a discussion of J. Edgar Hoover as a Progressive, see Powers, *Secrecy and Power,* pp. 145–46. Distinctions between 'responsible leaders' and 'agitators' abound in FBI files concerning Racial Matters. See Robert A. Hill, ed, *The FBI's RACON: racial Conditions in the United States During World War II* (Boston: Northeastern University Press, 1995) and the COINTELPRO-Black Nationalist Hate group file.

In addition, FBI countersubversive ideology never included conspiratorial anti-Semitism and it became less nativist and anti-union between 1919 and 1971. Klansmen on the other hand, 'continued to maintain that class lines were ethnic lines long after other Americans had replaced complex, progressive era racial taxonomies with the emerging conception of a monolithic white race'.[57] They retained atavistic notions of subversion regarding immigrants and Catholics into the 1960s and 1970s, even as they embraced more virulent forms of anti-Semitic conspiracy theories and fused these theories with the populist anticommunist discourses that had first risen to prominence in reaction to the New Deal.[58]

As Hoover's 1922 comments had made clear, his primary concern with regard to Klan activity was the integrity of the criminal justice system and law enforcement. When the FBI launched COINTELPRO in 1964 one of the first things FBI agents did was to provide Mississippi governor Paul Johnson with a list of law-enforcement personnel highway patrolmen, game wardens, city marshals, town constables and county sheriffs suspected of being Klan members. Johnson had the men fired and ordered the highway patrol to interrogate rural Klansmen.[59] Under the provisions of Section 122A of the FBI Manual of Instructions, Special Agents in the field offices advised state governors and heads of law enforcement agencies about Klan affiliation of law-enforcement officials.[60] FBI executives reasoned that the integrity of law enforcement was undermined by the Klan's use of vigilante tactics. They viewed vigilantism as an illegitimate, indeed counterproductive means for maintaining internal security.[61]

---

[57]   David E. Ruth, *Inventing the Public Enemy: The Gangster in American Popular Culture, 1918–1934* (University of Chicago Press, 1996) p. 73.

[58]   Evelyn Rich, 'Ku Klux Klan Ideology, 1954–1988', PhD, Boston University, 1988, pp. 56–79, 197–200 and 242–43.

[59]   James Dickerson, *Dixie's Dirty Secret: The True Story of How the Government, the Media and the Mob Conspired to Combat Integration and the Vietnam Antiwar Movement* (Armonk, NY: M.E. Sharpe, 1998) pp. 92–93 and 111; Don Whitehead, *Attack on Terror: The FBI Against the Ku Klux Klan in Mississippi* (New York: Funk and Wagnalls, 1970) p. 92; Gale to Tolson, 30 July 1964 (Section 1); Rosen to Belmont, 14 July 1964, in FBI file 44—25873-3 (PENVIC File); Keller, *Liberals and J. Edgar Hoover*, pp. 72–75, 86–92 and 130; Michal Belknap, *Federal Law and Southern Order: Racial Violence and Constitutional Conflict in the Post-Brown South* (Athens: University of Georgia Press, 1987) pp. 152–53 and 232–51; O'Reilly, *Racial Matters*, pp. 160–69 and 172; Powers, *Secrecy and Power*, pp. 407–11.

[60]   Director to Miami, 1 August 1967, 16 November 1967; Miami to Director, FBI, 2 August 1967, 26 September 1967, 7 November 1967, 4 December 1967.

[61]   Ibid; The House Un-American Activities Committee expressed similar concerns, US Congress, House Hearings before the Committee on Un-American Activities. *Activities of Ku Klux Klan Organzations*. 89th Congress, 1st Session, 1966, pp. 1962–2004, 2585–92, 2784–900, 3044–57, 3167–73 and 3187–239. See also Newton, *KKK Encyclopedia*, pp. 124, 276–77 and 393. For the FBI-HUAC relationship, see Drabble, 'To Ensure Domestic Tranquility'.

Bureau agents also worked with cooperative local officials and local news media to expose Klan sympathisers. In 1966 a situation arose that in FBI Director J. Edgar Hoover's opinion, 'could not be tolerated'.[62] Miami Police Chief D. Ray Pugh was offering guns, which he had confiscated during arrests, to Klansmen. The FBI considered framing him as an informant, but after agents provided a tip to a county solicitor, Pugh was quickly arrested for conspiracy to permit the operation of a house of prostitution and dismissed from the force.[63]

In another case, the Chattanooga, Tennessee Sheriff's department hired a Klan officer to act as a deputy sheriff in June 1967. The Knoxville Special Agent in Charge (SAC) alerted a police reporter at the *Chattanooga Times*.[64] The reporter wrote an editorial warning that 'the presence of KKK type individuals on the Police Force is a serious and contradicting matter at any time, but hate groups and white or black supremacy groups are a constant affront either to the letter or the spirit of the law'.[65] The deputy sheriff resigned from his position as Klan unit leader, but he continued to attend meetings. The FBI then applied more direct pressure, threatening to withhold the services of FBI crime laboratories from the Knoxville Police Department.[66]

The FBI also targeted Klan organisations because vigilante violence undermined 'domestic tranquility'.[67] Concerned that Klansmen might obtain rifles and ammunition from a U.S. Army Civilian Marksmanship programme, FBI agents informed the Military Intelligence services, the Secret Service and the Alcohol and Tobacco Tax Unit of the Treasury Department about a Klan-controlled National Rifle Association (NRA) chapter in North Carolina.[68] In 1967, FBI agents also sent

---

[62] Director to Miami, 28 September 1966.
[63] Director to Miami, 17 and 28 September 1966; 31 October 1966; Miami to Director, 16 and 30 September 1966, 3 and 18 October 1966, 5 and 23 January 1967, 28 March 1967; Iz Nachman 'South Bay Police Chief Dismissed, Then Jailed: Pugh Freed On Bond', *Palm Beach Times*, 10 January 1967.
[64] Knoxville to Director, 1 June 1967, 19 July 1967, 5 August 1967, 17 October 1967; Director to Knoxville 14 June 1967.
[65] Editorial, 'Klan and Patrol', *Chattanooga Post*, 3 August 1967.
[66] Knoxville to Director, 1 June 1967, 19 July 1967, 5 August 1967, 17 October 1967; Director to Knoxville, 14 June 1967; Martin Ochs, 'Why a Cyclops on County Police?' *Chattanooga Times*, 3 August 1967.
[67] Drabble, 'To Ensure Domestic Tranquility'; idem, 'From Vigilante Violence to Revolutionary Terror: FBI Covert Operations Against the KKK', Paper Presented at the American Studies Association Annual Conference, New Haven CT, October 2003, posted at http://geocities.com/drabbs/workingpapers.
[68] Charlotte to Director, 30 March 1967, 9 June 1967; Director to Charlotte, 25 April 1967.

anonymous letters to pro-gun ownership lobby alerting the Association that Klansmen were using NRA chapters as fronts for Klan activities.[69]

In addition to vigilante groups whose members stockpiled weapons, COINTELPRO also targeted racist agitators who incited breaches of the peace. National States Rights Party (NRSP) activists were targeted because they constantly vilified the FBI in their publications, because they worked with militant Klan organisations and Minutemen and because their incendiary speeches instigated riots.[70] Riots in Baltimore during the summer of 1966 resulted in an intensive effort to disrupt the ability of NSRP agitators to travel, as well as to encourage local authorities to prohibit rallies (see illustration 10.2).[71]

The American Nazi Party was another prime COINTELPRO prime target.[72] The FBI had investigated ANP leader George Lincoln Rockwell in 1958–60, in a brief neo-Brown Scare that had erupted over purported ties between intelligence agents of the United Arab Republic and domestic fascists.[73] ANP Stormtroopers deliberately courted media attention by engaging in publicity stunts and provocative counterdemonstrations against civil rights and anti-War demonstrators.[74] FBI intelligence reports on the ANP noted that violent disturbances arose in opposition to these counterdemonstrations and the violent

---

[69]   New Orleans to Director, 25 September 1967; Director to Charlotte, 25 April 1967; Charlotte to Director, 3 May 1967.

[70]   FBI Monograph, 'National States Rights Party', August 1966, ff. 27–28; FBI Monograph, 'WHITE EXTREMIST ORGANISATIONS, Part Two, National States Rights Party', May 1970, files in possession of the author. On the NSRP, see E.B. Duffee, Jr., 'The National States Rights Party', PhD, University of Maryland, 1968.

[71]   These efforts later overturned by the Courts on First Amendment grounds. Baltimore to Director, FBI, 27 and 29 July 1966, 23 September 1966, 16 November 1966, 4 January 1967, 29 August 1967; Los Angeles to Director, 28 July 1966; New York to Director, 29 July 1966; Director to Baltimore and Los Angeles, 18 November 1966; Baltimore to Director, FBI, 22 November 1966; Director to Baltimore, 30 November 1966.

[72]   See the Baltimore, Chicago and Los Angeles field office files. On the ANP, see William H. Schmaltz, *Hate: George Lincoln Rockwell and the American Nazi Party* (Washington D.C: Barssey's, 1999); Frederick James Simonelli, *American Fuehrer: George Lincoln Rockwell and the American Nazi Party* (Urbana: University of Illinois Press, 1999).

[73]   The investigation began after Rockwell made inquiries with the Foreign Agents Registration Section regarding his responsibilities should he undertake employment with the Egyptian government. WFO Report, 11 May 1959, George Lincoln Rockwell (FBI file 97–3835), 11–19, file in possession of the author,. See also the series by David Burke in the *New York Daily News*, 20–24 January 1959; David Lawrence, 'Nasser Seen Linked to Racists: Bombing and Propaganda Held Part of UAR Campaign to Knock Out Israel', *Washington Evening Star*, 26 January 1959; Drew Pearson, 'Haters Write to Nasser', *Washington Post and Times Herald*, 17 February 1959.

[74]   Leland V. Bell, *In Hitler's Shadow: The Anatomy of American Nazism* (Port Washington NY: Pantheon, 1973).

"Well, I'll Be Damned! I'm With the FBI Myself!"

Illustration 10.2   After one Richard J. Shelton was arrested in Chicago on
Marijuana charges and (falsely) claimed to be UKA
Imperial Wizard Robert Shelton's nephew, Birmingham
FBI agents found this cartoon in a newspaper, altered it by
adding the names of Shelton and an NSRP leader and
mailed copies to leaders of both organisations (Chicago to
Director, FBI 24 April 1966; Director to San Diego, 8 May
1966; Birmingham to Director, 30 April 1968, 11 September
1968). FBI executives launched the operation because the
cartoon 'shows that the FBI has infiltrated both
organizations, each of which already has shown
considerable animosity towards the other' (Director to
Birmingham, 24 June 1965).

reactions that ensued during Rockwell's public speaking engagements.[75] In FBI parlance, George Lincoln Rockwell's 'tongue and pen' were 'jagged weapons'. His 'invectives and vitriolic language', agents predicted, could incite his 'well armed' followers to commit 'physical violence'.[76]

Yet COINTELPRO-WHITE HATE did *not* target every high profile National Socialist or anti-Semitic group active in the United States during this period. The National Renaissance Party (NRP), which 'acted as a clearing house for anti-Semitic and anti-Negro individuals who might be prone to acts of violence were it not for the restraint placed upon them by their leader', according to the New York SAC, was not targeted. Rather, agents monitored the NRP so that the activities of potentially dangerous individuals could be monitored.[77] Indeed, a bomb plot involving a member of the Minutemen was uncovered through intelligence gained from informants in the NRP.[78]

Since local communities held little sympathy for vigilantism, prosecutions of Minutemen in New York were certainly more likely to succeed than prosecutions of Klansmen in the Deep South, yet this was not the only reason that the group was not targeted with covert action. The New York SAC also advised that

> ... if the American Nazi Party is revived in New York City, it will be under direction and control of individuals currently affiliated with NRP. ... in view of the fact that the NRP itself is so ineffective and since the New York Office obtains much intelligence

---

[75] See FBI files 9–39854 and 44–16407. It should be noted that NRP rallies were not always peaceful. A July 1967 rally at a Newburgh, New York courthouse had touched off two days of black rioting that led to seventy arrests. Newton, ed, *Ku Klux Klan Encyclopedia*, p. 417.

[76] Monograph, 'American Nazi Party', 64–68 [FBI file 3–39854: George Lincoln Rockwell], in possession of the author.

[77] New York to Director, FBI 29 August 1968. The NRP milieu attracted Northern UKA Grand Dragons Frank Rotella, Dan Burros and Roy Frankhouser. Newton, ed, *Ku Klux Klan Encyclopedia*, p. 417. Members of the NRP may have had some contact with German intelligence officials recruited by the CIA after the Second World War, but there is no evidence that such past associations in any way influenced the local FBI's decision not to target the group in the late 1960s. See Martin A. Lee, *The Beast Reawakens* (Boston: Little, Brown and Co., 1997) pp. 85–89 and 15–45.

[78] Ibid. The arrest and conviction of this Minuteman may have referred to either Paul Dommer or William Hoff, who were arrested in August 1968 for having given an undercover officer a can of dynamite to blow up the home of an antiwar activist. Dommer pled guilty in February 1969. Hoff, a Kleagle for the New York UKA and a member of the ANP and the NSRP, pled guilty to nine felony counts in August 1969. Newton, ed, *Ku Klux Klan Encyclopedia*, pp. 167 and 270.

information through the NRP, it is felt that any counterintelligence programme at this time is unwarranted and would not be in the best interest of the New York Office.[79]

COINTELPRO did not target the largely non-violent and non-secretive white supremacist Citizens Councils of the American south either.[80] In sum, vigilantism, violations of federal law and public agitation, not organised white supremacist activities per se, is what prompted FBI agents to launch covert action against any given white supremacist organisation.[81]

COINTELPRO-WHITE HATE and anticommunism

Scholars of Cold War countersubversion have established that the FBI was preoccupied with uncovering evidence of communist infiltration in civil rights and anti-war organisations.[82] The COINTELPRO-WHITE HATE file reveals that FBI executives also became concerned when Klansmen joined conservative grass-roots organisations, evidently because Klan ideology and vigilantism might thereby acquire legitimacy. In 1965, after members of the Association of Arkansas Klans gained control over a Chapter of the John Birch Society, the Little Rock Arkansas Special Agent in charge sent a letter from an 'interested reader' to the editor of the Birch Society's national bulletin. The writer explained that he was withholding his membership application due to the fact that 'riffraff' was leading the Pine Bluff Arkansas Birch chapter. According to this letter the local Birch Society president was 'using the Society for the benefit of the KKK', and this 'hurt the JBS in Pine Bluff and prevented it from building up into a good chapter'.[83]

In April 1966, National Knights of the KKK Imperial Wizard James Venable was invited to speak on 'Communism in the Civil Rights Movement', at a meeting of Robert W. Annable's National Christian Conservative Society. Since Annable had recently purchased property in a section of West Cleveland that might soon become integrated, the Cleveland SAC evidently furnished information to an

[79] Ibid. See also New York to Director 29 March 1965, 30 September 1966, 21 March 1968, 18 December 1968, 1 December 1969, 3 December 1970; Director to New York, 31 July 1969.

[80] O'Reilly, *Racial Matters*; Donner, *Age of Surveillance*; Keller, *Liberals and J. Edgar Hoover*.

[81] Drabble, 'From Vigilante Violence to Revolutionary Terror'.

[82] O'Reilly, *Hoover and the Un-Americans*; Keller, *The Liberals and J. Edgar Hoover*; Theoharis, *Spying on Americans*; Donner, *Age of Surveillance*.

[83] Little Rock to Director, 18 December 1964. See also Director to Little Rock, 23 September 1964, 16 November 1964, 7 January 1965; Little Rock to Director, 13 and 19 October 1964, 21 January 1965.

'extremely reliable source', this to discredit Annable by exposing his 'selfish interest'.[84] In September 1970, United Stand for America, Inc., a white group opposing the bussing of school children, drew several thousand whites to a number of Miami rallies. When a Klan officer attempted to take over the organisation, Miami field office agents leaked his identity to the *Fort Lauderdale News*.[85]

In each of these cases, the Bureau endeavoured to prevent Klansmen from influencing nonviolent, right wing or anti-integration organisations and thwart the Klan's efforts to gain a legitimate role in conservative politics. In keeping with such efforts, agents also went to extraordinary lengths to prevent a Klansmen from exerting influence over a war veterans' organisation, the National Marines Corps League. When Edward Twist III, a Klan organiser, was elected to the second highest position in the League, the Miami SAC arranged to have the *Fort Lauderdale News* publish a photograph of Twist at a Klan rally. Agents mailed a copy of the photograph to the Marines Corps League, along with a letter expressing 'disgust' over the 'disgrace that a despicable man' should gain such an honor.[86] Amongst the 'excellent results'[87] accrued from this operation, according to Miami agents, one was that someone made two bomb threats against Twist's bar, whereupon Twist resigned from the Klan and called it a 'subversive' organisation.[88]

The Bureau had little interest in the fact that a white supremacist continued to hold office in a Veterans' organisation. The important outcome, for Miami agents, was that Klan recruiting was no longer taking place in a legitimate patriotic organisation.[89] In general, those white supremacists that quit the Klan and

---

[84] A 'source' denotes someone in public life that confidentially provided information to and accepted information from the Bureau. Director to Cleveland, 3 May 1966. See also Cleveland to Director, FBI 27 April 1966, 2 June 1966; Atlanta to Cleveland, 11 May 1966. Annable has been described as a 'known Klansman' and the NCCS as a 'Klan affiliate'. In 1968 he was identified as the leader of the North American Alliance of White People and the George Wallace Christian Conservative Party of Ohio. The latter called for total segregation of races and for an immediate repeal of Ohio's fair housing laws. Newton, ed, *Ku Klux Klan Encyclopedia*, p. 18; Michael Dorman, *The George Wallace Myth* (New York: Bantam, 1976); Roldo S. Bartimole and Murray Gruber, 'Cleveland: Recipe for Violence', *The Nation*, 6 June 1967.

[85] Miami to Director, 30 September 1970, 6 January 1971.

[86] Director to Miami, 22 October 1965.

[87] Miami to Director, 8 November 1965.

[88] Ford Burkhart 'Ex-Member Calls Klan Subversive', *Miami Herald*, 5 November 1965.

[89] Miami to Director, 28 September 1965, 11 October 1965, 5, 8 and 16 November 1965, 28 December 1965, 15 February 1966, 24 April 1967; Director to Miami, 8 and 22 October 1965; Baumgardner to Sullivan, 21 October 1965, 10 November 1965; 'Klansman Quits But Eyed By Marine League', *Ft. Lauderdale News*, 5 November 1965; 'Bomb Scares

renounced violence were not targeted, even if they continued to espouse white supremacy.[90] This marks a major difference from FBI operations against leftists, in which former Communist Party members were assumed to hold subversive intentions when they joined civil rights and antiwar organisations.

Lest these examples leave the impression that the Bureau was only interested in insulating the political right from association with violence, one more operation may be cited. In November 1966, the Detroit SAC advised that Klan members, including the State Grand Dragon, were active at a General Motors Cadillac plant. To neutralise Klan recruiting activity, he composed a letter from a black worker and 17 year union member to local and national United Automobile Workers union officials. After noting a UAW fight for black rights, the letter declared that Klan activities at the plant had 'Negro workers ... scared for [their] jobs'.[91]

If the Bureau was concerned about Klan infiltration of legitimate social movements, the Bureau also jealously guarded its own countersubversive mandate. After Alabama Klansmen murdered civil rights activist Viola Liuzzo in 1965, the FBI stopped working with a Detroit policeman who sent Alabama authorities material which they used to discredit the victim. The Bureau also dropped a columnist who criticised the Bureau's handling of the Liuzzo murder investigation from their list of trusted journalists who received scoops from Bureau investigations.[92] An 'unscrupulous' author who had written a 'speculative' book, in J. Edgar Hoover's opinion, on the FBI's investigation of Klan murders in Mississippi, was denied access to Gary Thomas Rowe, the FBI informant who had been riding with the Klansmen who shot Liuzzo. A journalist who criticised the FBI because Rowe did not prevent the shooting, was also investigated and 'set straight' by Bureau agents.[93] The Bureau thus maintained strict control over its

---

at Ex-Klansman's Bar', *Miami Herald*, 5 November 1965; 'Second Klansman May Quit', *Miami Herald*, 5 November 1965; 'Calls Warn Twist Bar Bomb Target', *Ft. Lauderdale News*, 6 November 1965; 'Secret Klan Documents Name 4 Here', *Ft. Lauderdale News*, 4 November 1965; Patty Mummert 'Former Klansman Voted Reprimand: Twist Hearing Closed', *Ft. Lauderdale News*, 14 November 1965; 'Twist Reprimand Upheld By League', *Ft. Lauderdale News*, 2 August 1966.

[90]   See New Orleans to Director, 16 August 1966; Jackson to Director, 4 and 21 January 1966, 10 and 28 February 1966; Director to Jackson, 16 and 28 February 1966; Drabble, 'From Vigilante Violence to Revolutionary Terror'.

[91]   Detroit to Director, FBI, 22 November 1966. See also Director to Detroit, 7 December 1966.

[92]   Mary Stanton, *From Selma to Sorrow: The Life and Death of Viola Liuzzo* (Athens: University of Georgia Press, 1998) pp. 52, 94-102; Robert Conot, *American Odyssey*, (New York: Morrow, 1974) p. 467; FBI File 44-28601, VIOLA LIUZZO MURDER, PdF 8, pp. 60-65, 67-68.

[93]   Jones to DeLoach, 11 May 1965 (PdF 8b, 8), PdF 8B, pp. 73-75 *passim*, LIUZZO MURDER file, [Bufile 44-28601]. This file is downloadable from the FBI's Freedom of

files and informants, as well as media coverage of any cases in which its agents became involved.

The countersubversive response to Klan activity was to be covert, professional and under strict FBI control. In late 1965, a private detective named Eugene Tabbutt managed to convince United Klans of America (UKA) leader Robert Shelton to appoint him chief of the Klan Bureau of Investigation. Tabbutt had become responsible for investigating all UKA applicants as well as general investigative assignments involving the use of electronic equipment for surreptitious surveillance. At the same time, Tabbutt offered to sell tape recordings of Klan meetings to the Anti Defamation League of B'nai Brith (ADL) and the American Jewish Committee. He claimed that he could establish the existence of a relationship between the Klan and other far-right groups, including the Minutemen and the John Birch Society. He also asserted that the Minutemen had developed special weapons, which, resembling an ordinary pipe for tobacco smoking, fired a lethal cyanide pellet. Klansmen, he also alleged, were manufacturing and selling guns and silencers.[94]

From the perspective of FBI agents, Tabbutt had a questionable past. He had infiltrated the Klan during the late 1930s to uncover connections between the German American Bund and the Klan and to find out whether the German government had financed them. He had burglarised Pennsylvania Klan offices and sold copies of all Klan records from 1928–40 to the Philadelphia *Inquirer*, Jewish newspapers and the Anti-Defamation League.[95] Bureau executives alerted Philadelphia FBI field office agents that Tabbutt 'has an unsavory background and has been described as a con man, an opportunist and a person who would sell information to anyone'. They immediately launched operations to neutralise Tabbutt and cause the UKA to expel him.[96]

Information Act Website at http://foia.fbi.gov/liuzzo.htm. Bradford Huie, who wrote a book called *Three Lives for Mississippi* in 1965, and Inez Robb, were the authors in question. Stanton, *From Selma to Sorrow*, p. 52.

[94] These allegations resemble those of Minutemen informant Jerry Milton Brooks who fabricated a Minutemen cyanide plot against the United Nations and stories of a plan to use strychnine vials to knock off communists. Exposés by William Turner and Eric Norden included these claims, as well as those of Roy Frankhouser. John George and Laird Wilcox, eds, *Nazis, Communists, Klansmen and others on the Fringe: Political Extremism in America* (Buffalo: Prometheus Books, 1992) p. 291.

[95] Atlanta to Director, 7 December 1965; Director to Philadelphia, 25 October 1965, 1 and 22 November 1965, 1, 7 and 22 December 1965; Philadelphia to Director, 26 November 1965, 27 and 29 (two) December 1965; Birmingham to Director, 2 December 1965 and 5 January 1966.

[96] Director to Philadelphia, 25 October 1965.

Philadelphia field office agents alerted their contact at the ADL about Tabbutt's activities during the 1940s and instructed him to rebuff Tabbutt's advances. Reasoning that public disclosure of Tabbutt's double role would seriously impair UKA activity and cause Klan members to lose confidence in the UKA leadership, agents also alerted the Philadelphia *Inquirer* about Tabbutt's current offers to sell information. The Philadelphia *Independent* published Tabbutt's revelations. Agents also advised Philadelphia County Police of a plan, evidently involving Tabbutt, to drop Minutemen leaflets from a private plane. In an effort to prevent Tabbutt from renewing his firearms and detective licenses, agents also alerted them to an allegation by one of Tabbutt's former clients that Tabbutt had illegally installed wiretaps. One month later, Tabbutt was expelled from the UKA.[97] FBI agents moved to quickly neutralise Tabbutt's freelance activities, because they were not under the Bureau's direct control and threatened to disrupt the FBI's own efforts to neutralise Klan activity.[98] In early 1971, as the Bureau employed increasing numbers of informants in the 'extremist field', field offices conducted a review to insure that there were no 'plants' within racial informant ranks. Attempts to plant double agents, according to one FBI report, had been undertaken in the past.[99]

Anticommunists who argued that communist domination of the civil rights movement was enabled because of communist domination of the federal government also threatened FBI prerogatives. In 1965, Henry MacFarland's *American Flag Committee* newsletter contained a purported reprint of a 'Special Report of December, 1956' entitled 'The Lincoln Project – Blueprint for Chaos'. The Report pretended to have predicted the path taken by the civil rights movement since 1956 and to have proved that this was the product of a detailed

---

[97] Atlanta to Director, 7 December 1965, 14 January 1966, Section 2; Director to Philadelphia, 1 and 22 November 1965, 7 and 22 December 1965, 11 February 1966; Birmingham to Director, 2 December 1965, 5 January 1966; WFO to Director 30 November 1965; Philadelphia to Director 15 and 21 December 1965, and enclosed Bureau letter, 27 December 1965; Sullivan to Sizoo, 27 December 1965; Baumgardner to Sullivan, 18 March 1966 (Section 1); Harold Roberts, 'Undercover Agent Tells All, Exclusive KKK Expose', *Philadelphia Independent*, 12 March, 1966. See also the series of articles published during the following week.

[98] For a sociological analysis of informant typology, the activities of informants and the risks undertaken by their police handlers, see Steven Greer, 'Towards a sociological model of the police informant', *British Journal of Sociology*, 46 (1993) pp. 509–25. On agents provocateurs and double agents, see Gary Marx, 'Some Thoughts on a Neglected Category of Social Movement participant: The Agent Provocateur and the Informant', *Journal of American Sociology*, 80 (1974) pp. 402–42.

[99] Memorandum, Thomas H. George to SAC, Charlotte, 10 February 1971, Racial Informants, Racial Matters, in FBI File CE–170–963–55, in Folder 988, Collection # 4630, Greensboro Civil Rights Fund Records, Southern Historical Collection, Manuscripts Department, Wilson Library, University of North Carolina at Chapel Hill.

Communist Party-USA plan. When an FBI laboratory investigation revealed that the document had been created much later, agents informed one of their contacts in a New Orleans newspaper and MacFarland's ruse was exposed.[100]

Fighting communism, according to the FBI, required 'thoughtful, reliable and authoritative sources of information'. Indeed, 'irresponsible' citizens making 'reckless charges against each other', create a 'vital rift' which communists can exploit. According to FBI press releases from 1961:

> The job of curtailing and containing communism is one for legally constituted authorities with the steadfast cooperation of every loyal citizen. This is neither the time for inaction nor vigilante action; refrain from making private investigations. Report the information you have to the FBI and leave the checking of data to trained investigators.[101]

The FBI exposed McFarland because his conspiracy theories threatened to undermine the 'professional' countersubversives of the FBI.

In 1965, an FBI special 'expert' on the Communist Party-USA admonished an audience at Sanford University, Alabama that 'the fight against Communism should take place within the framework of law and order'. 'What we must avoid', he declared, 'is an over-emphasis on the Communist threat that is not factual, rational or intelligent'.[102] In 1963, J. Edgar Hoover characterised those 'rightist or extremist groups' which field office agents should monitor, 'reminding' them that 'anti-communism should not militate against checking on a group if it is engaged in unlawful activities in violation of federal statutes over which the Bureau has investigative jurisdiction'.[103] Similarly, a 1966 executive level FBI memorandum described the paramilitary Minutemen organisation as 'a militant and vehemently anti-communist organisation which has assumed a negative and unwise approach to the defense of freedom against communist aggression and thereby constitutes a threat to government authority and to law and order'.[104]

---

[100] Philadelphia to Director, 11 and 21 June 1965, 9 July 1965; Sullivan to Baumgardner 15 June 1965; Director to Philadelphia, 16 and 17 June 1965, 2 August 1965; 'Probe of Reds' Role is Urged', and 'When, Where MacFarland Wrote Letter is Question', *New Orleans Times Picayune*, 29 June 1965.

[101] 'To All Law Enforcement Officials', *FBI Law Enforcement Bulletin*, 1 April 1961; 'Internal Security', 17 April, 1961. ACLU Original Deposit, Box 50 Folder 13, American Civil Liberties Union Papers, Special Collections, University of Chicago.

[102] Andy Collins, 'Learn Facts on Communism, FBI Expert Urges Audience', *Birmingham News*, 22 March 1965, p. 6.

[103] Quoted in Theoharis, *Spying on Americans*, pp. 168 and 220.

[104] The Minuteman, according to J. Edgar Hoover, had 'an obsession for weapons'. Church Committee *Hearings*, p. 871.

The FBI's concerns about vigilantism were not merely about their tactics. Minutemen engaged in paramilitary drills and stockpiled illegal weapons, but their ideological 'approach' was also 'negative and unwise' in that they held that the main communist enemy resided not in Moscow, but in Washington DC.[105] The FBI conducted investigations for various American presidents, including the John Birch Society, which criticised Dwight Eisenhower, and Rev. Carl McIntyre's American Christian Action Council, which criticised Nixon administration policies.[106] An interesting counter example in this context concerns an anticommunist vigilante group called the Legion of Justice, a group that COINTELPRO did not target. In collusion and cooperation with the Chicago Police, the Legion engaged in raids, burglaries, harassment and assault against New Left organisations. The Legion received money from the 113th Military Intelligence Group in return for intelligence. Military Intelligence and the Chicago Police routinely exchanged intelligence reports and photographs, conducted joint interrogations and cooperated in counterintelligence against anti-war activities on the Northwestern University campus. Since the Chicago Subversive Activities Unit had a confidential relationship with the FBI, which included intelligence sharing, FBI briefings on Chicago area radicals for Unit personnel, local FBI agents presumably, were aware of police and MI collaboration with Legion activities.[107] Former FBI agent M. Wesley Swearington, who worked on the internal security squad in Chicago, remarked to this writer that local Special Agents in Charge would simply be advised, through oral instructions from FBI Headquarters, to ignore such groups.[108]

---

[105] William Turner points out that: 'De Pugh had driven an ideological wedge between himself and other paramilitary rightists ... who played ball with the FBI, ATTU, and CIA'. William W. Turner, *Power on the Right* (Palo Alto: Ramparts Press, 1971) p. 90.

[106] Theoharis, *Spying on Americans*, pp. 166 and 188. McIntyre was a fundamentalist preacher who maintained limited contacts with the anti-Semitic and paramilitary right from the 1930s to the 1960s and worked closely with HUAC in the 1940s.

[107] In 1970–71, Legion vigilantes bugged the American Friends Services Committee office used by the defense in the Chicago 7 conspiracy trial and gas-bombed performances by the Russian ballet as well as Chinese acrobatic troupes. Cook County, Illinois. 'Improper Police Intelligence Activities: A Report by the Extended March 1975 Cook County Grand Jury', 10 November 1975; Frank Donner, *Protectors of Privilege: Red Squads and Police Repression in Urban America* (Berkeley: University of California Press, 1990), pp. 146–50, 402 n.79 and 403 n.80. A 'symbiotic relationship' also existed between the Chicago Police and Congressional investigating committees such as the HUAC. O'Reilly, *Hoover and the Un-Americans*, p. 46. For more information on the Legion and its activities, see the American Civil Liberties Union Papers in the University of Chicago's Special Collections.

[108] M. Wesley Swearington, response to question by the author at Black Oak Books, Berkeley, California 4 March 1996. For similar accusations involving the sponsorship of Houston Police and KKK bombings, see Martin Waldron, 'Liberals Accuse Houston's Police', *New York Times*, 3 November 1970, p. 56; Martin Waldron, '2 Bombings Laid To 4 In Houston', *New York Times*, 12 June 1971, p. 35; Nicholas Chris, 'Bombs to the Right of

The Chicago-based United Patriots also engaged in vigilante harassment against antiwar groups. Unlike the Legion of Justice, their anticommunist propaganda asserted that 'Communism is Jewish'. Like the Minutemen, they engaged in paramilitary exercises. Perhaps most importantly, they were neither sponsored by the police nor by Military Intelligence. COINTELPRO did not ignore them. In order to curtail their activities, the FBI forwarded intelligence to sources in the Cook County, Illinois Sheriff's office and a local Jewish organisation.[109]

In a somewhat anomalous case in San Diego, the effectiveness of local vigilantes appears to have forestalled COINTELPRO operations against a local Minutemen unit. In San Diego, local agents harassed and disrupted leftist and antiwar groups under the 1968–71 COINTELPRO-NEW LEFT programme.[110] Howard Godfrey, who led the local Minutemen unit from 1969–72, acted as an FBI informant. As the Minutemen began to unravel following the incarceration of its leadership in 1968–69, the local Special Agent in Charge encouraged Godfrey to join an offshoot group, called the Secret Army Organisation. Members of Godfrey's SAO unit stockpiled weapons and explosives and engaged a campaign of harassment, vandalism and intelligence gathering against New Left and anti-Vietnam War organisations.

In January 1972, after the FBI shut down the COINTELPRO operations, an SAO vigilante shot into the home of a radical San Diego State economics professor, wounding a woman. Despite the fact that he had driven the car from which the shots were fired, local FBI handlers retained Godfrey's services. Godfrey turned the gun over to his FBI handler who, choosing to maintain informant coverage, hid the weapon and failed to inform local authorities about the informant's role in the shooting. Godfrey's role was exposed when another SAO member bombed a local theatre and San Diego authorities demanded that the FBI surface their informant to enable prosecution. Evidence presented in the resulting litigation collaborated Godfrey's allegations that local FBI agents had funded and trained members of the SAO. Bureau spokesmen attributed this activity to the actions of a rogue agent. Some of the more speculative journalistic accounts link the SAO operations to the Nixon campaign. Despite the compilation of voluminous

---

Them', *Nation*, 22 February 1972. The FBI only launched a few operations against the Texas UKA.

[109] Chicago to Director, FBI, 29 April 1969, 5 June 1969, 7 July 1969; Director, FBI, to Chicago 15 May 1969.

[110] San Diego to Director, FBI, 30 October 1970, COINTELPRO-NEW LEFT. For more COINTELPRO disruption actions in San Diego, see Director to San Diego, 24 July 1968, 12 December 1968, 18 August 1969, 8 February 1971; San Diego to Director, 16 July 1968, 31 October 1968, 14 and 22 November 1968, 30 April 1969, 15 August 1969, 4 February 1970, COINTELPRO-NEW LEFT file (available in Theoharis, ed, *COINTELPRO*).

evidence and testimony, the question of where ultimate agency lies in unfolding of the SAO affair remains quite murky.[111] FBI informant Joseph Burton made similar allegations about FBI sponsorship of violence, with regard to the Red Star Cadre, a Marxist-Leninist group set up by the Bureau in Tampa Florida, allegations that Bureau spokesmen vigorously denied.[112] Nevertheless, while it cannot be definitively proven that FBI agents instructed their informants in New Left and Black Power groups to engage in violent provocation, extensive testimony from such informants indicates that the FBI agents did little to discourage them.[113]

Particular Klan, Nazi and anticommunist organisations were targeted for neutralisation on the other hand, because public agitation and vigilante violence undermined domestic law and order, providing communists with propaganda opportunities and threatening to undermine the FBI's own countersubversive project. By discrediting reactionary populist organisations in the media and 'exposing' the leadership to the rank and file, as well as investigating terrorist

---

[111] Two SDPD vice officers were conducting surveillance in the theatre when the blast took place. Case files for *People of the State of California vs. William Francis Yakopec* (October–November 1972) and *People of the State of California vs. George Mitchell Hoover* (October–November 1972) San Diego federal courthouse; Case files for *Peter Bohmer; Paula Tharpe v. Richard Milhouse Nixon et. al.*, Civil Action 75–4–T, National Archives and Records Administration, Pacific Region (Laguna Niguel, California), Accession Number 021–81–0023, Box Number 32, NARA Location Number MB 29835. For interpretations of these proceedings, see Donner, *Age of Surveillance*, pp. 440–46; Peter Biskind, numerous articles in the *San Diego Union* 11–18 January 1976; Milton Viorst, 'FBI Mayhem', *New York Review of Books*, 18 March 1976; Stephen V. Roberts, 'F.B.I. Informer is Linked to Right Wing Violence', *New York Times*, 24 June 1974; Everett Holles, 'ACLU says F.B.I. Funded "Army" to Terrorise Anti-War Protesters', *New York Times* 27 June 1975. More speculative accounts include, Richard Popkin, 'The Strange Tale of the Secret Army Organization (USA)', *Ramparts*, October 1973; Peter Biskind, 'The FBI's Secret Soldiers', *New Times*, 9 January 1976.

[112] John M. Crewdson, 'Ex-Operative Says He Worked For FBI To Disrupt Political Activities Up to '74', and Ex-Operative's Account Called "Distorted or False" by the F.B.I', *New York Times*, 24 February 1975, p. 32.

[113] Gary Marx, 'External Efforts to Damage or Facilitate Social Movements: Some Patterns, Explanations, Outcomes and Complications', in Mayer Zald and John McCarthy, eds, *The Dynamics of Social Movements* (Cambridge MA: Little, Brown and Co., 1976); idem, 'Ironies of Social Control: Authorities as Contributors to Deviance Through Escalation, Nonenforcement and Covert Facilitation', *Social Problems*, 28, 3 (1981) pp. 22–246; idem, 'Some Thoughts'; Burton Levine, 'Professional Betrayers: The Secret World of Political Spies', PhD, University of Pennsylvania, 1995; Angus Mackenzie, 'Sabotaging the Dissident Press', *Columbia Journalism Review*, March–April 1981; Geoffrey Rips, *UnAmerican Activities: Pen American Centre Report The Campaign Against the Underground Press* (San Francisco: City Lights Books, 1981); Churchill, *COINTELPRO Papers*, Chapter 6; M. Wesley Swearington, *FBI Secrets: An Agent's Exposé* (Boston: South End Press, 1995) pp. 82–84.

operations for prosecutors in southern communities that abandoned sponsorship of vigilante violence, the FBI nurtured the politics of counter-extremism in the 1960s (see illustration 10.3).[114]

Conclusion

By accepting information from and maintaining good relations with the American Legion, the FBI deterred War veterans from conducting security investigations independently and promoted countersubversive anticommunism.[115] By disassociating white supremacist vigilantes from law enforcement and social movements as well as disassociating Klan discourse from countersubversive politics, the FBI also aided in the construction of political consensus during the 1960s. In the final analysis, the FBI targeted white supremacist vigilantes and irresponsible private countersubversive groups for covert action because they challenged the national security state's monopoly over the legitimate use of violence, as well as its dominion over the discourses of an American countersubversive tradition.[116]

[114] Drabble, 'To Ensure Domestic Tranquility'; idem, 'From Vigilante Violence to Revolutionary Terror'.

[115] Theoharis, 'The FBI and the American Legion Contact Program'.

[116] Keller, *Liberals and J. Edgar Hoover*, p. 5; Drabble, 'To Ensure Domestic Tranquility'.

Illustration 10.3   FBI agents mailed copies of this cartoon to 15 United Klans of America officers in March 1966 (Birmingham to Director, 1 April 1966).

Index